FLYING AND PRESERVING
HISTORIC AIRCRAFT

David Ogilvy passed away in July 2023, shortly before the publication of this book. His contributions to the world of general aviation are remembered and valued by many in today's aviation scene.

FLYING AND PRESERVING
HISTORIC AIRCRAFT

The Memoirs of David Ogilvy, Vice-President of the
Historic Aircraft Association

David Ogilvy OBE, FRAeS

FLYING AND PRESERVING HISTORIC AIRCRAFT
The Memoirs of David Ogilvy, Vice-President of the Historic Aircraft Association

First published in Great Britain in 2023 by
Air World
An imprint of
Pen & Sword Books Ltd
Yorkshire – Philadelphia

Copyright © David Ogilvy, 2023

ISBN 978 1 39904 444 8

The right of David Ogilvy to be identified as Author of this work has been asserted by him in accordance with the Copyright, Designs and Patents Act 1988.

A CIP catalogue record for this book is available from the British Library.

All rights reserved. No part of this book may be reproduced or transmitted in any form or by any means, electronic or mechanical including photocopying, recording or by any information storage and retrieval system, without permission from the Publisher in writing.

Typeset by SJmagic DESIGN SERVICES, India.

Printed and bound in the UK by CPI Group (UK) Ltd.

Pen & Sword Books Limited incorporates the imprints of Atlas, Archaeology, Aviation, Discovery, Family History, Fiction, History, Maritime, Military, Military Classics, Politics, Select, Transport, True Crime, Air World, Frontline Publishing, Leo Cooper, Remember When, Seaforth Publishing, The Praetorian Press, Wharncliffe Local History, Wharncliffe Transport, Wharncliffe True Crime and White Owl.

For a complete list of Pen & Sword titles please contact

PEN & SWORD BOOKS LIMITED
George House, Units 12 & 13, Beevor Street, Off Pontefract Road,
Barnsley, South Yorkshire, S71 1HN, England
E-mail: enquiries@pen-and-sword.co.uk
Website: www.pen-and-sword.co.uk

or

PEN AND SWORD BOOKS
1950 Lawrence Rd, Havertown, PA 19083, USA
E-mail: uspen-and-sword@casematepublishers.com
Website: www.penandswordbooks.com

Contents

Acknowledgements vii
Introduction: What is this all about? viii

Chapter 1	Why me? 1
Chapter 2	What now? 6
Chapter 3	More training 13
Chapter 4	A Squadron – at last 18
Chapter 5	The changing PR scene 28
Chapter 6	Freedom? 36
Chapter 7	Development 46
Chapter 8	Challenges away from the cockpit 59
Chapter 9	A.V. Roe Triplane 65
Chapter 10	Bristol F2B Fighter 70
Chapter 11	de Havilland DH51 76
Chapter 12	de Havilland DH60 Moth 81
Chapter 13	Avro Avian 88
Chapter 14	Avro Tutor 93
Chapter 15	Hawker Tomtit 100
Chapter 16	Parnall Elf 104
Chapter 17	de Havilland DH80A Puss Moth 108
Chapter 18	Spartan Arrow 113
Chapter 19	Comper CLA7 Swift 117
Chapter 20	de Havilland DH82A Tiger Moth 122

Chapter 21	de Havilland DH83 Fox Moth	124
Chapter 22	Avro Club Cadet	127
Chapter 23	BA Swallow	130
Chapter 24	de Havilland DH87B Hornet Moth	134
Chapter 25	de Havilland DH89A Dragon Rapide	138
Chapter 26	Miles M.3 Falcon	143
Chapter 27	Miles Hawk Speed Six	147
Chapter 28	Percival Mew Gull	150
Chapter 29	Gloster Gladiator	155
Chapter 30	Avro Anson	160
Chapter 31	Airspeed Oxford	168
Chapter 32	Miles M.11A Whitney Straight	173
Chapter 33	Miles M.14 Magister/Hawk Trainer	176
Chapter 34	de Havilland DH94 Moth Minor	180
Chapter 35	Percival Proctor	184
Chapter 36	de Havilland DH98 Mosquito	188
Chapter 37	Miles M.38 Messenger	197
Chapter 38	Gloster Meteor	200
Chapter 39	Miles M.65 Gemini	207
Chapter 40	Miles M.57 Aerovan	212
Chapter 41	Auster J/1 Autocrat and J5/F Aiglet Trainer	216
Chapter 42	Percival Prentice	223
Chapter 43	de Havilland Canada DHC1 Chipmunk	228
Chapter 44	Percival Provost	232
Chapter 45	Air racing in the 1950s	237
Chapter 46	In Closing	246

Acknowledgements

The author would like to thank Trevor Wilcock who has helped very substantially in enabling this book to be published. Trevor's aviation knowledge and interest has led to enjoyable and informative discussions which have helped to shape and finalise this book.

The author would also like to thank his daughter, Dr Jill Ogilvy-Scott, for her help with the editing process and for her encouragement during the latter stages of preparing this book.

Nearly all illustrations in this book have been provided by Philip Jarrett, to whom the author is very grateful. The exceptions are the last illustration and the author's photograph on the dust cover, reproduced with the kind permission of *Aeroplane Monthly*.

The author is grateful to Nicola Burrow for typing some of the text.

Lastly, the author would like to thank Pat Malone for agreeing to the use of material from the author's articles in AOPA UK Magazine.

Introduction

What is this all about?

When first I thought about assembling material for this book, I intended the contents to be little more than a collection of informal flight reports on a range of yesteryear's aeroplanes. However, others spoke, and I agreed to include an element of personal involvement, making it into a form of man/machine collection or, perhaps, an aerobiography; the idea was to cover a very varied selection of powered aeroplanes that contributed in some way to the progressive developments of the flying machine. The efforts of the very earliest pioneers barely qualified for the 'flying' element, but their work formed that essential foundation on which success was achieved. Britain was a slow starter and, following the achievements of the Wright brothers in the USA in 1903, we needed to turn to our neighbours in France to achieve sustained flight, but before long we accelerated the rate of development.

The start of the First World War in 1914 saw only small numbers of relatively flimsy machines with very limited military potential, but little more than two years later Britain produced the very effective and successful Bristol Fighter, which, unlike any other type, remained in production for eight years and in service for fourteen years *beyond* the end of hostilities, so I have stressed this as a prime example of what can be achieved when wartime pressure dictates the pace of progress.

The book works through the growth and heyday of private flying in the late twenties and through the later years until all this was halted with the outbreak of the Second World War in 1939. In the years shortly before this, the British aircraft industry shone well in the field

WHAT IS THIS ALL ABOUT?

of air sport, producing such machines as the de Havilland Comet that won the MacRobertson Air Race from England to Australia in 1934, the Percival Mew Gull in which Alex Henshaw gained the record to the Cape in 1939, the Miles Hawk Speed Six and the diminutive Comper Swift which played key roles around the race pylons of the time. It is fortunate that all four of these reappeared in the post-war skies and this has enabled me to include reports on the flying characteristics of the last three, all of which were specialist single-seaters. Also, I have included examples of the products of the many small aircraft manufacturers of the day, such as the Parnall Elf of 1929 with its unusual wing struts and its unique wooden engine bearers.

War was concentrating the attention of those in government – and elsewhere – leading to some rapid production orders and some much-needed new designs. Elementary trainers – the de Havilland Tiger Moth and Miles Magister, the Airspeed Oxford twin-engine advanced trainer and the Avro Anson that started life as a coastal patrol aircraft – are covered in the pages that follow.

Many other types, both Service and civil, are included in the overall text, but I move now to the end of the era that I am aiming to cover with reference to two special aeroplanes: the de Havilland Mosquito and the Gloster Meteor. For two and a half years of the Second World War the Mosquito was the fastest aeroplane in service in any air force, was the most versatile type in the RAF with thirty-eight designed variants and, by the end of hostilities, a late Mark 34 was the longest-range landplane on strength. No other aeroplane can claim such seemingly incompatible distinctions. By the end of hostilities the Meteor was in squadron service as the RAF's first jet fighter, which opened a new era. At first grossly underpowered, the type developed rapidly and by late 1946 a Mark 4 gained the world air speed record at 616mph.

No aeroplane can fly without considerable support and organisation. No background work can compare with taking a little Comper Swift in a tight turn around a race pylon, pointing a Meteor in a vertical dive to hit Mach 0.82, feeling the urge of 3,500 horses of piston power in a late mark Mosquito, or pottering in an open-cockpit biplane on a calm summer evening. However, I also briefly touch on some of the supporting activities that are needed to keep us in the air. I have been involved in several of the bodies that make their essential contributions to the cause, so I have seen some of the work concerned. Please remember that many people's unsung efforts enable the system – Service or civil – to operate. While there has been and still is the heavy hand of bureaucracy, the overall package gels and seems to hold together. Perhaps I have devoted too little space to this aspect of aviation activity, but almost certainly you will wish to spend more time delving into an aeroplane's flying qualities than into the complexities of airspace, licensing, airworthiness et al.

If you are a pilot and hope to fly an aeroplane with which you are not familiar, remember that all conventional types are broadly similar in response to control movements. You have no need to learn *how* to fly it, for you know that; you must be briefed on – or find from relevant notes – the type's idiosyncrasies, e.g. it may drop the port wing violently at the stall or there is a strong trim change when the last stage of flap is lowered. If it has dual controls, find a suitably qualified person to give you a check-out. If not, watch points while that person flies it. If it is a twin, in addition to normal practices, it is essential to make sure that you know how it behaves 'on one'. Have respect for the machine, but do not allow yourself to be frightened by it. The controls are for *your* use, so fly the aeroplane and avoid letting it fly you.

I have been amazingly fortunate to have enjoyed a life involved with a wide range of mainly historic aeroplanes. If I had failed to convince the RAF that I was determined to train as a pilot, just after the Second World War when they had far too many aircrew of all categories, I would have been unable to seek out the numerous opportunities that followed. I was able to start only through the favourable decision of one understanding senior medical officer, to whom I have remained indebted. Many subsequent events were possibly because I found myself in the right places at the right times – which happened with almost uncanny frequency – and these situations come to light throughout the book. I can take that theme

WHAT IS THIS ALL ABOUT?

even further, as I owe my life to two occasions on which something led me to avoid being in such places at the wrong times.

A few years ago I wrote handling reports on a number of aeroplane types and these were published in the house journal of the Aircraft Owners and Pilots Association. Several people suggested that they should have wider circulation and now edited versions of them form both the backbone and reason for this book.

David Ogilvy

Chapter 1

Why me?

Why am I writing this book? At the earliest age at which I could be seriously interested in anything, I developed an insatiable desire to find out as much as I could about aeroplanes and later learn to fly them. Unlike many people who had aviation ancestry that originated from the First World War or earlier, I could make no such claim. Neither my father, who taught music at a boys' school, nor my mother – a very good mother – had been anywhere near an aeroplane nor any desire to do so. So, somehow, I was a bit of an odd-ball self-starter. Soon I received some – possibly unnecessary – external encouragement when a Hawker Hart biplane light bomber of 1929 origin beat up my school and a little later a school friend and I were taken by his mother to see the flying at the long-lost aerodrome at Woodley, near Reading. It was the home of the Miles aircraft factory (owned by Phillips and Powis) and all the products were monoplanes, but in a corner of the field were three Gipsy Moths. These attracted my attention and the two events may have had an effect: to this day, although interested in all historic aircraft, I retain a strangely soft spot for open cockpit biplanes.

At my prep school there was little opportunity for anything directly related to aeroplanes, but I was the first and only member of the scout troop to gain an aircraft recognition badge. My interests needed to be put into practice at home, where we had a mainly unused Ping-Pong table. It was large and it was green, so clearly had one intended purpose. Soon it was occupied by a variety of non-flying $1/_{72}$ scale models, including some to a 'design' of my own. I sent detailed drawings to a government department, which I think was the Ministry of Aircraft Production. I received a very friendly reply, thanking me for my interest but regretting that it contained nothing new to the industry.

If no one wanted to use my youthful genius, I would put it into practice myself! I built several fairly small flying models, some of which were rubber-powered and others gliders. They were not desperately successful and I had insufficient money to buy a petrol engine, so I decided to concoct a large glider with a span of more than six feet. In the holidays I would help myself to the school's extensive grounds and eventually I launched this monster which, purely by chance, flew well. Too well, in fact, for on its third venture into the air it seemed to enjoy the experience, somehow catching a thermal and landing in the top of one of the many surrounding trees. There it sat, for many weeks, gradually disintegrating as it lost the war with the elements. That put paid to model flying but hit home with a lesson that I have not forgotten. However welcome in other ways, trees should keep as far away as possible from aeroplanes.

By this time the war had started and, understandably, protection for the Royal Family was stepped up. They were accustomed to attending Sunday services at St George's Chapel in Windsor Castle, open to the public, but they were advised to worship a little further from such a generally accessible spot. We lived in Windsor and my father was surprised to be appointed as honorary organist to HM King George VI. While I was still at home I was expected to attend to act as general dogsbody, especially as the instrument in St George's Hall, well out of public reach, was a rather elderly water organ that tended to run down at awkward moments, and I was called urgently to pump the liquid back to the top of the tank. My father was expected to train a choir, composed of randomly selected soldiers from the local Victoria barracks who were marched up the hill for the purpose. There was no attempt at selection or voice testing and most made no audible vocal sounds of any kind, but imagine my father's delight one Sunday when at practice he heard one of the crew singing a tenor part. Apparently, he had sung in a church choir before being called up and my father asked if he could attend on a regular basis, but no, the army made sure that no one could be retained.

The time came to move on. I went as a boarder to Aldenham School in Hertfordshire, where there was at least a chance to indulge in some form of aviation activity. There was a flight of the Air Training Corps, but before we could join we were required to have a year in the Junior Training Corps, which was the army version, to learn to march, use rifles, polish webbing and other alleged essentials before we were declared fit to specialise in more aviation-related activities. This was before today's Combined Cadet Force had been invented. Throughout more than three years at Aldenham I became increasingly impatient to join the Royal Air Force, train as a pilot and get into action. The best that I could manage was to commit a small untruth and tell the ATC CO that I had been selected for a gliding course and to inform his equivalent at No. 123 Gliding School, which was the nearest to my home, that my unit had nominated me for a course during the coming summer holidays. As I considered this to be a mutually beneficial arrangement I felt no bad conscience at this very minor dose of inaccuracy. It must have baffled the system, as very soon I was being dragged across Bray aerodrome in the almost flightless Dagling primary glider and then converting to the Kirby Cadet, which at least had no objection to getting airborne. At that time all training was solo from the start and the unfortunate instructors could fly only occasionally with a circuit or two at the end of the day's activities.

I had no claim to great achievement in either the academic or sporting field and I was given a beating for reading *The Aeroplane* magazine in a Latin lesson, but I did manage to be chosen for one task and I am confident that no other boy tackled it: to warn the entire school if a V1 flying bomb appeared as a potential danger. I could identify aircraft and I was a bugler in the school band, so I was sent to the cricket field with a bugle and binoculars, with strict instructions to produce the relevant sound if it appeared advisable to do so; no such situation arose.

Aldenham School is very close to Elstree aerodrome, where during the war Fairfield Aviation carried out repairs and conversions on Wellingtons and Lysanders. The work on the latter included modifications for special operations, transporting Allied agents into and out of enemy occupied territory, for which a conspicuous ladder was fitted on the port side of the fuselage and a massive underslung petrol tank increased the duration to eight hours. By 1943 this task had been completed and the resources were devoted to the 'cloth bomber', as the Wellington was known because of its all-over fabric covering. I made several unsuccessful attempts to get into the aerodrome until one day a US Army pilot landed and parked a Stinson Sentinel close to where I was standing just outside the boundary. He beckoned me over the barbed wire fence and shouted, 'Come and see my airplane.' However, I paid for my sins as trying too enthusiastically to get on to the site and hoping to progress to the works hangar, I cut my arm on a rusty barb and realised that I would need my first anti-tetanus injection. On returning to the school I concocted a tale to obscure the precise location of my incident and no more questions were fired at me.

There was no resident pilot at Elstree and when a completed aircraft was ready for an air test, sometimes we were treated to a unique sight and sound, when the sole remaining General Aircraft Monospar ST-25 would be flown over from nearby Hanworth by that company's chief test pilot 'Timber' Woods. This unique monoplane was powered by two 90hp Pobjoy Niagara radial engines that whined quietly like a pair of Singer sewing machines of similar age. Little could I know that, ten years later, I would be based at Elstree and keeping the little single-seat Niagara-powered Comper Swift racer G-ABUS in the hangar then occupied by Wellingtons.

There were several other unique viewing experiences during my time at Aldenham. The first shock that I received was in 1943 when I thought my eyes and/or head had suffered instant failures: lumbering along at low-level and low speed and almost over the school was a Vickers Virginia, a twin-engine biplane heavy bomber that had entered service in 1924 and had been withdrawn from squadrons in 1937. Naturally I checked and found that a lone specimen had been retained for parachute training at Henlow in Bedfordshire. Shortly afterwards it was grounded through lack of spares. Later in the same year I was not only surprised but wholly baffled when I saw a fast twin-boom aeroplane with no propeller and making a swishing sound. Naturally I was excited and mentioned this to several boys and even two masters, but no one seemed interested. What they must have deemed to be my fancy turned out to be the prototype de Havilland Vampire jet on its first or second full flight. I was quite pleased by my 'bag' of last Monospar, last Virginia and first Vampire in one year, but there my luck ended.

During my time in the ATC I had three flights in RAF aircraft. The first was from the long-lamented Hendon in a Dakota with no seats, but a bench down each side; this made me wonder whether flying was so good after all. Number two was aboard a Dominie – the military version of the famous DH89A Rapide biplane – which was only a bit better. The last flight turned the proverbial tables. It was in a Tiger Moth from the RAF Elementary Flying Training School at Panshanger. I was encouraged to do most of the poling and pedalling and I enjoyed every moment. Afterwards I had the cheek to ask if I could come again on a private venture basis and I was pleased to be told that I could do so if I appeared in uniform and if an aeroplane and instructor were available. Unfortunately, no such opportunity arose. By then I was a sergeant and my allotted tasks were to try to teach aircraft recognition to my fellow cadets and to keep their drill up to scratch. I enjoyed both but really wanted to get into the air.

It was time for me to leave school. Unfortunately for my youthful mind, but to my mother's sheer delight, the war had just ended and I had lost the chance to aim eight Browning machine guns at the enemy and knock him out of the sky; I had not considered the obvious alternative that he might get there first. I was aware that this would be a difficult time to be selected for training as a Service pilot, for hundreds if not thousands were to be forcibly 'demobbed', but my mind was set.

Chapter 2

What Now?

If I failed to train and qualify as a Service pilot what should I do? The RAF needed no more people, yet there was no way in which I could follow my aims and ambitions by any other route. I tried hard to convince myself that the training route would need to be kept alive, no matter how small the scale, as it would be virtually impossible to start it again from scratch, so I pumped up a totally unjustified dose of confidence, visited the Recruiting Office at Reading and said that I was reporting for training as a pilot. I was told that this was not possible, but there might be openings in air traffic control, engineering, and a few other tasks that I cannot remember. I insisted that I would be a pilot and would accept nothing else, but I made no apparent progress. I realised that I may have overstepped the mark, especially as the interviewing officer wore an air gunner's brevet, but imagine my disbelief when, a few weeks later, a letter arrived ordering me to report to the Aircrew Selection Centre at North Weald.

The tests occupied about three days, but the only one that floored me was the medical examination. I was ordered to stand on one leg with my eyes shut, but I collapsed in a heap on the floor. I was given a second chance but fell again. The MO regretted that he would be required to fail me on that. I appealed and he said there was no route for appeal, but – desperate, as this would thwart all my aims – I said that I would launch one and approach higher authority. To my pleasant surprise, he agreed to fetch the senior MO, who came in and said, 'Do it for me.' I did – and fell. He thought for a while and said, 'You are very determined and you have passed everything else, so I will turn a blind eye to that.' Phew!

WHAT NOW?

For a while I heard nothing, so spent a few weeks doing chores on a farm, which despite my impatience I enjoyed. Then I received orders to report to the Recruit Centre at the infamous Padgate in Lancashire. As Aircraftman 2nd Class all categories of entrant were gathered for intensive training. This was sissy stuff when compared with the workings of the Royal Marines, but it was hard enough for us to achieve the all-important toughening that did few of us any harm – my earlier experience at boarding school helped enormously.

During this initial recruit training, any of us who had been pre-selected for a pilot or navigator course (two of about thirty) wore white flashes in our forage caps, but quickly learned to remove them as we stood out as ideal candidates for unwholesome chores. The Station Warrant Officer (the RAF's equivalent of a Regimental Sergeant Major) had a specific dislike of prospective aircrew and delivered his 'AIRMAN!' shouts with especial venom. Our Nissen hut was cold. It was equipped with one lone solid fuel stove, but with no fuel. Perhaps, I thought, this was an intentional initiative test! I selected a long-deserted hut with a wooden door; it gave way fairly readily and soon was providing an element of warmth for the benefit of all, but the orderly sergeant, who arrived unexpectedly, asked how we had obtained the contents of the fire. I said that no one had provided any fuel and in that unacceptable absence I had looked after the welfare of my colleagues and had salvaged some waste material. The result was that I was given seven days' confinement to camp. Fortunately, this was of little concern as I had made one venture into the near neighbourhood and decided that inside was no worse than out. After about fourteen days in the Service, I had learnt lesson no.1: that initiative is not on the accepted menu for recruits.

At no time have I held any objection to strict discipline, so long as it contains some elements of practical common sense, but soon I learned that Padgate was not the real Air Force. In defence of the whole system, though, both then and in the years that followed, I found no sign of serious inhumanity or abuse of any kind.

Shortly after this we met a new life with the pilot grading school at Shellingford in Berkshire. Although the Tiger Moths and the instructors belonged to the RAF, this small informal outfit was operated by Air Service Training of Hamble in Hampshire, which was the UK's main centre for producing airline pilots. Life at Shellingford was unbelievably easy, but the work was serious. We had twelve hours of intensive flight training, with three tests, the last of which decided our futures. At the end about half the pupils were sent on their first solos, but I was not one of them. Those of us who had not made the grade indulged in much mutual commiseration, but imagine the surprise when we learned the truth: those who had gone solo were failed as pilots and were to undergo training as navigators, but they had been granted what might be their only chances ever to fly alone. This was a remarkable example of good thinking.

Whilst itching to continue the flying, we were faced with what I found to be the only intensively boring stage of my life: several months shunted between no fewer than six RAF stations (there were lots of them about in those days) with nothing to do at any of them. During some leave, my impatience led me to Denham Aero Club, where I carried out my first solo and a few subsequent hours in a Piper L4 Cub. This enabled me to maintain some small semblance of sanity.

The next 'proper' move was in the right direction, but offered no flying or even the sight of an aeroplane. It was to Initial Training School at Wittering. The nearest thing to live aviation activity for us was the work of the Chief Ground Instructor, who spent much of his time building, testing and modifying the first miniature jet engine – of his own design – for model aeroplanes. Our purpose in being there, though, was to spend twelve weeks on insights into theory of flight, instruments, navigation, organisation and administration, meteorology, airfield defence and other subjects judged to be of use when we tackled the real thing.

After a further but less prolonged gap, life returned, and fortunately, stayed put. The wartime two-tier system of attendance at a civil-operated Elementary Flying Training School with Tiger Moths or Magisters, followed by more advanced tuition at a Service Flying Training School using Harvards or Oxfords, had just been rolled into

WHAT NOW?

an all-through course at one unit; in this case it was to be No. 3 FTS at the large all-grass airfield of Feltwell, near Thetford in Norfolk. The RAF had no shortage of land, for the station had its own golf course and licensed clubhouse open to all ranks!

Now we come to the purpose of it all. At this stage all pilot trainees, ranked as Cadet Pilots, underwent similar courses, regardless of their subsequent roles. The first element, on Tiger Moths, covered about sixty-five flying hours and before going on official first solo it was a requirement to have three separate sessions on spinning and recovery. Two out of the twenty on the course had flown alone already, but this had been at flying clubs and in the interests of Service standardisation it was not recognised, so we did it again. Here I must record one of the very few real criticisms that I can offer: on my official third solo I was authorised to fly to the relief landing ground at Methwold and carry out an hour's circuits before returning to base. The distance was small, but I had received no navigation training and I became nervous when temporarily disorientated on the way back.

In addition to the exercises that anyone would have covered on an extended Private Pilot's Licence course, we received tuition in aerobatics and instrument flying (IF). Both of these were quite difficult, for the Tiger was reluctant to roll comfortably compared with its successors such as the Chipmunk and Provost, which went round smoothly almost before being asked to do so. More demanding was the IF, which was conducted almost in the dark under the canvas hood and all, including take-offs, on limited panel from the start.

Surprisingly we were not required to stop the propeller and restart the engine in flight, yet several years later, as an instructor, I was expected to teach this to ATC/CCF cadets on flying scholarship courses. Towards the end of this first stage I told my instructor how much I enjoyed my flying and wished that I could get more of it. He amazed me by saying that I was the first pupil to say that to him. As I explain later, this may have unintentionally saved my day.

At this time there was no differentiation between pilots destined for different tasks. In earlier years those earmarked for twins or multis would transfer to Airspeed Oxfords, but for some reason the type had been withdrawn and so were placed in storage, to be reintroduced several years later for training National Service pilots. At the time of my course, though, all who were going anywhere would progress from the Tiger Moth to the Harvard. Here, once we had managed to cope with the heavier and more powerful beast, we continued with more advanced phases of earlier exercises. Then things became even more interesting, with night flying, formation work, fighter affiliation with camera guns and dive bombing. There would be a marked target in one of the most remote spots in rural Norfolk, where a lone Range Officer would assess the accuracy – or otherwise – of our efforts at precision. Using 11lb smoke bombs, which had no lethal content, but which created conspicuous puffs on contact with the ground, the idea was to line up to fly almost overhead, letting the target disappear behind the wing root leading edge, count three, roll on the back and dive at what seemed a vertical angle, but which in reality was 60°. With a little practice, it was possible to become encouragingly accurate, but just when we reached this, there was no more to be had. At this stage, though, training was for all roles, with a smattering of each and no specialising; that would come later. One requirement that surprised me was a navigation exercise with one long leg at 15,000 feet with no oxygen. I doubt if that would be allowed today.

Most things on the course were pleasantly basic. The early stage, on Tiger Moths, had been wind-in-the-wires stuff, with no radio, while the Harvard provided a touch more sophistication with its retractable undercarriage, controllable pitch propeller, a full set of instruments and, of course, the added assets that went with VHF radio. Navigation aids were scarce, but two let-down facilities were available. My favourite was the continuous descent through cloud, or QGH, to use the code. On this, the controller in the 'Homer' would provide headings and heights to fly, leaving the pilot just to follow the instructions without the need to do in-flight calculations. The other aid that we could use if we returned to base to find it 'clamped in' was the Standard Beam Approach. On the earlier version of the kit, this would be set to the frequency of the home station and could not be used elsewhere, whereas the later, tunable, version could be used

WHAT NOW?

anywhere so long as you knew the approximate setting for the site. This was a wholly pilot-interpreted aid based on the dots and dashes of the Morse code. If you were far off beam you would receive a clear-cut dot or dash, as you neared the centre line you would continue to hear the same signal but with the other merging in; when you were on the line the dot and dash would merge completely into one continuous note. The only other sounds were from outer and inner position markers, at which you should be (if I remember correctly after some seventy-five years) at 800 and 300 feet respectively. If by this latter stage you were unable to see the ground ahead for a landing, you abandoned the approach and climbed away for a second attempt or a diversion to another airfield. We were required to practise both these aids throughout the appropriate stages of the course and I mention them here as examples of the facilities that were the best available at the time.

The course was well rounded, with half a day on flying and the other at ground school, exchanging mornings for afternoons each week. This was especially beneficial with winter weather and limited daylight. Each instructor had four pupils, with two in each group, so he had no undue pressure on time and this provided ample opportunity for briefings and discussion.

By the age of nineteen I was keen to learn more about certain elements of the civil world, so I put my foot in the proverbial water and concocted the name Thames Valley Aviation, operating from the cadets' mess but using my home address in Windsor through a box number. I placed a few inexpensive classified advertisements in the aviation press, announcing a new agency for aircraft sales. I had no expectation of commercial success and this would have contravened RAF rules, but it gave a useful insight into activities outside the Service fence. Clearly, an intruder into the established method of traders caused a minor rumpus and I was aware of several attempts to discover who or what TVA could be. Surprisingly and unexpectedly I sold a pair of Percival Proctors at £50 apiece and was rewarded with a commission of £5. There, though, it ended, as I needed to concentrate my time and attention on what I should be doing: training to be an operational Royal Air Force pilot. Nothing would be allowed to stop that.

Throughout this training supply exceeded demand, and there was no wartime need to produce as many pilots as quickly as possible. As a result, we needed to keep on our proverbial toes, for the 'chop' rate was high. Twenty pupils started on our Feltwell course; nine were removed quietly along the way and eleven of us were awarded our coveted Wings. Prior to that, though, at grading school, fifty per cent of candidates had been assessed as suitable for training as navigators rather than pilots, while at the very earliest stage, at the Aircrew Selection Centre, an unknown but substantial number had failed, usually for lack of hand and eye co-ordination, but also for medical or personality reasons. Educational standards had been checked at an even earlier stage. So we have no precise answer to the numbers game: probably, though, there were about eighty starters for the eleven of us who achieved our aims. Often, I wondered how I survived the many rejection procedures and, in retrospect, I believe it was that casual remark to my instructor, proving that I had enthusiasm if not any special skills or abilities.

At this stage, although we had our Wings, and a few more than 200 hours in our logbooks, our training was far from finished. We were asked what type of aircraft we wished to fly, with three courses available: Spitfires, Mosquitos or, surprisingly, Wellingtons. Although the old cloth bomber had been retired from squadron service, it was retained as a heavy twin conversion trainer for all who were destined for Bomber, Transport or Coastal Command. In common with many youngsters, I opted for the Spitfire, but there was no indication of where and on what we would go next. Even when I was instructed to report to Brize Norton, until after I had arrived I had no idea of what I would find. Just before leaving the train at Carterton station, I saw a lone Spitfire on the tarmac. My heart rose in tempo, but was this the type on offer?

Chapter 3

More Training

It was evening and there was little activity. The hangars were closed and the lone Spitfire sat there, unattended, until dark. Soon, though, I learnt the truth: No. 204 Advanced Flying School (AFS) was the unit for Mosquito training and, in the cases of rookies like me, for conversion to twins. To combine the two tasks at one time was quite a challenge to both a pupil and his instructor, for until shortly before this any pilot destined for multis would have completed a course on Oxfords and the big jump from Harvard to Mosquito would have been avoided.

Initially at FTS, I and others had looked at the Harvard as a large and potent beast, but we had coped, so perhaps we could master this much bigger move. On my first flight in the wooden wonder when my mentor – a slightly brusque but excellent confidence-building Scottish instructor – asked if it had been my first choice, I admitted that I was slightly disappointed as I had sought the Spitfire. Immediately he feathered the port fan and carried out a smooth barrel roll, singing that anything a Spitfire could do, a Mosquito could do better! Very quickly, although not yet 100 per cent convinced, I began to realise how fortunate I was to fly such a special aeroplane. Flying at 204 AFS was conducted on the Mark 3 trainer and the Mark 6 fighter-bomber, both early lightweight variants and, as I discovered soon, more pleasant to fly than the later, heavier versions. Slowly the type's significance dawned on me: it was the RAF's most versatile aircraft in the Second World War and for two and a half years of the conflict it had been the fastest type in service, clearly outperforming the Merlin-powered Spitfires of the time. At the other end of its active career, it became the longest-range aeroplane on strength; no other type in the history of aviation has achieved both those accolades, so clearly I was on to a good thing.

I will not attempt to assess why I was so fortunate to be where I was, but I had attained a reasonable assessment for handling ability, which would be the key requirement for a Mosquito pilot. Let me make clear, though, that I had no special claim, for at the other end of the skill scale, I scraped the barrel on instrument flying. Always I have appreciated its importance in the overall scheme of things, but I disliked it and found it very difficult. To me, to be pleasurable, flying must be a visual affair – perhaps one of several reasons for my aversion to becoming an airline pilot!

The course at 204 AFS was very thorough and comprehensive. We were expected to carry out our first solo on type after twelve hours of dual. Much of this was devoted to circuit work (which I enjoyed) and asymmetric flight, for the Mosquito had a powerful personality and stood no nonsense. It seemed to thrive by wanting to swing on take-off (which could be tamed by judiciously leading with the left throttle) and, more unpredictably, on landing, while on one engine the scope for error was very thin. The biggest problem in the latter case was allowing the airspeed to decay and running out of rudder control. This was most likely to occur on the approach, when applying power to correct an undershoot could lead to a rapid yaw followed almost immediately by an uncontrollable roll into the ground. In the 1940s and early 1950s there was no application of today's method of reducing power on the inactive engine and setting zero thrust: the propeller would be feathered and would sit there beside you in full view, as dead as a dodo. The accident rate was high and many years later the practice was banned, based on the argument that it was unnecessarily risky to practise for a situation (engine failure) that most probably would not occur. The present procedure might prove valid for modern twins with relatively tame asymmetric qualities, but for a type with a safety speed (V_{MCA}) range between 170 and 184kt (depending on mark) I remain convinced that the training we received was well worthwhile. I would not be happy to have a

MORE TRAINING

genuine stoppage and the need to face a feathered fan for the first time.

If I have given the impression that the Mosquito was a vicious and bad aeroplane, let me correct my mistake. Certainly it was hot, but in some ways that was one of its attractions; it performed admirably in the widest possible range of roles and its performance was unrivalled. The earlier marks with fighter-style broken sticks on which we trained at Brize Norton were delights to handle, while the later heavier variants with yokes were well suited to the long-haul tasks for which they were intended.

At most RAF stations Wednesday afternoons were (and, I think, are) devoted to sports, so while at Brize I invented my own version. I cycled to Kidlington, which then was the home of Oxford University Air Squadron, presented myself to the Chief Flying Instructor and asked if I could keep my hand in on light aircraft by flying one of his Tiger Moths. He agreed remarkably readily, arranged for me to have a dual check, which turned out to be a single circuit, and said that I could have a machine whenever one was available. For several weeks I took advantage of this offer and gave some unofficial instruction to my then navigator. Whilst sitting in the cockpit of a Tiger Moth might not be accepted as a sport, I was prepared to argue that my mode of transport to and from Kidlington was as good as any other activity, and I was not called upon to argue my case.

After leaving 204 AFS I was sent to 237 Operational Conversion Unit (OCU) at Leuchars in Fife to train as a photo-reconnaissance pilot. In view of the specialist nature of the work, this was a small unit with a Harvard, two Spitfire PR19s, a Mosquito T3 and two Mosquito PR34s. We shared the base with 120 Squadron and its white Coastal Command Lancasters and, for part of the time, the Tiger Moths of St Andrews University Air Squadron. Much of the time was spent at the conventional operating height of 30,000 feet (with only token pressurisation) photographing a range of targets, each usually covering a sufficient area to warrant completion of a mosaic map. For this, several parallel runs would be flown, with camera timing set to provide forty per cent fore-and-aft overlap and with each run positioned to provide fifteen per cent lateral overlap. The navigator would lie flat in the nose and would direct the pilot onto the appropriate start for each run and the pilot needed to fly as accurately as possible: the slightest bank would cause any resulting photo to be off track. This was work that needed a high level of mutual cooperation. At the start of the OCU course, pilots and navigators were teamed with the object of remaining as a crew when joining an operational squadron. I had considerable respect for the PR Spitfire pilots who needed to do the work singlehandedly and who were unable to see vertically down, but the two types were essential for the overall task as each tended to tackle slightly different commitments.

At high altitude the Griffon-powered Spitfire PR19 had a slightly better speed performance than the Mosquito PR34, but it lacked the range and endurance. Both types were unarmed and both were needed.

Here I must give one more credit point to the Mosquito's value. In early 1941 this private venture machine had entered production as a bomber, but the need for a high-performance PR type was more urgent and most of the early batches were converted on the line, with the result that the Mossie saw active service in the photographic role eight months before dropping any bombs on enemy territory. This may surprise some readers, but was evidence of the early adage that the country most likely to win a war would be the one with the best reconnaissance. (At the start of the Second World War the Germans were a long way ahead of us and their Junkers Ju86Ps photographed potential targets in England from heights that our Hurricanes and early Spitfires were unable to reach.) Less surprisingly, perhaps, the Mosquito remained in service in the PR role in the Far East until 1955 – three years after retirement from all other operational duties. Perhaps its only serious shortcoming was its high accident rate, with more coming to grief through pilots' handling errors than were destroyed by the enemy.

You may wonder why I have devoted so much space to the virtues of the Mosquito. The Spitfire remains with us in considerable numbers for all to see and hear in the air, so everyone knows that it was – and

MORE TRAINING

is – a great aeroplane, but the absence of an airworthy Mosquito in the UK has tended to make it lose its impact. Certainly, I would have enjoyed the Spitfire course at Chivenor, flying relatively lightweight Merlin-powered 16s, but it would have been followed exclusively by jets and unlikely to lead to any further opportunities in a specialised field. Mosquito experience, though, came to its own after I had left the RAF, with requests to fly the type intermittently over a total period of more than twelve years. I mention this to stress a point: the type that the Service dictates you will fly can have a significant impact on subsequent activities.

Although I had no intention of a light blue career, I would not have missed my time for anything. It gave opportunities that would otherwise have been impossible, and I enjoyed some flying that has left its mark on me to this day. I am not sure whether others agree, but despite carrying out far more flying over many more years as a civilian I feel that the adage 'once a Service pilot, always a Service pilot' is true. This is partly a matter of ethos but largely due to the training.

Chapter 4

A Squadron – at last

Now there was the move from the confines of the training world to the realities of a working squadron, but not the one that I had been expecting to join. I had been told that I was to be despatched to Singapore to join 81 Squadron, a mixed unit with a flight of Spitfire 19s and a flight of Mosquito 34s. I was planning the kit needed for such an overseas tour when, at very short notice, I was to forget all that and fill a gap for a Mosquito pilot on 58 Squadron at Benson in Oxfordshire. At the time I was quite disappointed at missing the opportunity to discover what flying and life in the Far East would be all about, but, as has happened so often, in the longer term my home posting had a strongly beneficial effect on my interests and on my subsequent career.

So far, so good. However, on arrival, fresh from two specialised courses on Mosquitos, I found myself on 'A' Flight, which was equipped with modified Avro Anson 19s. After one type familiarisation flight, I was put to work on an aerial survey of East Anglia, using the short-lived Decca navigation system instead of relying on the usual visual alignments. The hardest part of this was an almost daily call at 05:30 to ensure an early start, to catch what was known as first photographic light. The summer weather patterns were far more predictable than they are today, with a clear sky on about six of seven mornings and a steady build-up of fair-weather cumulus from about 11:00. Any more than about one-eighth cloud cover would put paid to our work and often we were back at base by midday. This meant that five very useful load-carrying Ansons and their crews could be available for other duties and many people in authority wasted no time in capturing this facility.

A SQUADRON – AT LAST

The Anson was a remarkably useful aeroplane. It was not a young man's steed and I sought a return to something with more spirit in its heart, but I respected it and its overall behaviour. It took a long time to get anywhere, but get there it did, and I can remember only one case of a flight being aborted due to unserviceability. The nine-cylinder Armstrong Siddeley Cheetah radial engines were not the world's smoothest and somehow they disliked being precisely synchronised, but they were friendly and I heard of more than one case in which a cylinder head would split and the Cheetah would continue to run to get the package home; I am not convinced, though, that it was a wise course of action. The Anson must have been the safest aeroplane in the Service and it was the only type that I met which we were authorised to fly without wearing parachutes. It could be likened to a small Dakota. It has an interesting development history, with an enormous difference between the original pre-war Mark 1 and the late variants, both of which I have had the good fortune to fly. In Chapter 30 I give the workhorse the space that it deserves.

After a few months the situation changed. The survey work was beginning to run down and I moved across to 'B' Flight and its Mosquitos. The work was very different, mainly high-level photo-reconnaissance and considerably more wide ranging. We had four PR34s, with a lone T3 for continuation training and Instrument Rating renewals. As always, the T3 was a delight to fly and the PR34 was not, but the latter had some serious work to do and it tackled its allotted tasks very capably. My main interest in flying was aircraft handling and I took considerable pleasure in endeavouring to assess the individual machines and their qualities. It is surprising how different one aircraft can be from another of seemingly similar origin, but eventually I found that their place of physical birth can have a marked influence. Without doubt PF669 was the most reliable and the smoothest to fly, whilst RG178 was a bit of a troublemaker and, as I discovered many years later, had an unhappy history. It had been one of two prototype 34s used by Boscombe Down for type acceptance trials, had gone out of control on one engine in cloud and suffered structural overstressing in the prolonged recovery. I knew nothing about this when I flew it many times in service, but I had wondered why it was the only 34 on the strengths of two squadrons at Benson that lacked 100-gallon drop tanks under its wings. Perhaps more importantly, a truth emerged: the RG machines had been built by de Havilland and the PFs by Percival. It is recorded that Geoffrey DH made a personal visit to Luton to investigate why the contractor's products were better than those from his own company, but I have been unable to find any reference to results of the investigation.

The work was mainly Benson based, but there were several deployments. I liked these, for PR work was largely an act of independence and a two-man crew could depart to places near and far to carry out specific tasks. Although most targets were military and in the interests of national defence, some were for civil agencies and I spent several weeks at Leuchars (again), mainly on seaweed research for the Department of Health for Scotland. During these 'away matches', so long as we produced the results, we had no daily responsibility to anyone. Frequent week-long detachments to Gibraltar or Libya were on a similar basis and provided considerable opportunities for initiative that relatively inexperienced two-man crews would be unable to enjoy in other roles. There were several testing situations, as on my second arrival at the Rock; after a flight of more than five hours, dusk was close, our Gee navigation system was producing no responses, we were told by the controller that the base's 'Homer' was out of action and low cloud was covering the area. Somewhere in that murk was a large solid rock protruding well into the circuit and it was unwise to wander from the prescribed pattern: I had learned from my previous visit that a Miles Martinet target tug had strayed a few hundred yards off track and had been fired at by the Spanish neighbours. If I could find the runway, most of which stood out into the sea with no land either side, I would remember my earlier fear that a tyre burst or swing on landing would lead to an unthinkable situation. However, somehow my excellent navigator, Larry Pope, managed to align us on the approach in cloud and the rest went well.

On our next visit to the Mediterranean, after almost six hours in the air, we arrived at Castel Benito, later known as Idris and now Tripoli

A SQUADRON – AT LAST

Airport. We were rather keen to touch terra firma, if only for comfort reasons, but as we approached the circuit the controller told us to 'hold' while his men cleared the runway: a herd of about thirty wild gazelle had chosen it for a form of tail-chasing party. Fortunately, they responded fairly quickly to the encouragement given to push off. I think that our fairly frequent short visits to the Middle East were twofold in purpose: to keep us in practice at operating far from home with only minimum support and to show that the British flag could still flutter in many places. Not all these events were successful, though, for when we were detailed for a two-day exercise with the Italian Navy, on neither day was there sight of or sound from our intended colleagues.

Back at home there was plenty of activity. On one side of 58's hangar (with its Mosquitos, Ansons and a Tiger Moth) was 540 Squadron with Mosquito PR34s, an Oxford and a Tiger Moth, while on the other, 541 had Spitfire PR19s and a brace of Harvards. A key place on the site was held by the King's Flight with the only four Vikings in RAF service. Another hangar was used for Lancaster PR1s of 82 Squadron, which was operating from Nairobi on a large-scale survey of Central Africa, with Benson as its home, to which their aircraft returned for major servicing. Also on the heavy side, the Radar Reconnaissance Flight operated a pair of Lincolns. By late 1952 a Meteor had been added to each of 58 and 540 Squadrons. Finally, in a rare quiet corner was 54 Group Communication Flight with an Anson 19 and a couple of Proctor 4s.

Benson was the long-term home of all UK photo-reconnaissance flying, with Leuchars used for detachments when longer-term commitments were in the north. Benson must have been the only RAF station on which, over a period of just three years, eleven types were based. If we add the civil vintage Avro Club Cadet that was hangared there for a few months (see the next chapter) the station can claim to have been the home for a round dozen.

Photo-reconnaissance crews, specifically navigators, needed to aim for considerable precision in their work and almost all were very conscientious. On the other hand, most pilots were not unduly enthusiastic about flying just for flying's sake. On 58 we had a 'hack' Tiger Moth, N9449, which had spent most of its time standing in a corner of the hangar, seemingly unloved. By the time that I had been on the squadron for almost a month I had managed virtually to commandeer it. By taking a fitter or flight mechanic on the occasional flight I was safe in the knowledge that it would be well maintained and no one in higher authority made any attempt to prevent me from doing my own thing. I had a conspicuous – and I think attractive – red flash painted along each side of the engine cowling and this extended along the fuselage almost to the roundel. Later, by which time I had other aims for the squadron's Tiger, I had the front windscreen removed and the front cockpit covered over. I think I can claim that N9449 became the RAF's only single-seat Tiger Moth, with its own non-standard colour scheme. I was twenty-one years of age, but at no time did anyone ask any questions.

The Service provided some excellent flying and gave me the pleasure and essential experience that would be impossible to obtain in any other way. However, soon I realised that I could add to this by trying to satisfy a growing interest in aircraft of pre-war origin. I would visit selected civil aerodromes on my little BSA Bantam 125cc two-stroke motorcycle and see what might be on offer. Among the early ventures was a nose-around at Blackbushe. Then an airport, littered with Lancastrians, Dakotas, Vikings et al, it was home also to a smaller number of private types. In one corner I found a small two-man organisation, based in two ageing Nissen huts, that carried out engineering work on light aircraft – all in the open! Imagine my enthusiasm when I saw a 1935 Miles Falcon, G-ADFH, undergoing a ground run. I waited patiently until the occupant switched off and then approached him for a chat about unusual aeroplanes. I told him that I was a Mosquito pilot in the RAF (a useful door opener in those days) and keen to widen my experience. He asked if I had a civil licence. Yes, I had. 'This machine needs an air test for the renewal of its Certificate of Airworthiness; can you do it?' Yes, I could. After checking the minimum of paperwork, I was aboard and away. Flying life was far more informal then and when I taxied to the runway holding point, with no radio, a Lancastrian pilot waved me on to take-off ahead of him; due to my slow speed this must have caused him considerable delay. On the other hand, if he had gone first, I would have needed to wait for his slipstream to disappear.

The flight went well and I declared the machine fit for purpose. I liked the Falcon, an attractive low-wing cabin monoplane with a neat trousered undercarriage, with seating for three: the centrally seated pilot with ample space and accommodation for two side-by-side behind. DFH was in its original Miles pre-war colour scheme of cream with red trimming and had a sporting look. It was the time to be bold. 'This would be a good aeroplane to enter in an air race,' I said, admitting that I had no previous experience in the field, but I was keen to start. The unexpected but very welcome response was, 'OK, put it in the Daily Express Air Race along the south coast and just pay for the petrol.' Clearly, he was unaware that at that time Shell provided free fuel for all air racing! That encouraging and affable engineer was Doug Bianchi, who had just started Personal Plane Services and who became well known and helpful to people who owned or operated unusual aeroplanes on tight budgets. Very shortly he moved his set-up to better premises at White Waltham; today the company remains active at Turweston Aerodrome. I'll leave details of the race until Chapter 45.

My 'day job' on Mosquitos had to take priority and by then I had realised how fortunate I was: gaining invaluable experience on a type that augured well for the future and being based in an area surrounded by other aviation activity. The work proceeded fairly smoothly with few unintended setbacks, but on one flight, at 20,000 feet, the starboard engine chose to indulge in a series of surges that were far from comfortable. At lower level the problem disappeared, so almost certainly it was a snag related to the two-stage supercharger. A specific item was suspected and this was replaced. I launched on an air test, but the trouble was still there. Other possible causes were sought and off I went again, but with no improvement. By the fourth abortive attempt the squadron commander entered the scene and ordered the 'chiefy', a flight sergeant fitter 1 of considerable experience who mistrusted pilots' technical assessments and who disliked flying, to go up with me. He was sceptical about the whole affair, but at the critical height I treated him to a dose of surging that he would be unlikely to forget. 'Alright, alright,' he spluttered, 'that's enough. Take it down.' The eventual outcome? The fitter who should have carried out the original change had placed the offending item and its replacement side-by-side on a work bench and he had put back the original one. This is a well-known error and over the years must have cost vast sums, but I was not unhappy: I had gained a little more valuable Mosquito time to put in my logbook! Throughout my time flying Service and, later, civil Mosquitos, spread loosely over a total of fifteen years, this was the only engine-related problem that came my way. Yet by the end, I had carried out about 200 practice single-engine landings – all real fully feathered events, as there were no simulators. In view of unhappy incidents in recent years, airline operators please note!

I am not sure whether this very little exercise had any effect on my thoughts for the longer term, but I decided to test the water. I had the cheek to write to Group Captain John Cunningham, of wartime night fighter fame and then de Havilland's chief test pilot, asking if he would be having a vacancy for an entrant to the profession. To my pleasant surprise, he replied stating that he preferred people with Mosquito experience and he would be willing to see me. At that early stage I was rather raw, with only three hundred hours or so on the type, so what could I do to make an impact? By this time Doug Bianchi had made his move to White Waltham and he had obtained the only airworthy de Havilland Puss Moth, G-AAZP, of 1930. I had flown it a few times and he agreed that it could take me to Hatfield for the interview. Might this do the trick?

The meeting was pleasant and relaxed. Yes, I had the right stuff in my logbook, but not enough of it. I should come back in a year or so and there could well be something available. Then John Cunningham accompanied me to my steed, admired it, swung the propeller, removed the chocks and waved me off. Before doing this, though, he had asked me to do a fly-by so that he could see this old DH aeroplane in the air. Obviously I obliged. I knew that I was some way

A SQUADRON – AT LAST

short of being available or ready for such employment, but it was encouraging not to have been totally rejected and I wondered how much influence the elegant old Puss had provided: quite a lot, I think.

Life on the squadron was quite varied. Much of the work was routine high-level reconnaissance, sometimes calling for several parallel runs to form a map-style mosaic. This called for some tight precision by the navigator, who operated the cameras from his prone position in the nose. He would call, 'Left, left, steady, right a bit' as appropriate and sometimes he would be tempted to shout, 'back a bit!' Rather unnaturally the pilot needed to do his minor heading changes keeping the wings level, as any bank would offset the result. By contrast, sometimes the task was at low-level, usually using forward facing F24 cameras, pointing the aircraft at the target – often a bridge – and pulling up over it. At only twenty-one or twenty-two this was my favourite part of the work and occasionally I would extend the task without using the cameras to provide any evidence of my guilt. The Mosquito was the ideal aeroplane for low flying as it was fast, with an almost perfect forward view. Once, though, someone disliked being disturbed by a pair of Merlins at close quarters and clearly he knew how and where to lodge a formal complaint. On return to base my action demanded the attention of someone more senior than my squadron commander and I was 'invited' to see the Officer Commanding Flying Wing, who was Wing Commander (later Air Commodore Sir) Hughie Idwal Edwards VC. He had received the highest possible award for leading a low-level bombing raid with Blenheims on the port of Bremen, which was one of the most heavily defended towns in Germany. He was a hard man with a tin leg as a result of a parachute accident and some people were openly afraid of him, but he could not have been more reasonable. Very calmly he explained that he had no desire to harm my enthusiasm and he was satisfied that there had been no danger to anyone, but that we needed to have discipline – and keep the public on our side. My punishment awaited me on the following morning: I was instructed to carry out a low-level navigation exercise that was far too long for comfort – to get it out of my system. My respect for the boss was even more pronounced when, a few days later, despite his handicap, I watched him carry out an immaculate single-engine approach and landing.

Not all the flying was routine and sometimes the PR34's unique range proved invaluable. We would go on long sorties over Russia and Russian-occupied territory with some key targets to photograph. On one occasion and on the longest trip of all, Larry and I were sent to cover just one obviously important strategic site – a bridge. At the time the work was highly secret and as mere operators we were not privileged to know why the pictures were so important. This work was carried out under the code name 'Operation Dimple', so, more than seventy years later, I entered this on the computer to see what the web would tell me, to be rewarded with pictures of several rather spotty female faces and instructions on how to have these unsightly growths removed! I tried another route to the web and found what is possibly the only written reference that exists: 'Finally, from the late 1940s it is understood that Mosquito PR34s from No. 58 Squadron took part in Operation Dimple where, after refuelling in West Germany, long-range reconnaissance sorties were flown over East Germany and the Soviet Bloc. Although official records on these sorties have never been released, there is no evidence that any Mosquitos were shot down whilst engaged in these activities.' By now I think I am safe in confirming that this information is correct. Still, though, I wonder what treatment we would have received if forced down on Soviet territory; nominally we were at peace, so we would not have been entitled to prisoner-of-war rights. Would we have been shot as spies? It is of no consequence now, but no one seemed prepared to tell us!

Later chapters will provide detailed information on a considerable number of aircraft types, both Service and civil, but here I must mention the Mosquito in relation to squadron activities. Without doubt it was an exceptional aeroplane and it fulfilled all its allotted roles admirably, but it demanded careful attention, especially when flying on one engine. During my three years at Benson, I witnessed three fatal accidents on asymmetric approaches to land, all in almost exactly similar situations. They were undershooting and in each case the pilot applied power on the live engine in an attempt to reach the runway. Hard as it may seem, the instruction was not to do this, but to land short of the airfield even if this meant crashing the aeroplane onto rough ground. At low speed, if more than a mere trickle of power was put on, the aircraft would yaw into the dead side and the increased lift of the faster wing would lead to a rapid roll and a dive into the ground. On one occasion I was at the runway holding position prior to take off, awaiting another Mosquito that was on finals on one engine. From my position it was clear that it was undershooting and slow. I called to Larry, 'Look. He won't make it,' and at that moment it yawed, rolled and flew almost vertically into the undershoot, about 100 yards from where I was parked. The whole uncontrolled sequence took little more than three seconds and I could not have seen more clearly or closely a Mosquito doing its one bad thing. More often than not these nasty accidents occurred to pilots of considerable experience and in this case it was my unfortunate squadron commander and his navigator who came to grief.

There is a well-worn expression about 'adding five knots for the wife and kids' on approach speeds. Although at that time I had no such responsibilities, I tended as self-defence to adopt this practice. The worst that could happen would be to run off the upwind end of the runway, but that was unlikely; one would be alive to face any wrath and be able to argue the case.

All twins have minimum control speeds on one engine and these vary enormously. At the low end of the scale was the Anson and its behaviour was as tame as it could be. By chance I watched a colleague on a practice asymmetric approach and, to my surprise, he decided to attempt a go-around. Wheels and flaps were down and I could see no hope of success, but the Annie at full power 'on one' struggled for the length of the 2,000 yard runway, very slowly losing height but remaining almost straight and upright. At the upwind end of the airfield was one lone tree and slowly but gently the pilot settled the aeroplane onto it. Quite quickly the Rescue and Fire Fighting Service (to use the official title) arrived, joined two ladders and enabled the lone occupant to climb down. He was physically unscathed and the Anson looked only a little worse. I am not sure whether it flew again.

Chapter 5

The changing PR scene

The PR scene was changing. No. 541 Squadron's Spitfire 19s disappeared and were replaced by Meteor PR10s, which for high altitude performance reverted to the longer-span wings of the early marks. Their range and endurance, though longer than on fighter variants, were less than those of their piston predecessors, so the squadron moved to Germany, where they were closer to the centre of their work. The 19s, though, continued to serve for a further three years on Singapore-based 81 Squadron and even today they have not disappeared, as two are on the Battle of Britain Memorial Flight. This was a unique mark of Spitfire, not only unarmed but with three of the leading-edge ribs on each wing removed to accommodate extra fuel. 82's little-known Lancaster PR1s were progressively retired and the final one was detained at Benson awaiting a spare component. This delay may have saved it from the scrapman, for even today it survives – it is the famous PA474 also of the BBMF. I had a very minor involvement when eventually it was ferried to the Maintenance Unit at Wroughton, as I was given the humble task of following in an Anson to carry back the crew!

No. 58 Squadron too, had its change, but not to any swishy jets. As late as 1951 a new Mosquito variant emerged: the rare and little-known PR35. This was a bomber version modified to carry out night photographic trials using a new form of photoflash; the work could not be carried out by PR34s as they had large fuel tanks in their bomb bays. Only four PR35s entered RAF service and these were allocated to 58 Squadron's B Flight, on which at the time I was one of four pilots. It was not my favourite job, especially when a photoflash chose to

THE CHANGING PR SCENE

ignite in the bomb bay, but I liked exchanges between flights as these enlivened interest in the various tasks in which the squadron was involved. Among these was one that occurred (fortunately) before the last Lancaster left. A summer-long PR detachment at Leuchars was ending and there were several men and much equipment to be brought home. A Lanc was sent to do this, but soon it became clear that the total load was too much and I went in an Anson to take whoever and whatever was left. No one quite knew the extent of this and I received a mildly nervous briefing by the squadron commander. Seemingly the Leuchars CO had insisted that the lodgers on his station must not leave anything behind. The Lancaster captain insisted that he could take no more and he departed southwards, leaving me the balance of load, which included numerous packages, large and small, with no information about the contents, together with a handful of airmen. Officers and NCOs had crammed into the Lanc and there was no one to consult. I was in a quandary, as I had been ordered to 'clear the deck' and yet I had no authority to fly the aeroplane beyond its permitted limits. I decided that as I had a job to do, I would do it and later face any consequences. I made sure that as much weight as possible was loaded in the front of the passenger cabin and then I set off.

Three things were in my favour and I convinced myself that between them they would see me through: the weather was good and reasonably calm, but with enough wind to be helpful on take-off, the conveniently into-wind runway 28 was more than 2,000 yards long and, thankfully, my mount was an Anson, with its second-to-none reputation as a willing load carrier. There would be plenty of space in which to abort the take-off if there was any doubt about getting airborne.

Even when taxying, the unusual weight was noticeable. Energetic effort was needed by the Cheetah engines to get the package moving and the ride was hard, but we went ahead and the take-off was the longest that I have experienced with any Anson. Retaining higher than usual climbing power we reached 2,300 feet and I decided to settle for that. I just hoped that each Cheetah would continue to growl – and both did.

Eventually we arrived overhead Benson. As old Annie had been reasonably controllable throughout the flight, foolishly I had overlooked the likelihood that, with so much weight at the back, it would be impossible to trim out on the landing approach. Very quickly, though, this happened, and I called the two airmen in the rear seats to rush forward and stand in the cockpit entrance. They were, of course, not strapped in, but it was the only way to ensure an organised arrival on terra firma. All ended well, but there were some surprised comments from the ground crew regarding the load to be retrieved from the passenger cabin. I explained the reason and asked them to keep quiet about it. I heard no more.

Now you will be wondering why I have written so much about what should have been an unexciting routine flight. My reason is to cover a situation that any Service pilot could face. On the ground, rank dictates who does what and I am sure that my squadron commander ordered me in good faith 'not to leave anything behind.' He was not aware of exactly what needed to be retrieved, but presumably he hoped that it would amount to a permissible load. When a pilot starts up for a flight, though, the order is reversed and regardless of rank he is in command of the aeroplane. He gives the orders and everything is his responsibility, so in this instance I could have refused to accept an overloaded machine. If anything had gone wrong, I alone would have carried the proverbial can; my CO's orders would have provided me with little if any defence. This, I feel, is an issue that may not be understood as well as it could be, but I am not implying that it should be altered: a pilot, i.e. the captain, must be in charge of his ship, however large or small it may be. I learned a lot from that little exercise.

I have always been keen to try my ham hands on any aeroplane on offer and if the 'offer' element was missing I would seek it out. With 54 Group Communications Flight on the station I decided to find the flight commander and ask if I could fly one of his two Percival Proctors. I was prepared to try some persuasion and, if necessary, say that if he needed a pilot and I was not required on the squadron, I would fly for him. All this preparation, though, was unnecessary, for as soon as he saw me he said, 'Thank goodness you are here. I have got to get Group Captain X to Wyton for a meeting, time is short and I can't find a pilot. Jump into 157, do a couple of circuits and by the time you are back I will have found a copy of Proctor Pilot's Notes! Then pick up the Group Captain and go.' All went well and I am sure that my passenger remained unaware of how close he was to missing his meeting. At least it enabled me to log another type. I doubt that this could happen today.

Long before this I had been keen to become a flying instructor. I could see no likelihood of an early course at the Central Flying School, so during a conveniently long leave before my posting to 58 Squadron, I had enrolled with the Wiltshire School of Flying at Thruxton. Due to the time shortage I had arranged for an intensive course and I emerged with a rating. When not required by the Service, I familiarised myself with the aviation world outside and became an (voluntary/unpaid) instructor when certain organisations needed some extra help. This included the Surrey Flying Club which, with a pair of Piper L4 Cubs, was based in the famous roundhouse at a nice aerodrome with two good grass runways called Gatwick! I spent more time, though, with the West London Aero Club at White Waltham, where I could see more chances for finding interesting aeroplanes. The wait was short and I had not even envisaged the first one to come my way: Hugh Scrope, Company secretary to Vickers-Armstrong and a keen amateur pilot, had taken the bold step of buying the well-known Percival Mew Gull single-seat racer G-AEXF in which Alex Henshaw had beaten the out-and-back Cape record in 1939. I had known Hugh for some time and he told me his story. He had bought 'EXF in Southern France where it had spent the war years in hidden storage; he had it brought up to sufficient standard to obtain a one-flight ferry permit and then courageously, with relatively little experience as a pilot, mainly on Austers, flew it home. Shortly after this he asked if I would do him a favour. He had not seen his new possession in the air, so would I be kind and fly it around for him? I obliged, but I was slightly disappointed in the Mew's handling characteristics. It was not until later that I discovered the reason: it had not been restored and was still on its one-flight ferry permit! I will tell you some more about this in Chapter 28.

A few more pre-war aeroplanes were coming my way and I was beginning to feel a need for some 'organisation' to look after the interests of their owners and operators, failing which these interesting machines might be lost. I wrote a letter to the editor of *Flight* magazine asking for any interested readers to make contact. Quite by coincidence, on the same day, a similar letter appeared in *The Aeroplane*, which in 1951 was a weekly competitor to *Flight*. The writer was Ron Gillman, a Senior Training Captain with British European Airways who, as a hobby, ran a four-man syndicate that had just restored the 1932 Avro Avian G-ABEE based at Denham. We agreed to meet and decided to form a body that would confine its coverage to aircraft that had been out of production since before the war – the Vintage Aeroplane Club. At that time the club and private flying world was awash with Tiger Moths and Magisters and both had been built in quantity until relatively recently, so they were excluded. Soon we needed to make exceptions, though, especially when Vivian Bellamy turned up at our first gathering in the sole-surviving Gloster Gladiator G-AMRK! Swiftly after this Hawker's own Hurricane G-AMAU appeared, so we decided to treat each type on its historical merits. G-AMAU became a frequent participant in VAC events, together with Tomtit G-AFTA and Hart G-ABMR, thanks to the positive support and enthusiasm of Neville Duke, Hawker's Chief Test Pilot.

A little earlier I described my interest in the squadron's Tiger Moth. At that time, in September each year, almost every active RAF flying station laid on a commemorative Battle of Britain air display. Also, the various fighter squadrons of the part-time Royal Auxiliary Air Force, equipped mainly with Spitfire 16s and 22s, raced each other around the pylons in the Cooper Trophy Air Races. If the part-time Auxiliaries could do their thing, surely the full-time Service could go one better and compete with Mosquitos? Not surprisingly my 'too innovative' suggestion was rejected, but, as a consolation, I was authorised to organise (and take part in!) a race with the station's three Tiger Moths. I was given a free hand to choose the course, so it was all inside the airfield boundary, using the windsocks as two of the four turning points. With N9449 slightly 'refined', I had an unfair advantage, but officially, the aim of the exercise was to entertain the public and apparently they enjoyed the opportunity to see the little show at close range.

I was no expert in the specialist art of aerobatics, but I endeavoured to maintain a very modest level of competence in the basic manoeuvres. As a result, with no competition, I had been asked to display the Tiger. I restricted my schedule to items in which I could be reasonably confident that I would finish pointing in the right direction and, for this reason I omitted even the genuine slow roll; most biplanes are reluctant to go round innocently and, for me, the old girl would perform perhaps reasonably smoothly for two out of three and fall out (not literally) of one – and that one could well be the first! By keeping it simple with loops, rolls-off-the-top, stall turns and wingovers I thought that I had kept the party reasonably clean, but I was cut to size when an experienced flight commander from the neighbouring squadron said, 'I liked your crazy flying.' There is a vast difference between an aerobatic display and a crazy flying act, so I was not sure how to interpret his comment. I just hoped that he was unaware of that difference!

Not very long after this the Tiger Moth was formally withdrawn from RAF service and without warning all were grounded. For several weeks my old friend sat in the corner of the squadron hangar, but one day it had disappeared; only recently I learned that it had been exported to Australia where it eventually went to the RAAF Museum.

I had assumed that the idea of keeping a private aeroplane on a Royal Air Force airfield would be the privilege of the Station Commander, but on investigation I found that 'subject to the availability of space, Service personnel may have hangar accommodation at no charge.' Following the formation of the Vintage Aeroplane Club (VAC), we found the sole surviving Avro Club Cadet G-ACHP of 1933 and bought it for £75 through our good friend Doug Bianchi. It was not quite flyable, but for a similar sum he brought it up to standard for a new Certificate of Airworthiness. The newly formed VAC needed several months' grace (willingly granted) in which to pay even £150! I took advantage of the newly discovered clause in King's Regulations and for a few months kept 'CHP at Benson. It has its share of space at Chapter 22.

My allotted time on 58 Squadron was coming to an end and I was looking ahead to what might happen. Then two examples of Service life came to the fore – one surprisingly considerate, the other decidedly less so. Very much to my surprise the CO of Bomber Command Communications Squadron approached me and said that he had been watching my involvement with the world of historic aviation and clearly I would need to remain in the London area. He had a vacancy for a pilot and he could fix it that I would fill that post. It was a quite large unit, based at Booker (now Wycombe Air Park) with about fourteen aircraft of five types. That last figure appealed, but it seemed clear that the bulk of the work, especially for a newcomer, would fall to the Ansons, which offered nothing new.

I was doing a spot of self-deliberation when, unannounced, a brand-new Meteor T7 arrived. This was for 58's pilots to gain some jet experience, with the promise of Canberras to follow. I decided not to accept the kind offer of a transfer to Booker, as I would like to try my hands on a pair of Rolls-Royce Derwents. However, during the negotiating stage I managed to scrounge my first flight in a Chipmunk that had just arrived on the unit.

To show a touch of enthusiasm, I went to my squadron commander and asked when I could have my first flight in the Meteor. His response was that as I had only two months remaining on his unit I would not be included. I pleaded, to no avail, but the CO went on fourteen days leave and on the first day the flight commander entered the crew room, whispering, 'Don't say anything,' threw a copy of Meteor Pilot's Notes into my lap and said, 'See you in an hour.' With the boss away I was able to make good use of the limited available time. I am pleased that my helpful 'encourager' was recognised for his virtues, as within a few weeks he was promoted and given command of 81 PR Squadron!

THE CHANGING PR SCENE

At this time many things seemed to be in a state of flux. In addition to my Service flying I had participated in numerous civil events, including air racing. One keen competitor was Ron Paine, who was Technical Director of the Air Schools Group with training establishments at Wolverhampton, Derby, and a not very active subsidiary at Elstree. The RAF Volunteer Reserve had just expanded and had enlisted almost all the available instructors, so there was a shortage in the civil field. I was told that Elstree needed a dose of energetic enthusiasm and Ron asked if I would like the job. There was just the matter of extraction from the Service, which was problematical as it was 1952 and a King's Year was in force. This was a form of statute that could (and presumably can still) be brought into effect when a national emergency exists. At such a time all members of the forces were required to stay on strength for up to twelve months beyond their planned time of release; however, somehow the company Chairman, who was Member of Parliament for Derby and a retired Group Captain, worked the proverbial miracle. I would be released early but required to remain on the Reserve and devote fourteen days to the Service annually for a maximum of four years.

Clearly, I would miss the ambience relating to military aviation and I was resigned to flying light aircraft only, with progressively less of it and more time devoted to organisation and management. I reported for duty, to be met by my predecessor who had a severe dose of flu and greeted me with, 'So you're here at last. I feel awful and I am off.' That was my first and last meeting with him and I needed to learn the new job as a solo exercise. I had no idea that in the longer term some very welcome opportunities would arise. I was to be more fortunate than I deserved.

Chapter 6

Freedom?

This was a new world. Although, on a spare-time basis I had faced the very different ways of light aviation, clearly there was no organised control system to ensure any form of standards or standardisation. Behind me I had only six years of Service flying, but it was enough to enable me to invent my own ideas about the pros and cons of both forms of aeronautical life. I was only twenty-three, unattached and free to devote what seemed like 24/7 to developing my plans. Most probably my relatively youthful enthusiasm and determination caused me to jump ahead of reality, but I was not going to let go. I could see lots of scope ahead.

The place was scruffy, with the minimum of available office and general working space. The small fleet was in much better condition: three Auster Autocrats and a brace of Miles Hawk Trainers – the civil name for former RAF Magisters. We had no on-site servicing facility, but fortunately we had a contract with a 'two men and a boy' organisation named Light Aircraft Maintenance Services; they were conscientious, reliable and their charges were reasonable. That was about the best part of the local set-up. However, we had one strong line: we were a very small part of a long-established organisation. Throughout the Second World War, Air Schools Limited had operated Elementary Flying Training Schools at Wolverhampton and Derby (Burnaston) which had trained more than 14,000 pilots for the RAF. Although much scaled down to peacetime needs, the company continued to manage two RAF Reserve Flying Schools. Associated firms operated charter services, carried out extensive light aircraft maintenance and were branching into airline work, initially with

FREEDOM?

Rapides, as Derby Airways, but many years later becoming British Midland. Knowing that I was not restricted to the resources of the local candle-stick maker, I saw this as a chance to forge ahead with confidence.

Flying clubs and schools fell into two categories: their courses were either 'approved' or 'not approved'. For the former, an organisation needed to operate on a full-time basis, have certain minimum training facilities and be subject to an annual inspection by the local office of the Ministry of Civil Aviation. This gave a club the authority to train a candidate for a Private Pilot's Licence in only thirty flying hours, provided that it was carried out within a total time of six months. Not many people qualified in so few hours, especially as spinning and recovery were on the syllabus and, generally, the tail-down trainers of the time were more difficult to handle than most machines used today. Anyone learning on a non-approved course needed a minimum of forty hours. One advantage of the day, though, was that controlled airspace was virtually non-existent and there were far fewer other restrictions.

A significant advantage in running an approved course was that an organisation could apply for a contract with the Air Ministry to train ATC/CCF cadets for their PPLs under the Flying Scholarship scheme. The syllabus needed to be completed in thirty hours and only in an exceptional case could this be extended to a maximum of thirty-three. To avoid struggling in the later stage, a cadet would be assessed at nine hours and if he was not at or very close to first solo he would be suspended. Only selected aircraft, mainly ex-Service trainers, could be used, parachutes were worn, and the course included stopping the engine in flight and diving hard to restart the propeller. Instructors needed to be tested and approved by examiners of the RAF Central Flying School. This may sound a bit restrictive, but it was disciplined and provided a source of additional income. A by-product allowed a private pilot with at least 100 hours as pilot in command to apply for approval to give air experience flights to cadets who were not selected for PPL courses. About half the cost was covered by the Air Ministry, but few pilots were keen to take advantage of the cheap flying and the scheme was abandoned.

Many other favourable benefits existed. The Government was keen to encourage airmindedness and all flying training for the PPL was exempt from fuel tax. Sensibly, this was handled in a manner that made it impossible to fiddle the system: petrol at the pump was bought at the full price and the tax relief was claimed in arrears on the basis of an average consumption for each aircraft type used. The scheme was an initiative of the Association of British Aeroclubs and Centres, which handled the administration. This enabled training organisations to sell flying at little more than £3 per hour!

Bringing the cost to some individuals even lower was the result of another brainwave for the ABAC. The so-called works flying scheme allowed any company to claim exemption from tax on money used to subsidise staff to learn to fly. One condition was that the facility must be available on an equal basis to anyone in the organisation from the Chairman to the cleaner. The only stigma was one that would not be tolerated today: people flying under this scheme were not made members of the related club and were not permitted to use the social facilities, so, in some cases, basic huts were provided in which they could carry out their 'works' habits! Some companies continued to subsidise their employees' flying, but many years ago the whole idea was scaled down extensively.

The future seemed bright. Central London was only about twelve miles away, but little effort had been made to capture the inhabitants and get them into cockpits. Quite rightly I needed to work to a firm budget, but one early expenditure produced disappointing results. I had 100 double-crown posters spread all over the underground rail system and awaited the crowds, but despite the design winning a London Transport direct-sell award, clearly the commuting public preferred other ways to spend its money. I was reluctant to risk real sums on national newspapers as my little insert would be lost amongst the many other attractions, but I gave it a try with some inexpensive classified advertisements. Fortunately, these fared better than I had expected. Quickly I learned that getting people into the air was a more fickle task than it should be, but soon I realised the value of press releases. The wastage rate is enormous, but by soaking the market regularly the occasional take-up

FREEDOM?

can generate very worthwhile results. Although largely overtaken by new technology, I am pleased that some organisations continued to place value on the hard copy of the written word.

The overall task was both interesting and challenging. Although I had gained limited experience with the world of private and club flying, mainly I had been accustomed to the organisation and standards of the Service. Despite my occasional and youthful break-away from laid-down practices and procedures, I had gathered a strong feeling towards the importance of flying discipline, and I took the risk of introducing some of this to our civil pupils; whether an aeroplane had military roundels or G-A... on its skin, it used the same airspace, often the same aerodromes and flew over the same inhabited areas.

Intentionally we charged similar rates for flights with or without an instructor, for as part of our campaign for safety and standards we called for students, and especially recently qualified pilots, to have fairly frequent check flights with instructors and they tended to accept them readily. I had considerable sympathy for the self-payer. Many private pilots are heavily under-trained, but many are not aware of it and yet for their own sakes I would resist any official demand for a longer course.

Elstree was not an easy place at which to learn (or teach) on tailwheel types, but in those days it had not only the present east-west (27/09) hard runway, but also a north-east/south-west (04/22) grass strip; this was short and rough with handicaps at each end in the form of a reservoir literally touching one aerodrome boundary and a row of tall electricity pylons too close to the other end. However, the alternative take-off and landing directions enabled us to continue training when the crosswind on the main runway would have proved too severe for aircraft types designed to operate from omni-directional grass sites. Also, the Auster Autocrat had brake pedals for the left-hand occupant only, so a newcomer needed to have the first few lessons in the right seat and transfer to the correct side when (s)he had grasped the basic principles of taxying.

One of many changes from Service life was the need to find and pay for one's accommodation. My work at Elstree occupied most hours of the day and occasionally into the night, so I needed to live close to the job. Almost by chance I found that my former housemaster at Aldenham had retired to a nice house next to the Battleaxes pub, about 200 yards from the end of the runway, so I approached him, still as 'Sir', to see if he could accommodate me. He could. His wife had not lost her culinary skills, so when I was free a good evening meal compensated for snacks that were grabbed during the day.

I stayed there for about four years and one evening in the third of these, relaxing over a newspaper, I was called to the telephone. 'Are you sitting safely? Don't jump off your chair,' said the familiar voice of Ron Paine, the group's Derby-based Technical Director and my boss. 'Would you like to fly Mosquitos again?' – short pause – 'Yes or No?' 'Of course I would,' I replied, wondering what it was all about and whether I could cope after flying only singles and the Miles Gemini light twin since leaving the Service. Derby Aviation had won a contract to collect ten Mosquitos from the RAF Maintenance Unit at Silloth in Cumberland, fly them to Derby, overhaul and convert them for specialist air survey work and deliver them to Prestwick, from where a professional ferry pilot would take them to Canada via Iceland. I would do the internal ferrying and flight testing, but I must not forget that I had a flying school to run. Fortunately, by then, the little unit at Elstree had expanded and I could leave the routine work to a very capable deputy. My main concern, though, was the gap of three years since I had handled a brace of Merlins and all that went with them. However, the influential company Chairman managed to arrange for me to have a refresher check flight on a T3 with the RAF Home Command Examining Unit at White Waltham. The day came and I was making progress but seeking more when after just three circuits my one-off mentor said, 'You don't seem to have forgotten how to do it. That will do.'

Before long I was at Silloth to do the first test/acceptance flight on a recently released B35, still in its Service camouflage but with the Canadian civil registration CF-HMN splashed over the fuselage roundels. All went well and later in the day I took it to Burnaston, then a pleasant but not very big grass airfield. Surprisingly, the arrival marked the first occasion on which a Mosquito had landed there. From my viewpoint the whole programme went smoothly and I had no serious problem on any of the batch, but the trans-Atlantic ferry pilot was not so fortunate, as on one machine a supercharger disintegrated when over the ocean and he needed to do an asymmetric landing on Iceland in far from favourable weather conditions.

The task was spread over about five months with the time devoted roughly equally between the Mossies and the school at Elstree, often leading to a series of seven-day weeks, but the great variety of the action suited me, so I was quite happy with it all. The ten Mosquitos served for several years with Spartan Air Services of Ottawa and one of the batch became a bit special to me. Registered CF-HMS, it had been RS700 which I had flown on 58 Squadron several years previously. Surprisingly, someone discovered this, presented me with an accurate scale model and departed without revealing his name. To this day, approaching seventy years later, it remains on display in my bedroom.

Although Spartan carried out a successful and extensive survey of some remote parts of Canada, progressively the Mosquitos came to grief, with four destroyed in flying accidents, three fatal. Long before this, though, I had returned to my normal work at Elstree, which continued to expand, although occasionally I went back to Burnaston for some interesting ventures. A subsidiary of Derby Aviation known as Derby Aerosurveys had a contract to carry out a magnetometer survey in central Africa and for the purpose had acquired the last remaining airworthy Anson 1. Registered G-AMDA (formerly N4877) it was based at Blackpool, and I went to fetch it. I had some experience on late mark Ansons and assumed that this, together with a briefing from the chief engineer there, would suffice. However, I was baffled to find four (unlabelled) fuel levers on the old bird, whereas the more recent versions had only two. My mentor told me not to worry as he would set them for the flight with no need to change until I turned them off at Derby. I had checked that there was more than enough petrol in the centre tanks and set off.

The Anson 1 called for 160 turns of a handle in order to retract the undercarriage. I had left the wheels down and was about to begin the long process when the port engine stopped. I called that I was returning on one, soon to discover that the elderly bird was not very willing to maintain height in this wheels down condition, but fortunately the airfield was close and a steadily descending circuit and approach produced a reasonable result. I was just criticising the machine for being unfair to a pilot on his first flight on the type, when the engineer came running across the airfield, entered the cockpit and apologised profusely: despite several years' experience with the machine, he realised that he had set the fuel levers wrongly and that my port engine had been on the outer instead of the almost full main tank. He convinced me that his re-setting was correct and I tried again to get 'MDA to Derby – this time successfully. You may think that I had been remiss not to try changing tanks and you may be right, but I had been unable to discover what each lever did and I had visions of the other engine stopping. Later I found that the fuel controls were not in a logical order!

This uninspiring introduction to the world's only remaining Mark 1 Anson was the start of an unexpected and long relationship. After it was overhauled and equipped for its task in Africa, I was asked to do the first flights with the magnetometer and I experimented with dangling 'the bird' at different positions and with varying lengths of cable. The scientific side of this was way beyond my understanding and I did just the flying, but it enabled me to look more fully at the qualities of this first mark of Anson.

Back at Elstree the pilot training activities continued to grow, as did the aircraft fleet. I and one of my colleagues were authorised to conduct flying instructor courses and as these called for working to higher standards than were required for training private pilots, I enjoyed them. One day a young lady appeared and said that she had sufficient experience as a pilot to train to be an instructor and could we provide the course. I replied that I would need to give her a flying test to see if there were any rough edges to smooth off, but was pleased to find that she flew very well and could start straight away. I preferred to train instructors in pairs so that they could carry out some 'mutual' exercises in which they could practice on each other.

FREEDOM?

Fortunately, a young man appeared seeking similar advanced training and he, too, flew well. Both completed their courses and passed their tests and I was able to take them on strength, each in a part-time capacity. They had 'day jobs', so they would come at weekends and on summer evenings. And Reader, I married her!

One very welcome but unintended reward with the job was the number of opportunities to try my greedy hands at visiting aircraft. The first of these was when a helicopter instructor arrived in a Bell 47 and asked if I would like a spot of dual. This was to be my first attempt at handling a rotary-wing machine and I was aware that several pupil pilots had gathered outside in the hope that they would see me make a hash of it. They were not disappointed! Soon one of Derby's Rapides landed and was due to wait for an hour or so before picking up some charter passengers. The pilot was happy for me to fill the gap and give me my first opportunity to fly this delightful twin-engine biplane. Unfortunately, in an unwise attempt to do a three-pointer I endured the type's wing dropping tendency on touchdown, but no harm was done except to my pride. As CFI/Manager I was not expected to do embarrassing deeds in public! I learnt my lesson though and was more cautious on several subsequent Rapide flights.

A bulbous Miles Aerovan landed and taxied to the pumps. I was determined not to miss this and I made a bee-line to the pilot before he stepped out. Yes, I could take it for half an hour while he went for some coffee. He showed me the fuel cocks and sent me off. I tell you what this was like in Chapter 40. Less straightforward, though, was the arrival of an Italian Piaggio P136 amphibian. The English sales pilot came straight to me and asked if I had done any flying from water and, if not, would I like to have a go on the River Medway? I managed five take-offs and landings, under strict guidance, which became my total experience of needing to remember not to lower the wheels on the downwind leg!

The most exotic of the visiting aircraft that came within my reach was sent by intent. By this time I was on the Pilotage Committee of the ABAC and the Chairman thought that I should see how other countries designed and built trainers. The subject was the Czech Zlin

Trener, which in appearance was not unlike a Chipmunk. However, when a demonstration pilot fired into action he rolled inverted immediately after take-off and climbed to about 2,000 feet before reverting to the erect. From there he carried out a lively sequence of aerobatics – some conventional and others far from it – before returning to terra firma and saying, 'Your turn now.' I was pleased that I had not been with him during his performance as almost certainly my stomach would have failed to cope, so I climbed away (the right way up) to a spot well out of sight and made my own very personal mistakes while discovering what the Zlin was all about. The feature that was new to me was the ability to fly inverted with the engine running as happily as it did in the normal attitude. Despite its special qualities, for normal flying I preferred the Chipmunk.

I insisted that these appearances by visiting aeroplanes were useful in broadening my experience, but equally I was aware that there was some serious work to do.

My mind was strongly geared to the work on hand and I forgot that I had a Reserve commitment to the Royal Air Force. I received instructions to report to No. 187 (Ferry) Squadron at Aston Down and was surprised to learn that, if I wished, I could be taken there by air. In those days there was little concern about cost and at the allotted time the statutory Anson arrived and I was the sole occupant of the passenger cabin. I was not much use to the unit as I was not in current practice on Service types, but I was asked to collect a very early production piston Provost from the Percival factory at Luton (then a grass airfield) and deliver it to Ternhill, the first RAF station to receive the type. There were no Pilot's Notes, a Percival fitter did his best and I set off. The rate of climb was surprisingly good, though it was found some time later that at high power settings the Alvis Leonides shed cylinder heads, which was not conducive to happiness on a pilot's first solo, so the take-off boost was reduced. At later dates I flew the Provost at the lower output, but it was pleasant to have this one experience in the machine's original form.

During my time with Air Schools, based mainly at Elstree, there were several outside activities that helped to keep me occupied with aviation activity. Starting in 1950 I participated in the majority of available air races, all of which in the UK were operated, or at least supervised, by the Royal Aero Club. The majority of these were handicap events over a variety of lengths and laps, but a few were scratch races in which all entrants were of one aircraft type and were flagged off at the same time. I have devoted Chapter 45 to the subject in detail as it is a specialist subject and one about which most aviation people have little or no knowledge. I have participated in races with as few as three or as many as seventy-five entries and as usual I was very fortunate to be able to do so when I feel that there was no better time to have the experience: many of the machines that competed in 1938 survived the Second World War and reappeared with the return of peace. Such single-seat stalwarts as the Comper Swift, Miles Hawk Speed Six and Percival Mew Gull regenerated the earlier atmosphere and I have included handling reports that I hope will be of interest to today's readers.

Chapter 7

Development

Many things were changing. Following a main spar failure on a Proctor, most wooden aircraft were subjected to some severe restrictions. Our Gemini, G-AJTL, on which we had provided twin-engine conversion training at little over £5 per hour, failed a glued joint test and repairs would be unacceptably expensive, so it was grounded. More seriously, though, all Magisters were declared unsuitable for further use on public transport work (which, wrongly, pilot training was considered to be) and we had less than a year, to the expiry date of each machine's annual Certificate of Airworthiness, to find successors. Fortunately, the RAF declared its first batch of Chipmunks for release and without doubt this would be an ideal type to use. However, the airworthiness authority of the day thought otherwise, calling for extensive and expensive modifications before the military machines could be declared safe for civil use, as explained in the next chapter.

We were becoming busier. Clearly there was plenty of business to be captured and we needed to expand the resources. Perhaps this would be a good time to introduce a firmer regime and stress more positively the responsibilities that any pilot – private or professional – should accept. This involved strengthening the importance of flying discipline. Understandably, some people disliked this and moved away to find more of a 'club atmosphere', but before long we were able to welcome others who appreciated that all flying should be taken seriously. It is a fallacy that discipline and enjoyment are incompatible, and there is no need to adopt 'the customer is always right' policy. We explained that this was in the pupil's interest,

DEVELOPMENT

especially for the longer term, but also in the early training stages. An instructor welcomes a trainee's mistakes, so long as (s)he learns from them and avoids frequent repetition of the same errors. This could be brought home very readily by holding a Bank note (in those days just £1) and saying that in effect you have just thrown this overboard, so think about what you have done and avoid wasting this next one. Whatever anyone may think about this policy, on most people it worked.

Progressively my work became more desk-bound, but I made my best efforts to maintain some cockpit time in instructional and testing roles, to which I added some activity in support of my lifelong interest in historic aircraft. After a while I needed to resign from running the Vintage Aeroplane Club (VAC), as my paid work and this voluntary task together required more hours than I could muster, but I was very fortunate to receive an almost unbelievable and unrefusable offer: a gentleman named Jack Linnell was the owner of the diminutive Comper Swift G-ABUS and was reluctant to dispose of it, so he sought someone younger to take it on, treat it as his own and return it when he had finished with it. Would I like to be that person? This attractive little single-seat aeroplane called Black Magic had become well-known in air racing circles and the kind owner hoped that I would continue to pace it around the pylons! I had enjoyed racing in a number of mainly borrowed mounts, but here was a chance to keep at it in one of the only two active survivors of a 1930 machine designed specifically for the job. I will return to the Swift in later chapters.

Although the VAC had a short life, solely because no one was willing or able to fill the essential posts when vacancies arose through pressure of work, after a fairly short break the Vintage Aircraft Club was formed. While this introduced slightly different aims it flourishes today and long may it continue to do so. Though I have the privilege of an honorary position, I cannot claim credit for its success and I am concentrating my attention in this book on organisations with which I have had some form of front line involvement. In the main these will be the Vintage Aeroplane Club, the Derby Aviation/Air Schools

Group and the Shuttleworth Collection, although I have ventured into a writer's ramble into the overall world of general aviation.

Back to work. By now business was buzzing, but margins in the pilot training world were small and it was difficult to explain the potential value of a large investment in expansion. However, we needed a more professional face and I was challenged to find a suitable name for the operation. The best that I could offer was the London School of Flying Ltd and this was accepted, together with the Midland School for the then smaller training unit at Derby. New facilities were essential and after some delay I was authorised to design and place an order for a compact building that would combine offices, lecture rooms, D4 Link, catering facilities and sleeping accommodation for the growing number of professional pilot trainees now coming on strength. By now the ageing Maggies had gone, and, although we needed to charge a higher hourly rate for this slightly more refined machine, people took more readily to the Chipmunk.

The whole organisation, from the Chairman down, worked on the principle of having just enough staff to carry out the required tasks, but with no employed passengers. Throughout my working life I have liked and supported this, so why not extend it to the aeroplanes? Checking other users' figures, most Chippies on flying clubs and schools, also those in the RAF, were being put to work for between 350 and 450 hours per annum. This, I thought, gave us an opening to take on much more business without the need to acquire more aircraft. The Chipmunk made no objection to the idea and proved itself a willing workhorse. In one calendar year we monitored each Elstree based machine's achievement and, of five aircraft, the best topped 1250 hours and the slackest 960. The only drawback to this high intensity of use was that if one aeroplane was out of service for any length of time there were some mildly unpopular operating problems, but these were economically preferable to having, perhaps, twelve Chipmunks each at the high end of the national average of, say, 450 hours.

The Austers on the training fleet fared less favourably, for they were more wind sensitive and became in less demand once the Chipmunk became the centre of attention. They had been upgraded, though, as they had started life as Autocrats powered by 100hp Cirrus Minor IIs and had been converted at Derby into Alphas with the ubiquitous and more reliable Gipsy Majors of 130hp. Although there was relatively little increase in speed, the climb rate was improved substantially and with three people aboard a full flap go around became much less stressful! Before the conversion, though, our parent organisation had worked with Auster Aircraft and Blackburn Engines to solve an uncomfortable tendency on Cirrus engines to suffer crankshaft failure on the climb. This was overcome by removing the original relatively coarse-pitch wooden propellors and replacing them by Fairey Reed metal units. With the older equipment, 2,200rpm, obtainable at almost full throttle, was regularly used and, for reasons beyond my ken, this setting created excessive crankshaft whip leading to failure. The metal propellors were happiest at 2,300 and as far as I am aware there were no further failures.

The Austers continued to serve a useful purpose, for we had an agreement with an Elstree-based company called Photoflight to provide an aeroplane and pilot whenever they were required. One machine, G-AGXT, had been modified with a removable panel in the rear perspex, for the benefit of the sideways facing photographer. In due course the owner of Photoflight retired, so we bought his small firm and its work.

For some time we had no facility to provide twin-engine conversions and this was becoming increasingly critical. The extensive magnetometer survey in Africa had been completed and the ageing Anson 1, G-AMDA, was given the training task. Not surprisingly, this rather cumbersome veteran was of considerable attraction to onlookers but was not suited to the work. Reluctantly I insisted on its withdrawal, and it was replaced initially by an Anson 19 and later by a more practical but far less interesting Piper Apache.

I was becoming concerned about the likely future for the old Anson. It was the world's only airworthy Mark 1 (of 9000 built) and it might fail to find a good home. Fortunately, though, a very determined and dedicated Welshman named Peter Thomas, who already had played a significant part in saving a Sunderland flying boat at Pembroke Dock, was taking the bold step of opening his own aviation museum at Staverton (now Gloucestershire Airport). He intended to acquire some appropriate former military machines and keep them flying, but he had very limited financial resources. My overlords at Derby agreed to sell the Anson to him for a nominal £50 and somehow I found myself involved in the overall deal, to be one of his two honorary display pilots. The other was John Schooling, one of the two people mentioned in the previous chapter whom I trained as instructors and who started teaching at Elstree in part-time capacities. John, though, had joined the staff and now was the CFI.

Peter called his new venture Skyfame. We helped him to acquire an exceptionally clean Airspeed Oxford, which was an important feature as the type was very sensitive to dents and bumps on the engine cowlings, the wing root fairings and the small area of wing in between. In Chapter 31 I deal with the handling qualities and explain why I think that a good Oxford is one of the most satisfying of all aeroplanes to fly in a display. As with the Anson 1, this was the world's only remaining airworthy example. A third but essentially key aircraft in the Skyfame collection was a Mosquito B35 that had been used in making the film '*633 Squadron*'. I was privileged to serve as a display pilot on all three Skyfame aircraft. Also, when the flying sequences for the film had been completed, the makers discovered that the sound from some take-off and landing sequences was missing, so I spent an enjoyable day 'bashing the circuit' at Bovingdon, including attempts to make wheel contact immediately alongside the recording microphone. As I could see that almost certainly this would be my last opportunity to fly the wooden wonder, I may have stretched the task just slightly!

Throughout my time with the Derby Aviation/Air Schools Group I was able to enjoy ample variety. In addition to the school machines and various aeroplanes that visited Elstree, I was (happily) asked to fly some interesting machines on behalf of the parent company. These included several air tests and ferry flights, on a rare Fairchild Argus, taking an Airspeed Consul to Derby from the sadly but inevitably

DEVELOPMENT

dying Croydon Airport, testing a Chipmunk for the Irish Air Corps, and flying a Mosquito from Shawbury to our works for a lady who intended, but due to sponsorship withdrawal failed, to tackle a speed record over the Pacific Ocean. This machine, G-AOSS, sat forlornly for a couple of years on a corner of the airfield and, alas, then was burned on a Guy Fawkes night.

Perhaps the best 'catch' was a historic machine that I had yearned to fly, owned by my boss Ron Paine. This was the 1935 Miles Hawk Speed Six single seat racer G-ADGP that I had met around the pylons at several events, but which its proud owner kept strictly for his own hands. Imagine my disbelief as I walked along the front of the main works hangar, to be called by the Chief Inspector asking if I had time to do an air test for a C of A renewal. I said that it depended on what aircraft needed testing. With a look of glee he opened a hangar door, revealed the unique racer and said, 'Will that do?' Of course I had time. Apparently, the airworthiness inspector was coming that afternoon, the flight test results needed to be available for him to see and my boss was away. I am convinced that this was an intentional and kindly act by a fellow staff member who knew of my earlier frustration.

By now the set-up had expanded further and I was responsible for three training units, with the London School at Elstree, the Midland at Derby and a small offshoot of the London School at Denham. All three were equipped with an interchangeable fleet of light blue Chipmunks and Auster Alphas, and the single Apache at Elstree. Major maintenance work was carried out at Derby, which also was the base of the airline operations of Derby Airways, itself becoming a substantial operation with an eventual name change to British Midland. As evidence that the whole operation was a tight package and used any staff member on any task that might seem appropriate, in the early days of scheduled services I was asked to see the Chairman in the London office, to be told to prepare the publicity and promotional material for a new midweek route between Derby and Glasgow. It seemed a strange choice of destination, but it was to be subsidised by Rolls-Royce who would buy a number of seats each day whether or not they were used. The whole operation was gloriously informal, using the first of the company's eight DC3s, G-ANTD, with a husband and wife (Captain and stewardess) team forming two-thirds of the crew, operating from the grass airfield. Twice a day an accountant would leave his office and climb into the miniature control hut to provide the air traffic service. In winter the evening return flight would arrive after dark and a gooseneck flare path was laid out on the grass by hand. This basic vintage service proved very reliable, without any known incident.

Throughout my years with Derby Aviation and later, I endeavoured to keep my roving mind on anything that I had the nerve to think should be changed. Flying remained a key part of the process and closely related activities played important roles. Whilst I accepted that bar talk could be interesting, in general terms it served little in the way of getting things done. I became deeply involved with the Association of British Aero Clubs and Centres and its absorption with the aviation side of the Royal Aero Club to form the British elements of the, till then, American-only Aircraft Owners and Pilots Association. A Board comprising six members from each side set to work and I was by far the youngest, with the background of the former Vintage Aeroplane Club to help me look after the needs of owners and operators of machines that had been produced before the Second World War.

After almost fourteen years in the post, during which, progressively, the job had changed enormously, I was looking ahead to see where we could go next. I had enjoyed organising an annual flying display, nominally as a public relations move to keep the local residents on side, and I made every effort to include whatever I could find in the way of veteran and vintage aircraft. On most such events I finished the show with the Spitfire 5b AR510, which for much of the time – owned and operated by its makers Vickers Supermarine – was the only flyable specimen of its type. Today this machine serves with the RAF Battle of Britain Memorial Flight, and airworthy Spitfires number in their dozens!

The Derby based organisation, of which pilot training was a relatively small part, seemed to me to be functioning as well as any

DEVELOPMENT

private group of aviation companies could expect, but the airline side, by then British Midland Airways, was being prepared as a saleable business. After considerable discussion, the then Board decided to put the whole package on the market and this would include the schools. The Directors were far from young and I think they were seeking more peaceful lives.

The Midland School was phased out and the London School was in new hands as a stand-alone body. There was no technical or other back-up facility and the new owner had no practical aviation experience. I was not happy with the attitude towards flying training and although I was retained as a Director, I could see clashes of standards on the – not so distant – horizon.

For the 1966 display at Elstree, I had hired a couple of historic aeroplanes from the Shuttleworth Collection at Old Warden and Air Commodore Allen Wheeler, the Aviation Trustee, appeared. He attended the pilots' briefing and could be seen taking a strong interest in all that was happening. It was in the days before the Civil Aviation Authority ruled that a display organiser must not fly in the show, so I gained some pleasure from demonstrating the Skyfame Oxford. I should add that the organiser's post had not been abandoned, for I insisted on a formal temporary handover to my deputy, and I always found this to be a satisfactory course of action. When activities quietened down, I was approached by the Air Commodore, who said that Shuttleworth's manager was about to retire and would I like the job?

This came as a great surprise. Naturally I had taken an interest in the Shuttleworth Collection, but this had been at a distance. It had been started quite privately by Richard Ormonde Shuttleworth, son of a successful maker of steam engines who had built aeroplanes during the First World War. Richard developed a deep interest in veteran cars and built up a worthwhile range of very early vehicles, most of which have been retained to this day and participate in a parade as part of what has developed. The Collection has its own workshop in which restoration, maintenance, and operational tasks are conducted mainly by a team of devoted volunteers.

FLYING AND PRESERVING HISTORIC AIRCRAFT

The bulk of the earliest aircraft in the aviation collection had been built up by Richard Shuttleworth in the very late twenties and through the thirties as a very personal project alongside the cars with which he had started. Some of these were incomplete when war brought it all to a halt and others were dismantled to save space. The hangars were mainly used for repairing military Harvards and Richard joined the RAF to qualify as a Service pilot. Although he had obtained his wings he was not quite ready to join an operational squadron and was carrying out a night navigation exercise in a Fairey Battle light bomber when he flew into the hill at the back of Old Warden aerodrome and was killed outright. The precise details of the accident have never been revealed, but immediately after the war this led to the formation of the Richard Ormonde Shuttleworth Remembrance Trust, a charity to be devoted to aviation and agriculture. Unfortunately, due to the vast land-owning element of the new organisation, the latter and the Shuttleworth Agricultural College attracted all the attention and the funds, so there was a heavy task ahead to get the priorities reversed.

Despite their significance, the aeroplanes were a relatively unloved entity. Most remained dismantled so that they could be transported by road when booked to appear at displays. There was very little flying at the aerodrome, which had been reduced in size and was very rough; the Collection was not even open to the general public, but the then manager, Leonard Jackson, who had been Richard's first paid employee and had been there for most of his working life, except for the war when he served as an engineering officer, would take selected groups on conducted tours. He refused to accept visitors other than people with aviation interests, such as students at the nearby Cranfield College of Aeronautics, now Cranfield University.

All this needed to be changed very quickly and at that time the only, very limited, income came from companies who subsidised their earlier products, but as the established aircraft industry was about to be closed, or absorbed in the new more impersonalised group, I was told that my key priority must be to put the Collection on a self-supporting basis. I accepted the job on these terms, but was unsure how difficult this would be; the retiring manager came in two or three

DEVELOPMENT

times a day and put up a CLOSED sign at the entrance, and this was designed to obliterate any publicity material that I had prepared. This went on for several weeks until, in desperation, I persuaded the Air Commodore to threaten to stop my predecessor's pension unless he ceased to be obstructive. Fortunately, that worked.

The big disadvantage of the Shuttleworth Collection General Manager position was the unbalanced structure of the Trust with a concentration of funding and operation on farming. With Allen Wheeler as the only aviation representative among the six Trustees, it was hard to get things done. All efforts were in favour of Shuttleworth College, even to the use of land. The College Principal physically moved fences to the extent of reducing the size of the aviation environment, especially the landing run. One day I happened to be out on the manoeuvring area and saw that a wire fence had been placed across the landing run – unlikely to be noticed by a visiting pilot – so I removed it one evening when all others had gone and tucked it in a safe area, but the next day found it resurrected. That evening I dismantled it again, put it into the back of my car and took it home. It was still in my garden shed ten years later. Before this I had got the Royal Engineers to reroute Aston Brook to extend 04/22 runway by around 180 yards as a training exercise! There was a constant battle of College vs Collection and one of the Principal's favourite habits was to place cattle on the aerodrome just before a flying event. After much argument I managed to get a ruling that by arrangement he could graze sheep but not cattle on the airfield.

Although infuriating, the overall unbelievable (mis)management enabled me to tackle many tasks without, I learnt quickly, any approval from anyone. When fairly new in the Shuttleworth job, I felt that I would miss the Miles Magister trainer on which I had instructed for several years; one specimen was still flying and I tracked down the owner, who was quite willing to sell it. It was in poor condition and I knocked a little off his asking price, bought it for the Collection and slotted it quickly into the workshop programme to prevent the deal backfiring. No questions were asked and after about two years it emerged, fully restored, with its Service serial P6382. The only order regarding flying given to me by the lone Aviation Trustee was that whenever I intended to include the First World War Avro 504K trainer in a display programme I should ask him if he wanted to fly it before allocating it to any other pilot. He had trained from scratch on original rotary-engined 504Ks very shortly after that war. The only general limitations imposed on me regarding all flying carried out by the Collection's aircraft was one with which I agreed wholly: that if there was any doubt about the weather as to whether or not a specific machine should be flown, the answer should always be dictated on the safe side. Before I took the job I obtained the Air Commodore's authority to fly any type whenever I could see a reason, but no machine was to be flown purely for personal pleasure. After all, almost every aircraft was the world's sole surviving flyable specimen of its type and I placed much value on this.

Keeping a fleet of historic aeroplanes in airworthy condition called (and still calls) for many disciplines: a small team of conscientious and caring aircraft engineers skilled in wood and metal; a supply of useable components for types up to 100 years old, or the ability to reverse engineer, making a new component from the worn components of an old item; a wide knowledge of what may be where for possible exchanges, and an ability to negotiate – tactfully!

Then we must consider pilots who have good judgement as strongly as flying ability, flexibility and a strong respect for the often sole surviving specimen of a machine that they may be called upon to fly. When I joined the Shuttleworth Collection staff in 1966 I was a relative junior in the flying world as we had no fewer than seven professional test pilots, mostly in senior positions in the airframe manufacturing industry, who happily devoted considerable time and attention to the cause, all entirely voluntarily. All that I could offer was some experience with historic types because I had been co-founder of the Vintage Aeroplane Club and I was particularly grateful to Wing Commander Dicky Martin, then Chief Test Pilot for the Gloster Aircraft Company; soon after I came aboard, he became the Collection's Senior Pilot. He had the knack of familiarising someone with a rare, strange type and doing so with the minimum of fuss.

DEVELOPMENT

Another case of help from Dicky was on one summer evening when we were in an upstairs office that overlooked the aerodrome, about to 'shut the shop', appreciating the calm conditions of the moment, when, purely by chance, we spoke simultaneously with the precise words, 'This is the time that we should be flying these aeroplanes,' and decided, there and then, that we would put this into practice. We wasted no time, but fixed a suitable date, agreed to fly just four wind-sensitive aircraft, circulated our intentions to the Shuttleworth Veteran Aeroplane Society membership and other appropriate parties and launched the first-ever flying evening. That was over fifty years ago, and it has remained a unique regular feature in the Collection calendar.

One main factor in my work with the Shuttleworth Collection, and with Air Schools in the preceding years, was the lack of organised management structures. It can lead to frustration, but meant that I was left virtually alone to do what I thought to be right. I am not an engineer and I need advice from others when considering whether a substantial technical task should be tackled, but I have been fortunate. Whilst I was aware that the true veterans were the intended mainstay of the Collection, I was keen to extend the age range and bring it through its later development years at least.

Shortly after joining the Collection in 1966, looking for other appropriate historic aeroplanes with which to build up the range, I heard stories about five Hawker Hind light biplane bombers of 1935 that were ending their days parked in a hangar in Afghanistan. Apparently, they were left there to deteriorate as there was no active scrap activity in the country. Rumours abounded about aircraft abandoned around the world, and eventually I received irrefutable evidence that about ten of these machines existed and I was determined that somehow I would acquire one to add to the flyable fleet.

The news spread among people who wanted to help to bring a specimen back to its country of origin and I received several offers of help, but eventually there were so many well-intentioned but impracticable schemes on offer that I tended to ignore them. One day, though, I was close to losing a genuine opportunity, when someone claiming to be ready and able to tackle the task rang and I was tempted to fend him off. However, he offered an impressive proposal and I believed him. Within forty-eight hours I met Bill Collard, the Operations manager of the Ford Motor Company based at the company's headquarters at Dagenham in Essex, who explained that a new heavy vehicle needed extensive testing on rough roads, and it could bring the Hind home.

It was all go – there was a need to finalise a deal with the then Royal Afghan Air Force, but this was not easy, as there was no British representative in the country and correspondence remained unanswered, so I contacted the British Air Attaché in Tehran, who fortunately was enthusiastic in his support of the project. Ford was more than well equipped for the exercise, providing a coach for the crew comprising a medical officer, photographer, and a total team of six. Also, Shuttleworth sent the Trust's two senior engineers, Malcolm Frazer and Wally Berry, to do the specialist work and ensure that the aeroplane was as complete as possible. The C-in-C of the Air Force, General Gulbahar, insisted that the Hind would fly in Afghan markings for the first two years of its reactivated life, and this was honoured. Today it has an appropriate Royal Air Force paint scheme of 1935 and, in company with the majority of Shuttleworth aircraft, it is the only specimen of its kind that flies anywhere in the world.

Another serendipitous evening moment was when Wally Berry and I met by the record-breaking de Havilland Comet racer G-ACSS, which had been added to the Collection in 1966 in very far from airworthy condition. One of us said, 'Well, why don't we...' And some sixteen years later 'CSS was airborne once more, unfortunately too late for me to fly her, so there is no report in this book. However, the unique stories of 'CSS and the other Comets justify – and have been given – a book of their own.[*]

---

[*]. Ogilvy, David: *de Havilland's Racing Comets*, Airlife, 1987

Chapter 8

Challenges away from the cockpit

Very early in aviation life it became clear that unacceptable levels of bureaucracy and self-protecting actions were serious handicaps to the much-needed freedom affecting some sections of what should be a flying community.

Amongst the first that I met was the vast overreaction by the Air Registration Board relating to wooden aeroplanes. Certainly, a Percival Proctor suffered a main spar failure through problems with glued joints, and to prevent recurrences some action was necessary. However, most of the older and some not-so-old types were made of wood and a vast number of machines had their lives terminated prematurely and unnecessarily. One that came to the fore was the ex-RAF Miles Magister, in civil guise known officially as the Hawk Trainer 3, which in the later 1950s was continuing to give good service with flying schools and clubs. All were inspected and most were proved to be trouble free, yet the type was condemned and restricted to private use. Whilst the checks were related mainly to the spars, many of us who operated fleets of Maggies knew that this was not the main source of any likely problem. In practice the offending dampness would creep downhill to the lowest part of the aeroplane, leading to a standing but meaningful joke: on a pre-flight check, take a pot of glue, and squirt some of the stuff around the sternpost and you would be OK.

At this time the Maggie was in the late stages of its career as a trainer, but the Chipmunk was not. In 1956 when the first batch was released by the RAF – not through any fault in the aeroplane but following closure of the RAF Volunteer Reserve flying schools – some machines were fewer than four years of age and were sold by the Air Ministry for about £300 each. Yet as soon as the roundels were removed the type that had proved its capability in its intended role was considered unsuitable. Only one of the demanded changes was sensible: the cartridge starter was considered to be unsafe in the less organised and less disciplined private and club environment, so electric starters needed to be fitted. Unfortunately, this created a separate problem, as the low capacity batteries were unhappy when required to take on an added heavy duty. This though, was not anyone's fault.

The overall problem, though, extended far beyond this. When the first thirty machines came on the market as military Chipmunk T10s, the type was not even eligible for a civil Certificate of Airworthiness, but many purchasers were not aware of this: official policy was that unless the type and specific mark had been approved it could not be flown again once it left the Service. Small numbers of Chipmunks (known as 21s) had been built as civil machines, so with the general feeling that a Chipmunk was a Chipmunk very few people foresaw the bother that lay ahead. A civil-built 21 was fine, but the 10 was a military machine and therefore not safe, even though the Duke of Edinburgh learned to fly in one and, seventeen years later, so did Prince Charles.

735 Chipmunks had been built for the RAF and had flown many thousands of hours; our first of these, G-AOSY, was classed by the ARB as a virtual prototype so we needed to face all the investigation and development charges as well as the costs of the required new items. The official fuel capacity of 18 gallons (although in practice twenty could be accommodated) was considered to give a less-than-safe endurance, yet the military Auster 5, with its more thirsty Lycoming engine, had been cleared for civil use with tankage for only 15 gallons. The authorities were unable to offer an answer to that, so after much dispute and desk hammering we were permitted to retain the pair of 9 gallon tanks. Night flying, though, was not permitted, as the gauges were not sufficiently luminous and were not easily visible from the rear (instructor's) seat.

CHALLENGES AWAY FROM THE COCKPIT

The metal fixed pitch propeller (i.e. without any working components) needed to be sent away to obtain an expensive tag of approval. All the instruments needed to be removed, overhauled and given a civil release. Even the engine – a Mark 8 version of the very well proven Gipsy Major – was allowed only 500 of its 1,000 hour life, so if one had run for 520 hours in the Service it must be removed and reconditioned or scrapped. Some items that needed to be removed for inspection were not to be returned to their original and safe working positions: the reservoir for hydraulic fluid, which had carried out its task satisfactorily just ahead of the firewall (where its contents could be checked with ease), must be moved to a position behind the wall where any leaks would drip directly onto the voltage regulator!

The aviation press of the time devoted several pages to this absurd situation, including several letters of complaint from people trying to use the machines that they had bought. In the end, though, after we had wasted a substantial sum, expended considerable time and energy, and lost several months of what could have been constructive use of the Chipmunk, the following official notice appeared:

> 'Regarding the civil certification of the surplus Air Ministry Chipmunk T10s, the requirements are to be very much reduced with the introduction of a new civil series, the Mark 22. Very few modifications will now be necessary to convert the military Chipmunks to full C of A standard for this new mark, and the costs should be little more than the normal overhaul costs for similar light aircraft.'

This outcome of such a frustrating experience served at least one valuable purpose: there is no need to sit back and accept unjustifiable demands that may be put forward. The result served as a useful tool in the years ahead during which there have been numerous opportunities to challenge the system – with confidence!

Airworthiness is by no means the only source of problems for the operator of lighter or historic aircraft. There have been – and still are – organisations and individuals with no regard for general aviation (GA) or its needs. In this, the main cause of misunderstanding is the use and availability of airspace. To keep a finger or two on the pulse I served for more than twenty-five years on the National Air Traffic Management Advisory Committee and during this time I heard much that incensed me and others representing GA's various interests. There was much reference to the seriousness of commercial air transport, with implications that the lighter side was all just fun flying. Whilst those who take to the air purely for personal pleasure deserve a sensible share of freedom, which often is missing, we need to view the overall scene in a realistic perspective.

The figures that I am about to quote are a few years old, but there cannot have been a vast change since I obtained them. Taking all scheduled airline operations, eighty-seven per cent of passengers were flying to or from their holiday destinations and even Heathrow confessed to eighty-four per cent of its customers falling into this category. Yet when the whole of GA is considered, more than seventy per cent of flights had some business, safety, or other serious purpose. I am not pretending that there is anything wrong with this balance, but the 'lighter' element warrants more consideration, especially where airspace availability is concerned. On three occasions I have objected to proposals to make carriage of radio compulsory, yet every day thousands of vehicles on our roads cross each other at three-figure closing speeds and at only a few feet distance. Would a plan be accepted that compels every car driver to have and to use radio – with an appropriate licence?

Possibly the single subject in which the most nonsense has been perpetuated is that of congested airspace. Apart from a very few places at certain times there is no such thing. We hear of the perpetual increase in the numbers of passengers travelling on the world's airlines, but for its protagonists there is no mention of the fact that larger aircraft lead to the need for fewer machines. It may surprise some people to learn that in 1950 there were more commercial air transport aircraft (i.e. airliners) on the UK register than there are today. Many of these were quite small, including a number of eight-seater

Rapides, so the passenger figures were very low, but one aeroplane is one aeroplane and regardless of its capacity each needs its own right of way. Also, other aviation activity took place on a much larger scale than has been seen for many years. In the extended London area alone there were four fighter squadrons of the Royal Auxiliary Air Force and six RAF Reserve flying schools. All these operated at their peaks at weekends, sharing the airspace with the club and private aircraft. On one clear Sunday afternoon, well clear of any airfield and viewing from the open cockpit of a Magister, I counted fifteen aircraft just going about what they were going about. These included two that were spinning (at safe heights well above most others) as, then, this was an essential part of the syllabus for the Private Pilot's Licence. I was told by older colleagues that I was too young to have experienced any real activity, but I have seen evidence that when pressure was at its wartime peak, the RAF Elementary Flying Training School at Burnaston had 110 Magisters on strength, with the use of just one relief landing ground, with no radio and no form of air traffic control. I am not suggesting that we should go back to that, but it puts in perspective the current term marked on charts as 'Area of Intense Aerial Activity'. I feel that this should be recorded before there is no one still around to put the truth on paper.

When, at NATMAC meetings, I tried to put forward the fact that without GA the industry would collapse, some people tried to ridicule me. The fact, though, is that the majority of pilots joining the airlines entered the profession by the club and private flying movement. A high percentage started by learning to fly at their local clubs, often for pleasure and later deciding to go ahead for careers. So, many of the Tiger Moths, Magisters, Auster variants et al were not just getting in the way of the serious brigade but helping to ensure that the latter could continue to operate.

Much nonsense was spoken, including false claims by the larger airlines' delegates that they refused to take new pilots who had trained by that 'casual' route but either they failed to admit or were unaware of the truth: that they relied on the smaller operators to take on the inexperienced newcomers whom, after they had two or three years' experience, they would 'pinch'. It was all a part of a not very satisfactory chain, in which the minor airlines were always the sufferers. My point here is that all these trainees needed to have access to airspace and have available aerodromes within reach of their homes or workplaces, without which they would take up other pursuits and not start to fly.

I received one form of encouragement, which helped to persuade me to keep trying. To my complete surprise the then Director of Airspace Policy, who chaired the NATMAC meetings, handed me a piece of paper on which he had handwritten 'How refreshing to hear someone talking sense about airspace.'

There were almost limitless opportunities for negotiation – and if necessary, battles – with the relevant authorities. Sometimes there were pitiable disagreements between those in power in the Service and those outside. In the early days when the Ministry of Civil Aviation was striving to prove itself and its independence, I was preparing a working plan for a course for the London School of Flying. I hoped to be on a safe surface when I said that I was following broadly the methods that I had learned in the RAF, but I was taken aside quietly and told that I should aim to avoid that as much as possible.

No doubt you have read enough of this and wish to get closer to the cockpit of some of the aircraft you have met in the previous pages, which I welcome you to do now. Fortunately, today the Historic Aircraft Association, Light Aircraft Association and other organisations are using their experience and influence to remove some of the restrictions that have applied in the past, and we must all hope that this excellent work will continue for many years ahead.

As well as my assessment of the various aircraft from the pilot's perspective, I have given a little of the history and evolution of each type – space prevents me from being more comprehensive, but if you want to know more, the Internet is your oyster! I have given them largely in birth order, bar for some limited grouping of related types. Read on to see how things have evolved over some forty years!

Chapter 9

Wot! No Ailerons?
A.V. Roe's Triplane of 1910

The early development of the aeroplane was a painful process, due partly to the frustrations experienced by pioneers when their hard work resulted in failure to fly and, when a machine did manage to get into the air, on or before landing it could put paid to the project by collapsing into a mangled heap. Then there was the personal injury that might go with it. To those more fortunate among them, we must honour their persistence in building, flying, crashing, rebuilding and so on, often repeating the process until they achieved something approaching sustained flight. Without these stalwarts of the early twentieth century, where would we be today, considerably more than a hundred years later?

I may be too impatient, for although I understand the significance of the essential evolution process, I cannot arouse much enthusiasm for staggering across the field in an attempt to get a couple of feet of air under the wheels of a Bleriot. Quite wrongly, it reminds me of my days as an ATC cadet, with ground slides and low hops in a Dagling glider, which was almost as reluctant to take to flight. I accept that this is a personal failing and not realistically comparable, but for me an aeroplane must qualify for both halves of that word and at least climb towards the circuit, however slowly or badly it does so.

To put this to the test, the Shuttleworth Collection's Avro Triplane proved to be an ideal mount. As there was no flyable original specimen anywhere in the world, the Trustees took on board the replica of the Triplane IV that had been built in 1965 for the famous film *'Those Magnificent Men in their Flying Machines'*. It is not a precise copy of the machine that had been constructed in 1910 by Alliott Verdon

Roe and, thankfully, with a Cirrus Hermes of 1927 it has a touch more power than its predecessor, but it fully reflects Mr Roe's design theory: that most of a wing's lift is produced by the first portion just behind the leading edge, so the span should be as large as practicable and the chord (or width) no greater than needed for structural integrity. Also, such a layout produces less induced drag, which leads to a better performance for a given power output. Although only four steadily developed experimental Roe Triplanes were built, the theory proved itself on the extremely successful Avro 504, about 9,000 of which were built for the Royal Flying Corps and early years of the RAF. Anyone who thinks that aviation happened only in small doses during the 1914-18 war is invited to try again!

Looking around and through the Triplane on a pre-flight check, even a regular biplane pilot must remember that there are more wings to look at than the accustomed ration, but the most noticeable feature is the absence of any movable controls – ailerons – which shakes the mind. What will this strange structure be like to handle in the air? We had heard about wing warping, but had to put it to the test, remembering that the whole idea had been short-lived, so presumably was not ideal. For the Triplane, to allow some flexibility without twisting the spars, hinges were fitted to the rear spars on the two upper wings, each of thirty-two feet span. The lowest main plane, of only twenty feet, has no intentional warping.

For my initiation into three wings without any ailerons, a seat without a surrounding cockpit and an engine that sits outside and above the nose I was fortunate to have a relatively calm summer evening. Despite that, little time was needed to confirm – as expected – that it had a rooted objection to responding to normal management. Before proving this, though, I had a strange feeling of insecurity, perched in the open fuselage with a need to stretch one's legs almost fully to place feet on a pair of small wooden blocks that double as rudder pedals. A greater surprise, though, came when exercising the wrongly named control wheel fore and aft for full and free travel, for when displaced from the centre it fell fully forward or backward at its own will. Testing laterally, there is no precise stop as there is when checking full aileron movement, but just a growing resistance when the cables controlling the wing warping tauten as they approach full deflection. It seems sensible not to try this too enthusiastically as excess stress might lead to a sudden twang; this, though, would be less harmful than having a similar experience in the air.

All this pre-flight angst removed some of the normally inherent desire to fly a 'new' aeroplane, for the whole package was stranger than anything that I had met previously. However, now was action time. As part of the priming process, a petrol-soaked rag was placed in the carburettor intake. I have heard other pilots feel very worried about this, but, for once, I was unconcerned, as I had experienced a similar need on the much later (1932) Comper Swift which also refused to fire into life without such artificial aid.

The remainder of the starting process is more conventional and, usually, only one hand-swing is needed. However, once all four pots are in action, the immediate view is a mild mental deterrent. Not only is the engine bulk both immediately ahead and exposed to the breeze, but most of its working parts are to be seen, with rocker arms, valve springs and push rods doing their stuff, sending oil all over the pilot. To this is added water from condensation on the intake manifold, so the magic liquid mixture provides a shower of slowly increasing temperature.

A fair percentage of the available power is needed to persuade the beast to move forward, but once it gets going it rides the ground smoothly; turning, though, is a privilege that it offers only reluctantly, so wing-tip help is almost essential to get into the right position for the experience to come. Surprisingly, the take-off is very easy, although a positive pull is needed to persuade a transition from floor to flight.

Once in the air, the Triplane reverts to taking control of the situation. To obtain any climb it is essential to try to maintain balanced flight, but this is difficult to achieve as there is no device with which to determine the precise direction of the airflow to measure slip or skid. This is exacerbated by the bare fuselage, as with very little keel area behind the centre of gravity there is no lateral or directional stability and no beneficial secondary effect of using either the rudder or wing warping. In pitch, the situation is little better. Even in favourable conditions, slight turbulence upsets the system when each bump becomes two bumps as each hits the wings and, a little later, the tailplane.

Before I experienced the practical peculiarities of Mr Roe's fourth Triplane design I was given a very scanty pre-flight briefing on the basis that very quickly I would discover all that I needed to know. I doubt if the 'all' bit can ever apply, but certainly the brain was working hard seeking solutions to what one would expect to be easily solved situations. Yet even a mild wing drop, which occurred sufficiently often to provide ample opportunity to try different answers, could lead to a minor mental disaster. Later I heard from others who were able to provide valuable insights into the machine's idiosyncrasies, so here I quote that well-known doyen of test and display pilots, the late Neil Williams: 'the same wing drop in the Triplane has the makings of an incipient disaster from the pilot's point of view as he winds the wheel with the energy of a London bus driver taking a sharp corner. All to no avail, as the wing continues to go down and one has the horrifying impression that the whole lot is about to turn turtle like a small yacht in a gale.' This includes a touch of journalistic licence, but it provides a clear message! Whilst in normal flight, if the Triplane can be persuaded to indulge in such an activity, it is possible, but not very encouraging, to look around and see what it is all about. A look downward confirms that there is nothing between the seat and the ground beneath, so perhaps it is better to spend any available time endeavouring to learn more about the aeroplane's behavioural tendencies. Unlike most conventional light aeroplanes, where after closing the throttle one leaves the nose where it was until the speed decreases to the required gliding figure, due to the high drag and low structural density Mr Roe's machine seems to stop immediately and a positive forward push is needed to set-up a glide at about 40 knots, which is about 5kt lower than the normal cruise figure!

One fact that I failed to find until some time later was the safe limit of bank. For my first approach I made a rather ragged final turn that upset me and the aeroplane. Attempting to line-up on the into-wind landing path, I used too much bank and for a stressfully long time the lowered wing refused to come up. When eventually I had the relevant bits pointing in roughly the right direction for a powered approach, the touchdown itself was smooth and straightforward, except that an almost aggressive pull back on the wheel was needed to persuade the package to adopt the required landing attitude. The resulting ground run was the shortest – probably little more than two aircraft lengths – that I have ever experienced. Also, in accordance with its determination to be difficult, the Triplane is the only machine that I have flown on which the take-off and touchdown are the easiest parts of a flight, with the bits in between that cause the problems.

Long after this intriguing experience, which seems much more worthwhile now than it felt at the time, some very enlightening research was carried out on the machine's serious wing dropping habit. The results showed that up to about five degrees of bank it has neutral lateral stability and above that very modest figure it is unstable in roll, so the bank just continues to increase almost regardless of pilot input. This has caused serious concern to several other pilots, including one with far more flying experience than I could ever have hoped to achieve, who was authorised to fly the Triplane to a display at a nearby aerodrome, but shortly afterwards he rang to admit that he had frightened himself and could someone else take it back to Old Warden? Another's main comment after his first flight on the type was that the only rule the machine was likely to obey was the law of gravity.

The difficulties that modern pilots have experienced flying the Avro Triplane of 1910 bring home the problems that faced the aviators of the time. More importantly, though, it proves the extent to which we should show our respect for those early pioneers, who provided the essential stepping stones that have led to the aeroplanes that we take for granted today. Despite my comments, in retrospect I would not have missed the opportunity to do battle with this unusual piece of aeronautical kit. It was a unique experience that remains alive in my mind today.

Chapter 10

'A topping fighting two-seater'
Bristol F2B Fighter

Pressure – or the threat – of a major war has created efficient operational aeroplanes within remarkably short time frames. This was especially noticeable in the 1939-1945 upheaval, during which the Spitfire, among others, improved in speed and overall performance at a pace that would be economically impracticable in more peaceful times. The trend, though, was born long before this, and in 1916 a large and powerful two-seater emerged to become what many people have described as the most effective fighting machine of the First World War. This was the Bristol F2 popularly known as the 'Brisfit'.

The first prototype took to the air in September 1916, powered by a Rolls-Royce 12-cylinder liquid-cooled Vee of 190hp, which later became known as the Falcon 1. Subsequently, this engine layout proved right, for the pattern was retained with the Kestrel, Merlin and even the Griffon that powered Shackletons well into the post Second World War era. As the F2A, the Bristol prototype went to Orfordness for armament trials, which included fitting Constantinesco gun-synchronising gear to allow a Vickers gun to fire forwards through the arc of the propeller and a Scarff ring for the observer's Lewis gun in the rear cockpit.

All production F2As had redesigned wings and on 8 March 1917 – only six months after the prototype's initial flight – the first examples went to 48 Squadron Royal Flying Corps in France. Initially the results were disastrous, with unacceptably heavy losses, two being shot down by the renowned Baron Manfred von Richthofen. The troubles, though, were short-lived and instead of relying on the observer to engage the enemy with his Lewis machine gun, the

'A TOPPING FIGHTING TWO-SEATER'

Vickers gun was used offensively as in a single-seat fighter, leaving the observer to operate in a defensive role. Once the new crew co-operation procedure was established, the results were excellent.

Many pages have been written about the Fighter's exploits and achievements, but here we are concerned more with the virtues of the aeroplane itself. Within two months of receiving the new aircraft, 48's Commanding Officer wrote: 'Regarding the Bristol, she is a topping fighting two-seater, the best here. She is faster than the Hun two-seater but cannot match the latest Albatros Scout for speed. Where she does score tremendously is in her power to dive. In this she is above many English or Allied machines.' He continued: 'Many Huns who have dived on the tail of one, missed and gone on diving, have been dived after, overtaken, and destroyed. They are dived plumb vertically for thousands of feet until the noise is like that of a million sabres cleaving the air. The indicated speed then is 60 to 90mph the second time round the dial. The indicator reads normally to 130mph then a space, so probably the speed is well over 230mph. She loops well. She stands an enormous amount of punishment in the way of being shot about and several have been hard hit and come home, to be written off charge as beyond repair.'

Despite this encouraging assessment, the original F2A had a short operational life and soon was replaced by the F2B, which had several improvements. These included changes to the wings at the roots and a modification to the fuselage, the latter mainly to allow the pilot a better view. Also, the very sparse cockpit of the earlier version was upgraded with a simple but recognisable instrument panel. Several engines were used, but by far the majority had the very successful Rolls-Royce Falcon III V-12 that developed 275hp and remained the key power unit throughout the F2B's long and active life. Perhaps its reliability was partly because it attained maximum power output at only 2,000rpm.

By the war's end 3,100 had been built. Unlike its contemporaries, though, this was not the end of the line, as production continued until the 4,469th in December 1926. In the post-war years F2Bs served mainly on army co-operation work, both at home and overseas, with final withdrawal in 1932.

During the early post-war years several F2Bs were released on to the market. My near namesake C.P.B. Ogilvie bought D8096, which became G-AEPH; it was kept in his Primrose Garage at Watford with the intention of restoring it to flying condition. He failed to do so, and as late as 1946, with youthful cheek, I persuaded him to let me see it. It was almost complete, but dismantled, and in a generally sad state. I had no thought that eventually it would take to the air again and that, twenty-one years later, I would be privileged to fly it.

Ogilvie had an understandably stubborn desire to retain his prize piece, but he was eventually persuaded to part with it by the late Leonard Jackson, then manager of the Shuttleworth Collection. Subsequently, the airframe returned to its original home, the Bristol Aeroplane Company, for restoration, while its Falcon III engine received comparable treatment at its Rolls-Royce birthplace. The two were re-united, and the born-again Bristol Fighter flew from Filton on 14 February 1951. It remained at Bristol until June 1952, when it was transferred to its new home at Old Warden.

I believe very firmly that, whenever practicable, historic aeroplanes should be flown. It is important, though, to prevent unnecessary wear, tear, or strain, that their use should be under tight control and restricted to essential air tests, a safe minimum of pilot familiarisation flights and short careful demonstrations. As evidence that this practice has been followed on D8096, the logbooks reveal that between its installation on 20 December 1950 and its removal for major work in September 1982, the Falcon had run for 168hr, or about 5hr each year. In later life even this modest average was reduced, for between March 1993 and December 2004 the total was 36hr, or little more than 3hr per annum. This reveals sound housekeeping, an essential ingredient in the responsible operation of any ageing aeroplane.

Now we move a long way forward to Denham on a warm evening in May 1967, where D8096 was to spend the night after participating in a display. As Shuttleworth's relatively new General Manager I was slowly gaining experience on some of the Collection's very special aeroplanes, but, very rightly, opportunities were scarce. However, Dicky Martin, then the organisation's senior pilot, invited me to taxy the machine across the aerodrome to the hangars, adding, 'and, to keep the engine cool, do a circuit or two on the way.' I should add that I had taken considerable prior interest in D8096 and had digested some facts and figures prior to the succinct pre-flight briefing that Dicky gave me. After this short familiarisation flight, during which I endeavoured to assess what it must have been like to operate the machine in anger, I had to wait eighteen months before another opportunity arose; it is on this second, and subsequent flights, that I base my thoughts and findings. Hours were very tightly constrained and my third experience on the type was a demonstration at a public display. Shuttleworth pilots need to get a grip quickly!

Two features sunk in. The very large two-bladed propeller left relatively little ground clearance, so it would be important not to lift the tail high on take-off; and below the instrument panel was a complex of pipes and taps that controlled the pressurisation of the fuel system. The former was easily manageable, but the latter took time to assimilate. I wondered how, in stress of battle, a pilot finding a drop in pressure would be able to think sufficiently clearly to play the taps in the right order.

Following thorough external and internal checks, starting the engine, after pumping up the fuel pressure, calls for two or three prop-swingers operating in harmony with linked arms, as the Falcon's compressions are too strong for one person to overcome. The pilot's procedure involves energetic winding of the handle for the starter magneto, but this needs careful co-ordination with the workers outside. Alternatively, the engine may be fired into life by means of the Hucks starter, a mechanical device mounted on a Ford chassis. Once running, the Falcon sounds, feels and is purposeful. The only difficulty is the position of the magneto switches, which are not only outside the cockpit but out of view!

Taxying calls for wing-walkers, as the F2B's large slab-sided fuselage gives it a strong determination to turn into wind, with no brakes to prevent it from doing so. Take-off is impressive, with a rapid acceleration, and less tendency to swing than one might expect. It is airborne after a very short run, especially if care is taken to keep the tail fairly low to prevent a propeller scrape. Although rate of climb is one good measure of an aeroplane's value as a (useful fighting) machine, in the interests of the Falcon's age, I avoided a full-throttle ascent and turned to published records for the answer, but the results were frustrating. I found figures varying from 875 to 1,300ft/min, but, as no weights were quoted to check whether these were comparable, I was barely any the wiser. From 'feel' I am sure that the higher figure is nearer the truth.

In normal flight the rudder is relatively light and the elevators are even lighter, but the ailerons are unexpectedly heavy, needing two hands for manoeuvring at higher speeds. Perhaps the most noticeable feature of the Brisfit's handling, though, is its behaviour in turns, which must come as a surprise to any pilot with a relatively modern mind. On more recent aeroplanes the ailerons operate differentially, which means that a down-going control (on the outside of the turn) moves less than its opposite partner travelling upwards, but there is no such luxury on the Brisfit. As a result, an attempt to turn on ailerons alone, or with insufficient use of rudder, causes the machine to bank correctly but to change heading in the wrong direction. This is because the full-travel down-going aileron generates drag where it is least needed; so to keep the aircraft in balance and achieve the desired result calls for generous use of the feet, preferably applying into-turn rudder slightly before moving the control column in the same direction. This must have added to the problems of accurate gun sighting, but the successes achieved prove that the pilots of the day knew what they were doing.

From several styles of approach to the stall, a gentle buffet preceded an equally mild breakaway, with only a modest tendency to drop a wing. As a high-drag aeroplane the Brisfit is not very fast. The published maximum speed is 125mph at sea level, only 5mph below the permissible limit on the Shuttleworth machine, but this is no handicap in the relatively gentle demonstrations that are the order of the day. A large trim lever on the right side of the cockpit serves well to relieve fore-and-aft load between different airspeeds. It is important throughout a flight to keep constant checks not only on the oil pressure, but also on the fuel pressure and coolant temperature, the last of which is controllable from the cockpit by use of radiator shutters.

The landing is critical, and it is important to do this as nearly as possible into wind. The final over-the-fence approach speed is a very modest 55mph and, with a touchdown at about 40mph and a helpful tailskid, the subsequent ground run is very short, though still long enough to display a tendency to swing into a ground loop. The Brisfit gives its pilot a pre-flight visual warning of this, for there are hoops under each lower wingtip to prevent it from scraping the ground on the way round.

The Bristol Fighter leaves a favourably positive mark on the memory. In a critique of its pure handling qualities, it lacks well-coordinated flying controls, but this is compensated by a number of matching virtues. By measurements of its time it was (and fortunately still is) a big and powerful 'adult' aeroplane that called for and received a high level of respect. Its record as the most effective fighting aeroplane of the First World War and its unique continuation in RAF squadron service for fourteen years afterwards provide better evidence than words can offer. This is even more surprising when we consider that when, in 1915, Frank Barnwell started designing the Bristol R2A, it was not intended to be a fighter, but an artillery spotter.

For fifty-six years D8096 was the world's only airworthy Bristol Fighter. However, two other long-term rebuilds emerged in mid-2006 to enable a three-ship formation to appear once each at Duxford and Old Warden. I was very fortunate to be commentating at the latter event, so I had the opportunity to absorb the unique sight and sound that most probably will never occur again. The two newcomers have departed to owners in the USA and New Zealand, so now the old stalwart has the honour of being Europe's sole flying example of one of the most famous and successful fighting aeroplanes of its time.

Chapter 11

Before the Moth
de Havilland DH51

Not all good aeroplanes gain worthwhile production orders. Before the Moth series became established as the most historically significant mass-produced light aircraft of all time, much heart-searching must have been carried out in the de Havilland stable at Stag Lane, Edgware. The Moth did not just happen to happen, for immediately before it were two designs at opposite ends of the light aeroplane range. Between them, these machines showed clearly that neither quite filled the bill to serve the needs of the prospective private owner and amateur pilot.

Despite its design number, the DH51 surfaced later than the diminutive DH53. The 53 first saw daylight under its wheels in late 1923 and made some impact at the *Daily Mail* light aeroplane trials at Lympne in October that year. It covered 59.3 miles on a gallon of petrol, but with a weight of only 565lb it was too small, too low-powered and proved generally inadequate for serious touring. Its 750cc Douglas motorcycle engine gave constant trouble.

By contrast, the DH51 was relatively large, with a span of thirty-seven feet (more than a Spitfire) and a permitted weight of 2,240lb. Everything about it was big, with a sensibly roomy cockpit and accommodation for three in tandem, although it became more established later in a two-seat configuration with a detachable fuselage panel over the front 'hole'. It was powered at first by a 90hp RAF 1a engine, this had only single ignition and failed to suit the airworthiness authorities of the time; greater success came with the V-8 Airdisco.

This engine is quite interesting. Basically a war-surplus Renault, it was acquired, modified and marketed by the Aircraft Disposal

Company (ADC). Producing 120hp in its civilian form and ideally suited in power output for a machine of the 51's size and weight, it was of greater overall calibre than needed for the popular-to-be light aeroplanes of the twenties. As a result, the Airdisco was virtually sliced down the middle and each half produced the basis for the ADC Cirrus 1 which, with its four upright cylinders in line, produced 60hp in return for a weight of only 290lb. This powered the first DH60 Moth in 1925.

The first DH51 to fly, in July 1924, was exported to Australia and converted to a floatplane, it capsized in Sydney Harbour at the age of seven. The second survived only a little longer, to be scrapped at Hanworth in 1933. The third and last (in all senses) had – and indeed has – a much greater claim to a place in the history book.

G-EBIR first flew in September 1925, and early in 1926 went to Nairobi, the first aircraft to be registered in Kenya, where it stayed for some forty years. Through a co-operative venture which included considerable help from Hawker Siddeley Aviation – later absorbed into today's BAE Systems – (as successors to the de Havilland Aircraft Co) it was airfreighted home to England in a vast Blackburn Beverley for permanent preservation by the Shuttleworth Collection at Old Warden in Bedfordshire. H-SA refurbished G-EBIR at their Hawarden works and, after a long time away from home, the last DH51 came back to live only about forty miles from where it had been built nearly fifty years previously.

As a two-bay biplane with a relatively shallow fuselage, the DH51 has a strong external resemblance to the famous DH9 of the First World War, which proved so successful in a variety of post-war civil roles. A large four-bladed wooden propeller gives the 51 a certain added character, helping to augment the impression of size. With a V-8 engine, the 51 has long pipes running down both sides of the cockpit, but at different heights to ease cockpit access. There is a hinged flap on the left side of the front cockpit to make passenger entry more straightforward than that for the pilot, who has no such facility. The bucket seats have fixed upholstery and these provide a level of comfort that I have not met in any other open-cockpit type, while the spade-grip control column (surely not original?) wrongly gives an almost fighterish impression. Vintage-style instruments, few in number but with large traditional dials, cover the basic needs of airspeed, height, engine power and oil pressure. Other trade tools within easy reach are a cheese-cutter for fore-and-aft trim, acting via a spring balance directly on the elevator, and a pair of pull-for-on fuel cocks for main and reserve supplies, which just come from different levels in the one tank of thirty gallons capacity.

Start procedure is unusual for a light aeroplane intended for private use. Although the propeller can be hand-swung, the rapidity with which the four blades follow each other creates an added hazard. The Airdisco boasts a third (starter) magneto; current for this is generated by energetic winding from within, whilst engineers perform a rather similar external cranking operation in slightly slower motion. Although an established method for getting some of the heavier engines into action in the twenties and thirties, it is one that is more normally associated with military aircraft.

Once running, the Airdisco is a smooth operator when within its 'happy' range. G-EBIR has insisted on retaining a flat spot near the low end of the rev scale, for although adjustments to carburettor balancing have moved the trouble area both up and down the scale, it refuses to be eliminated. Yet many engines have settings that are best avoided and this one makes no bones about the bits that it dislikes.

On a cold start, oil pressure rises to a bare 30lb. To a modern mind this is cause for concern, but once the engine gets warm the situation seems serious. However, there is no need for alarm, as the Airdisco (like its successor, the Cirrus) has a splash as opposed to a pressure-fed oil circulation system and a data plate provides consolation by quoting 5-8lb as the normal operating range. This, however, is at the front of the engine and cannot be seen by the pilot. The engine heats quickly and prefers to avoid long ground running. When long runs are essential for test purposes, a special ground-use cowl can be fitted to deflect an increased air supply to wherever it is needed.

Most tailskid, brakeless aeroplanes can create taxying problems and the DH51 generates its own. Normally a skid is fixed to the sternpost (as on the DH60 Moth) or it is movable with the rudder (Tiger Moth) and the latter arrangement makes the taxying task much easier; G-EBIR though, has neither of these, with a floating, bungee-balanced skid which points in the direction in which one has been, but offers little hope or help for where one wishes to go. In practice, though, this behaves more effectively than it feels.

Once the problem of alignment has been overcome, take-off is easy. There is very little swing tendency and when it is ready the 51 unsticks on its own, which is quite soon. Climb performance is creditable, with a return of nearly 800ft/min. It is during the early flight stage that a modification, or more correctly a re-conversion to original, shows to great advantage. When G-EBIR arrived at Old Warden, it had the most immovable and purposeless set of ailerons imaginable. One pilot described the feeling as though they were set in concrete, while I feared on my first flight that I had taken off with control locks in position. This, I thought, must have been a prime reason for the type failing to sell.

How wrong I proved to be. During a routine inspection, a Shuttleworth engineer discovered that all the fittings existed for setting-up differential ailerons, although at that time they were set to travel in equal amounts both ways. What a transformation. With no handbook or other guidelines, the sensible solution seemed to be to use Tiger Moth figures. These worked admirably; through no fault of the designer, what had been a dull and uninspiring machine to fly became a living thing. If flown in proper biplane tradition with sensible rations of rudder, the newly activated ailerons provided a control balance that made turn entry and exit into remarkably smooth sequences.

There is nothing very special about the DH51, except that it is unbelievably docile, except in rough conditions, when it reveals a marked lack of control response. Unlike the little DH53, which indulged in some sharp practices including aileron snatch just before the stall, the larger machine seems to have no aerodynamic vices. The stall, which provides one of the best indications of any aeroplane's manners, is almost indefinable as a precise occurrence.

From a leisurely entry, the 51's nose eventually finds its way down at a figure below the minimum reading on the ASI (where there is a +10mph position error). Clearly a modern altimeter would show signs of unwinding, but only by using a bit of determined effort and 'entering with intent' can a positive and pronounced break-away be induced. Even then the wings remain on the level.

Performance is unexceptional, but adequate. With 1,800rpm the cruise is about 90mph, but to achieve this the eight cylinders drink about eleven gallons per hour. Range and endurance, though, are adequate, with a maximum flight time of about 2½ hours.

With an approach at 55-60mph, the landing holds no surprises, but the large wheels and low pressure tyres offer a far more comfortable touchdown and subsequent roll than the first DH60 Moths that followed so soon after. Certainly the 51 will not tolerate a crosswind, and the natural weathercock tendency is accentuated by the strange tailskid attachment that I have already mentioned.

As my original assessment of the reason for the DH51's market failure was so grossly wrong, I must assume that sheer size maimed its chances. By the volume of materials alone, it must have cost a lot to build; hangarage bills would be high; the large engine drank fairly heavily. All these misfortunes add up to tell a tale that is easy to understand, but as G-EBIR really is such a likeable flying machine, it is unfortunate that customers failed to materialise. The DH51, though, was definitely not a failure. It proved the need for a smaller, less expensive and lower-powered aeroplane, and from this was born the DH60 Moth. Without that original Moth, which initially was supplied on a heavily subsidised basis to six flying clubs, the private flying movement would have taken many more years to gel.

Chapter 12

Where club flying began
de Havilland DH60 Moth

And now to the Moth: although people had been involved with the private side of flying since the very earliest days, before the First World War, it all began to come together in 1925 when, in an attempt to make the nation more air-minded, the Air Ministry sponsored the opening of, and the equipment for, five geographically spread flying clubs. Types previously available were surplus military machines that were not economically suitable for the task. Among the first DH60 Moths delivered from the de Havilland factory at Stag Lane was G-EBLV, which went to the Lancashire Aero Club; fortunately, both that aeroplane and the club remain alive and well today. Other recipients of the new aeroplanes were the Midland Aero Club, Newcastle Aero Club, the Yorkshire Aeroplane Club and, not surprisingly, de Havilland's own London Aeroplane Club. These were Cirrus Moths, with the four-cylinder upright engine developing only 60bhp.

There were several variants of the basic design and, during its development, the available power output ranged from 60hp in the earliest models to more than twice that figure in the last – the Moth Major – with eight different engines and a time spread of seven years between the initial flights of first and final variants. So there were many Moths, in both character and production: 2,112 DH60s were built between 1925 and 1934. With all these variations, it is impossible to report more than generally on the handling qualities of the type, so now we will look at a few of the features that are common to the overall design. Firstly, entry is not very easy, especially to the front seat, for which it is necessary to climb over – or seemingly through – a flying wire. Not until 1930 did Moths have hinged flaps on the cockpit sides to ease entry and exit. Throughout this exercise care must be taken to step only on the narrow strengthened walkway on the lower wing, which is on different sides on different variants; any error of judgement here leads to a foot going through the fabric and close of play for the day. Solo flying, though, is carried out from the rear cockpit, as the front seat is on the centre of gravity, so there was no trim change for a student pilot (then called a pupil) when the instructor got out. This was common practice for almost all tandem two-seaters of the day, reversed only with the introduction of the DHC-1 Chipmunk in 1950.

In the early fifties I was secretary of the Vintage Aeroplane Club and I made myself sufficient of a youthful nuisance to get my hands and feet on a range of interesting light aircraft of an earlier era. Perhaps a key among these was G-EBLV which I flew in 1952. With a maximum weight of only 1,240lb – 600lb lighter than a Tiger Moth on which I had trained and subsequently had flown on many occasions – the difference was very marked, as was the much lower power. However, perhaps the feature that hit me most – literally – was the very hard undercarriage with a straight-through axle and large thin wheels with high pressure (40lb/in^2) tyres which, on later Moths, gave way to a more tolerant split unit with wheels of smaller diameter and lower tyre pressure. Certainly, the earliest Moths knew how to bounce on an imprecisely judged landing, and I admit to experiencing this at first-hand.

Clearly there is insufficient space to provide detailed handling reports on all the DH60s, so I have selected one in the middle of the range: the DH60X Hermes Moth, using G-EBWD as the test case. Built in 1928 as a Cirrus Moth, 'WD became Richard Shuttleworth's first aeroplane and, sensibly, he converted it to a Hermes of 105hp. With this and the much improved split axle undercarriage (hence the 'X' designation), 'WD was (and, fortunately, is) a delightful aeroplane to fly.

The cockpit is small, both in width and length. It is very much more cramped than that of the later Tiger Moth. There is insufficient room to put a worthwhile cushion behind one's back and still have the stick and instruments sufficiently far ahead for comfort. However, this is a petty penalty to pay for a machine with so many virtues. An uncluttered panel, or dashboard as it would have been called, contains essentials only: an airspeed indicator graduated from 40mph to (optimistically) 160mph, rpm and oil pressure gauges, a cross-level and a non-sensitive altimeter complete the picture. An early P-type compass graces the floor, while a generous rear hatch holds sufficient kit to make 'away matches' practicable. The person in the front is allowed to read height and speed only, but has the added benefit of a large clock with which to criticise the pilot for failing to reach his destination on time!

During and after the hand-swing start, the pilot is treated to visual entertainment, as the moving rockers and valves of the uncowled upright engine are exposed for all to see, and these can generate an almost hypnotic effect. Unlike the earliest splash-fed Cirrus engine which offered about 5lb of oil pressure, the Hermes operates at a more comforting figure and jumps to about 60lb after starting, settling to an average of 38-42lb in normal flight. It produces a unique sound, with a series of rapid hollow 'pops' from the end of the long pipe, which runs along the right side of the fuselage and can burn an unwarily misplaced hand.

Taxying calls for a touch of the fast-dying traditional skill. Unlike the later Tiger with its steerable skid connected to the rudder, the pure Moth has a fixed skid attached rigidly to the bottom of the sternpost. This offers little help in negotiating corners, for which generous rudder, accompanied by careful bursts of engine, may need to be supported by the use of appropriate aileron and, on windy days, a wing walker.

The take-off is most satisfying, for the Hermes Moth's weight/power ratio is good, and after an immediate tail-rise it is airborne more rapidly than most other conventional light biplanes. It is impossible to record a precise unstick figure, as the ASI comes to registered life at 40mph, but I am convinced that G-EBWD takes little persuasion to fly happily at about 5mph below this.

One of the first tests for any type is to check its conduct at the stall. If it shows unhappy qualities at the low end of the speed scale this serves as a warning, calling for added caution, but the Moth emerges with an entirely clean health record. In fact, there is little to report except to state the expected: the ailerons become as sloppy as one would anticipate, there is a lot of waffling and wallowing, and eventually the nose drops (at a speed below the lowest ASI graduation) in an unhurried manner. With the usual variations and a few built-in tricks, a wing can be persuaded to go down, often to the tuneful accompaniment of a whistling in one or more of the wires. At this stage any minor irregularities in the rigging make themselves seen, heard, or felt – sometimes all three. But the machine behaves impeccably.

What is the Moth really like? Although very capable of serving a fully functional purpose and with some very long, famous historic flights to the type's credit, it is in another sphere that it really shines. To enjoy the purest pleasures of flight just for the sake of flying, the Moth is hard to beat. The ingredients must be available and the time must be right, but let us choose a calm, clear June evening, about an hour before dusk, and with nowhere particular to go. With the Hermes throttled back to provide a gentle 1,500rpm (the data plate quotes 1,900 as normal) and the ASI offering a little less than 70 to match, I will leave the rest to the imagination of the reader, except to add one personal point: to gain the full rewards of such a situation, this needs to be a solo affair and an empty front cockpit adds a certain flavour to the scene. That may sound ungraciously unsociable, but there is something special about flying alone and many pilots will understand what I mean.

Moths lived at the peak of the era of sideslipping, which provides the most effective way of killing surplus height on the approach. The Moth slips well, which is a useful facet as its normal glide is far from steep. Crossing the boundary fence at about 55mph IAS sets up 'WD nicely for a steady hold-off. With the earlier large wheels, high-pressure tyres, and straight axle undercarriage, the Moth bounced energetically after only a minor misjudgement, but the later system is more tolerant. Nevertheless, if one must err – and who doesn't? – it is advisable to round-out a little early; the subsequent drop on to three points is far less embarrassing than the bounce that is given free of charge in exchange for a slightly premature touchdown during the hold-off. The rudder remains moderately effective almost to the end of the landing run, but although the fixed skid helps to provide braking, out-of-wind landings should be avoided if possible.

Clearly, a biplane with all the usual array of struts, flying and landing wires and other excrescences that make it what it is, will not gain much performance on the level with power increase, but a bigger engine offers positive benefits in the rate of climb. A direct speed comparison between the first and the last of the DH60 series brings home the point: the original 60hp Moth claimed a book maximum of 91mph while the later Moth Major, with its 130hp, offered 112mph – or roughly a twenty per cent improvement from a 100+ per cent power increase. This means, of course, that 'WD is little faster now than it was when built with a Cirrus, but its get-up-and-go climb performance (it clocks more than 650ft/min) vastly improves its overall qualities as a flying machine. It loops very neatly and can be flown all the way round positively from about 110mph, but it does not invite manoeuvres in roll.

Now let us look closer at the later Moth Major. The upright engine of the earlier Moths furnished a fair amount of metal above the horizon and therefore created a poor forward view when on the ground, so in 1931 the next development – the 120hp Gipsy III – was designed to run inverted. Fitted to the DH60 airframe, this created a virtually new aeroplane, yet one that retained the many virtues of its predecessor.

Known as the DH60GIII, the prototype emerged in March 1932. The extra power and improved view were very welcome, and demand came from private owners and clubs, with eight of the latter equipping with the type from new. From the fifty-eighth machine, the GIII engine was replaced by what became the ubiquitous Gipsy Major of 130hp. Although with this engine the machine then became known as the Moth Major, inexplicably it has retained the handle DH60GIII to this day. 154 machines were built from scratch, including one by students of the then famous de Havilland Aeronautical Technical School, with several others created by conversions from older DH60s with upright engines. Additional fuselages were constructed and used on the military Queen Bee target aircraft.

The cockpit layout is much as would be expected, with a selection of basic instruments comprising from left to right, a non-sensitive ICAN altimeter, rpm and turn and slip gauges, airspeed indicator, oil pressure gauge and a large P-type compass on the right wall; the trimmer is on the left wall. There is no carburettor heat control, but the traditional Gipsy Major flame trap allows warm air to do the necessary work which, in my humble opinion, it does more effectively than the troublesome modern devices. Fuel is gravity fed from the 19-gallon tank forming the centre-section between the two top all-folding wings.

The suspension, provided by a combination of oil and rubber blocks within the main legs, (the latter developed so successfully on the DH98 Mosquito), provides a firm but comfortable ride. The standard pre-take-off checks are more than covered by the long-established but now discarded TTMFFGHH (trim, throttle friction, magnetos, fuel, flaps, gauges, hatches, harness) and away we go, expectedly calling for a medium dose of right rudder. Acceleration is vastly superior to that of its predecessor and very shortly the alert machine flies itself off the floor at about 45mph. A gentle delay to reach 60mph IAS leads to a very creditable climb rate of almost 900ft/min, which gives it a head-start of more than 200ft/min over its successor the similarly powered DH82A Tiger Moth. Levelling into cruise mode, the 60GIII purrs along quietly due to the under-fuselage exhaust pipe, which provides a marked change from the admittedly pleasant burble from the normally exposed four stubs. A setting of 1,950rpm produces about 90mph.

The GIII's overall handling is very likeable but, as expected, there is little directional stability; this calls for realistic use of rudder at all times, including changes of power setting and, especially, when leading into a turn, in which adverse aileron drag is relatively modest. Steep turns can be held very contentedly.

Low-speed flight leading to the stall holds no surprises and the break-away is very tame, but this should not be treated as an invitation to avoid positive recovery action; for it is possible to remain in the stalled condition with wings level and losing more height in the process than appears from the relative comfort of the cockpit. Nearer to the other end of the speed range, despite the absence of strakes, aerobatics are permitted, and the loop is a smart, happy event. As with most biplanes of the era, though, rolling manoeuvres are less benign and, out of respect for a vintage aeroplane which, at the time, was the sole UK survivor, I refrained from venturing far into this realm.

The Major trims out happily on the glide approach at 60mph and provides very good experience in judging precision for a three-point landing. Doing so into wind is a very satisfying exercise, but out of it there is much wisdom in setting out for a wheeler. As with all brakeless machines, subsequent taxying calls for a sense of airmanship covering aerodrome (or airstrip) surface, ground gradients, wind strength and direction and available manoeuvring space.

In 1954, through my involvement with the then Vintage Aeroplane Club, I had the good fortune to be invited to fly Moth Major G-ADHE, based at Denham and owned by Peter Hindmarsh. I grew quite attached to this intriguing machine and had the opportunity to fly it in the Southend Trophy Air Race. My main recollection of this event was flying almost wing-tip to wing-tip for what seemed like several minutes with Neville Duke as he overtook me by about 2mph in what was then his Hawker Tomtit G-AFTA.

I liked the Moth Major and, although 'DHE came to grief long ago, I am pleased to report that the type has not disappeared from the UK scene. Mainly through examples being re-imported, there are six on the register and currently two of these are airworthy. With good fortune, before long, perhaps another two will join that status. Here is an aeroplane that warrants a future existence; if I dare say so, and if it was better known, the Major could become a more popular possession than is the Tiger Moth!

Chapter 13

A close second
Avro Avian

When we consider the best of pre-war light aeroplanes we tend to think of de Havilland and Miles, yet many other designers and manufacturers became well established in the field and some excellent machines emerged from A.V. Roe & Co, a name amongst the very earliest on the aviation scene. The Avro 504 series should need little introduction to even the most recent flying recruit, for its almost legendary fame as the type on which pilot training really became established has lived on. After the 504 followed several other two-seat tandem, open Avro biplanes established themselves, and a very fine breed they were.

The prototype Avian, G-EBOV, flew in 1926 behind an Armstrong-Siddeley Genet of only 75hp. The type developed in the following few years and, among the progressive refinements, the early circular 504-type rudder gave way to a more modern-looking, angular, vertical tail surface.

Avians were produced in various forms and with quite an array of power sources. They achieved many successes, including H.J. (Bert) Hinckler's mere fifteen days solo flight from England to Australia in February 1928. Before this a lady pilot, Mrs Elliott Lynn, had achieved a light aeroplane height record of 19,200 feet in an Avian powered by the little-known Avro Alpha radial. However, perhaps the most frequently documented of the Avian's successes on the home front was in 1930, when another member of the fair sex, Winifred Brown, won the King's Cup Air Race in G-EBZV.

Strangely by today's standards, when Britain imports so many aircraft from the United States and elsewhere, the general flow in the early thirties was the other way. British machines were acknowledged as the best in the world and many new Avians were exported to America, with others sent to almost every country that one can name. Still, the type developed and the later machines to be built, known as the Mark IV, forsook the traditional wooden fuselage for a stronger structure of steel tube. One Avian, G-AAXH, was used by British Landing Gears Ltd to develop an early form of tricycle undercarriage.

There are few records of Avians serving with the RAF in an active flying role, for most machines at the start of the war in 1939 were impressed for use as ground instructional airframes. Four emerged with peace in 1945, but only two flew again. G-ACKE operated from Baginton, Coventry, until it lost an argument in a collision with a Tiger Moth.

G-ABEE had a happier, though far too short, reactivation in the hands of a group of four members of the then Vintage Aeroplane Club; this organisation held flying meetings in the early fifties for owners of pre-war light types and it operated the Avian's successor, an Avro Club Cadet, G-ACHP. Experience of G-ABEE provides the basis of my comments.

It had been used as an unofficial 'hack' for the CO at Bassingbourn (how this happened so late in the type's career is impossible to determine) and in 1948 found its way, in sick state, to Denham. It lay there, forlorn, for two years when a group set to work to restore it to full flying health. With the help of parts from G-ACKE, which by then had met its Tiger Moth, a rejuvenated G-ABEE emerged in mid-1951 complete with overhauled Gipsy II engine.

Like the original DH60 Moth, the Avian was not the easiest aeroplane to enter. With a long exhaust pipe down the port side, running near the top of the fuselage to a point behind the rear cockpit, entry was possible only from the other side. The walkway on the lower wing started well forward of the trailing edge and, to enter the front cockpit, a passenger needed not only to reach this but to work round a flying wire in the process! I cannot confirm the state of play on other Avians, but 'BEE offered little in the front other than, strangely, a pair of large, typically-Avro, electric-light type ignition switches which lived on even to the last mark of Anson.

The rear cockpit offered a reasonable scale of kit, including a trimmer without a gauge. However, by levelling the two ends of the chain that wound round the trim wheel, neutral was engaged! This was correct for take-off. Points of interest included a generous tank holding 24 gallons and a facility for priming without the need to raise a cowling.

Taxying was in the true vintage style. Tailskids attached to the rudder had not become the norm so, with the skid fixed to the rear of the fuselage, some energetic efforts were needed to persuade 'BEE to go round any corners other than those that led straight into wind. She had a pronounced weathercock tendency, which one would expect from her fair expanse of slab-sidedness, but with realistic use of the throttle, opposite aileron when needed and a reasonable manoeuvring space, movement on the ground was adequately controllable.

If there was one crime that the upright Gipsy II of 105hp would not tolerate, it was rapid throttle movement. Fuel supply was by gravity and there was no fuel pump, a feature common to most biplanes with tanks fitted in the centre-section of the top wing providing a good natural head of fuel. The early Gipsy spluttered quietly but decisively with any harsh power increase, which was a mild problem on the ground when a good rush of slipstream was needed to bring the rudder into business.

Take-off was uneventful if carried out reasonably into wind. With the relatively low power, there was hardly any swing; acceleration was tame, too, but with a low wing loading the run was short and 'BEE was soon climbing smoothly and quietly at 65mph. Vertical success was at a rate of about 600ft/min, despite an imaginative range of figures better and worse, published in a number of different documents.

The most noticeable features of the climb, which the Gipsy performed very comfortably when slightly throttled back to give 2,000rpm, were the high nose position and the lack of draught. The first, of course, contributed largely to the second. Goggles could be raised and kept raised throughout the climb; this was possible with some other biplanes fitted with upright engines and, consequently, low-slung propellers, but the Avian was more comfortable than most.

Lowering the nose for level flight created (not surprisingly) a very marked increase in draught round the face and a first feeling of being mildly cold. The engine was unexpectedly quiet and smooth at all times except when suffering from the odd cough already mentioned. A verbally advised cruise of 1,850rpm provided an indicated reading of 84mph, which was about what I had expected. Again, textbooks quote cruise figures for various versions of the Avian between 82mph and 105mph, but these were not accompanied by comparative rpm references; as by this time 'BEE was at least a mild hybrid, I doubt if it conformed precisely to the specification of any particular mark. Nominally it was a (Sports) Avian IV.

One of the first qualities that I hope to find in any aeroplane in level flight is a set of ailerons that are lively and, preferably, light on the touch. Here the Avian could not claim to shine, for they were slower in response than that of any Moth in the straight-winged DH60 range; but I viewed the Avian as a tourer and certainly not the type of machine on which to try anything ambitious in roll. There was some cable play fore-and-aft and the stick could be moved an inch or two before any elevator response came to light; however, I was assured that this was a temporary elastic condition as a result of a new elevator control cable, so to criticise this as a type characteristic would be unfair.

Turns needed to be of the traditional biplane variety. The drag of the ailerons was accentuated as they were not differential, so into-turn rudder to maintain balanced flight played a major part in the turning process. This, of course, is much more satisfying than the present-day turn carried out almost on aileron alone.

The stall was straightforward but, as from the level, it called for a marked show of nose and very pronounced backward pressure, it was not a condition that a pilot would have been likely to meet inadvertently. My old notes record that the power-off breakaway occurred at 43mph, but I am inclined to challenge this: I would have expected a lower reading.

The Avian looped contentedly from 120, even though a little more energy from the elevators would have made the over-the-top arc feel a shade more decisive. Perhaps the manoeuvre that it liked best was the stall turn, which it performed admirably; but I have never been a confirmed aerobat and leisurely, early biplanes have better things to offer. What, among aeronautical activities, can be more pleasant than a gentle potter, with the throttle well back, and the calm of a summer evening to go with it? 1,400rpm produced virtually no mechanical vibration or noise (except a satisfying burble from the end of the long exhaust pipe behind one's left ear) with an indicated 65mph on the level. Only rationed daylight brought this happy state to a close.

The landing, with no wind at all by this time, offered no special features other than an expected need to hold the nose very high in order to achieve a bona fide 3-pointer. The subsequent run seemed slightly longer than I had expected, but all aeroplanes roll-on in such calm conditions. The undercarriage, of a fairly soft nature, always seemed to provide a smooth ride but, again, taxying towards the hangars at Denham, the engine reminded me that it would not tolerate inconsiderate treatment. Full rudder, a burst of throttle and a cough told me that this Avian, at least (and there were no others) was not the machine to try to manoeuvre in confined spaces.

What is the final verdict? With a markedly soft spot for an open cockpit biplane, obviously I liked the Avian. By direct comparison with two other types of similar configuration, the DH60 Moth and the Spartan Arrow, I put the Avian between the two. I have not yet found anything that beats the real Moth as an aeroplane in which to enjoy the purer pleasures of flying, but the Avian came a fairly close second. It was docile, quiet, relatively draught-free, but still decidedly 'open'.

A handful of Avians still exists, and two are presently earmarked for restoration in the UK. Perhaps after sixty years we will soon see one airborne again!

Chapter 14

Can the Tutor teach?
Avro Tutor

In the very early days of flying there was no organised pattern of training for pilots; not until 1915 did the Smith-Barry system, introduced on Avro 504s at Gosport, bring into use some form of set sequence. This was the start of serious dual as we know it and the manuals of the time provided laid-down 'patter' for instructors to blow down their rubber Gosport tubes, hopefully into the ears of their suffering pupils.

Flying in the First World War happened on a far larger scale than most people realise; almost 9,000 Avro 504s were built, which is far more than any British Service trainer since then. When the need came for a new machine to replace the 504, two types entered the field. One was Hawker's Tomtit, which was produced in small numbers, but the overall winner of the contest was the Tutor from the Avro stable, whose designers had a solid background on which to build. By the early thirties the RAF had settled into a relatively small peacetime organisation and the requirement was fulfilled with the production of only 394 machines.

The Avro Tutor entered service in 1932 and soon equipped the majority of RAF flying schools. Training of the time concentrated on pure flying, stressing the need for good judgment. Very sensibly the normal way to land was from a glide approach, which was useful in establishing sound practice for forced landings, while aerobatics and formation flying held high places on the priority list. The aircraft had no radio, navigational aids were mainly in a pilot's head, instrument flight was at a relatively rudimentary development stage and there were few complications in the cockpit. Even the much heralded (and very successful) British standard panel of six flight instruments had not been introduced.

Despite its relative simplicity, the Tutor was ahead of its time with efficient brakes, a tailwheel that usually faced the right way, surprisingly roomy cockpits with adjustable seats and rudder pedals and an all-flying variable incidence tailplane. It was a tough horse, with a span of thirty-four feet, an all-up weight of 2,400lb (tare 1,722) and a generous fuel capacity of 32 gallons to feed a seven-cylinder Armstrong-Siddeley Lynx radial engine developing 215hp. Economically, regarding both initial purchase and operating expenditure, this relatively large beast must have been unpopular among those whose lot it was to protect the Service purse, but for others who instructed on it the Tutor could have produced few complaints. Certainly, its successors – the Tiger Moth and Magister – were lighter, less sophisticated and less expensive, yet each fulfilled its allotted role admirably.

Today, only one Tutor remains. As K3215 it served from 1933 until 1936 with the RAF College at Cranwell and then moved to the Central Flying School; it was the last machine of the type to be retired from RAF service, somehow remaining on strength until December 1946, which most probably was two years later than any other example. Perhaps some fortunate station commander managed to keep it under his watchful eye; at that time such a commendable practice was not uncommon. After demob, this sole survivor was registered G-AHSA, but whilst being used for the film *Reach for the Sky*' it suffered a crankshaft failure and subsequently was grounded for a considerable time. Eventually, though, a nationwide search revealed three specimens of the Lynx in various states of disrepair and, from these, Armstrong-Siddeley of Coventry built up one good unit. Then G-AHSA/K3215 started a new life with the Shuttleworth Collection at Old Warden, where I was fortunate to be able to fly it on more than twenty occasions spread over almost twenty-five years.

From outside, the Tutor can offer several features of practical merit. Basically, it is an all-metal aeroplane with a fuselage structure of welded steel tube with fabric covering on wooden stringers; the one-piece side panels, each running along the entire length of the two tandem cockpits, can be removed for ease of inspection and servicing. The engine, too, is easily accessible and much routine maintenance can be carried out without taking off the Townend exhaust ring that surrounds it.

Once aboard, the aeroplane's relatively massive bulk again comes to the fore, for I know of no other light aeroplane with individual cockpits that can offer such an enormous amount of space and comfort. Yes, comfort! The rudder pedals are easily adjustable for distance and the bucket seat travels up and down through a range to suit the reach of any pilot of any size. An enormous trim wheel and a thick brake lever, which can be set up on the notched basis, add to the atmosphere of size and solidity that accompanies everything about this machine.

Starting offers the first and only inconvenience, for in keeping with the traditions of the time, and in common with most other Armstrong-Siddeley radials, the Lynx is brought to life via a starter magneto (which necessitates a third ignition switch) and some energetic hand-cranking from within. If, as has happened many times, a pilot straps himself in tightly before this stage, he may have difficulty in reaching the cranking handle, which is on the right wall in front of, and reached from under, the instrument panel. The Tutor offers a choice of three alternative starting methods, including a dog on the front of the propeller to engage the crosshead from a mobile Hucks starter, but the standard method is far more basic. Two men, with hands linked, prepare for a hand-swing and, after all the normal setting-up has been completed, the pilot calls 'one, two, three, go.' On this last word, the swingers swing; the pilot turns the crank as energetically as its inaccessible position allows, and he keeps turning until the engine fires steadily. Then he switches off the third magneto. As an alternative to hand-swinging, an engineer can activate things by winding an external cranking handle. There are, of course, a few other things to do, such as remembering to switch off the priming cock, which cannot be reached at all from the rear cockpit without standing upright! An intriguing feature of the Lynx and its sister engines, including the earlier Mongoose in the Tomtit, is that they will run happily whilst turning either way; it is not uncommon for an unsuspecting pilot, who at first sound thinks all is well, to see the engineers' hands waving for him to switch off and try again in the hope that it will obey its left-hand tractor specification at the next attempt.

At this point we revert to relative normality. Oil pressure rises to about 90lb/in^2 and on a radial it is particularly important that it should do so fairly quickly; then we wait for some positive action by the oil temperature gauge before the run-up, for this engine likes a heavy oil (straight 100 is used), which keeps the consumption to an acceptable figure. As with most radials, the Lynx runs slowly and a full-power check gives only 1,675rpm or so. Once on the move the efficient brakes, which are as good as those of a Chipmunk and far better than those of the Magister, which is one of the types that replaced the Tutor, provide a pleasant surprise to anyone who has flown other (mostly brakeless) machines of the period.

The weight reveals itself on take-off. Despite an alleged 215hp, acceleration is remarkable for being so unspectacular; the entire ground run is fairly ponderous, but only a little guidance is required for keeping straight and once the Tutor is airborne it seems to be relieved of its troubles and settles into a tolerable climb rate of 750ft/min against a book figure of 1,000. It beats its way commendably through the bumps and behaves best if left alone.

The cruise is comfort itself. The cockpit provides scope for an airborne picnic, if required, but equally it offers really worthwhile space for the more conventional pastimes such as furling and unfurling maps. It is sensible to keep goggles on as a secondary windscreen, but the one fitted to the aeroplane is sufficiently workmanlike to permit periodical doses of bare-eyed flight. The makers' very precise setting of 1,620rpm for the cruise gives 90mph.

At lower speeds the handling characteristics are not outstanding, and despite ailerons on all four wings, certainly not crisp. Understandably, this is most marked at 65-70mph in the climb, but an airspeed increase of about twenty per cent produces a response that is much more alert. Throughout the speed range, though, control displacement is unusually marked and in snappy reverse-direction turns the control column really moves across the width of the broad cockpit. However, there is more overall control improvement with speed increase than the unwary pilot might expect from the initial sluggishness, for from a little more than normal cruise of 90mph the machine can be rolled into and out of turns with some spirit. This must have been a marvellous asset for any ab-initio instructor whose task was to teach the varying effects of controls and subsequent exercises at different airspeeds.

In the interests of long life of both airframe and engine (which must always be to the fore in a pilot's mind throughout any flight) aerobatics are kept to an absolute minimum and manoeuvres that involve negative G are banned. As a result, one does not indulge in prolonged series of aerobatics either for practice or personal pleasure; no doubt those who flew Tutors regularly when there were plenty of them reached high standards (and certainly the CFS team members, who specialised in inverted formation, achieved this) but from the odd few loops and some rolls-off I can claim neither expert knowledge nor a clear conscience to investigate. The machine is extremely pleasant to fly and, of all the earlier types held at Old Warden, it is by far the most practicable and satisfactory specimen for general and cross-country work; it is the oldest machine of all that can tolerate a fair cross-wind for landing and can be taxied anywhere without help, but it does not ask specifically to be aerobatted, especially when compared with, say, the Chipmunk, which does. As the Tutor is a heavyish aeroplane, airspeed diminishes rapidly in the first part of a loop, and it is easy to run short of it at the top; if one makes this mistake – as, alas, I know from experience – nothing drastic happens, but there is a strange and protracted feeling of empty nothingness as the machine seems to flop its way round into the descent, still very considerately facing the right way.

A feature that finds the underlying truth in any aeroplane is its manner at and near the stall. Here the Tutor is very kind, perhaps too much so for a trainer. As airspeed decreases, a marked control woolliness displays itself, especially with the ailerons, but despite this they are usable down to the breakaway, which occurs at 42mph. From a gradual, level approach to the stall, the result is very tame, with a fairly positive nose drop but almost no tendency for a wing to go down. If put to the test in slightly less textbook conditions, such as a more rapid movement in pitch and a spot of built-in yaw, slight spirit displays itself and I have no doubt that if left alone, it would enter a spin; respect for the Tutor's age, though, has meant not waiting to find out.

The big trim-wheel is heavily geared and a lot of winding is needed to produce a small change in tailplane incidence. This means, of course, that large movements are called for in order to remove stick loads, which are more than moderately pronounced with changes in airspeed. Not surprisingly, this is most noticeable between level flight and a glide approach, and shows most at the end of a demonstration flight when the average operating speed has been a little higher than that of a routine cruise. Alterations in power, too, create moderate load changes.

Generally, the view is good in all directions, but the exhaust collector ring and its external cowling protrude well outside the fuselage line and this creates some visual obstruction on the final approach and hold-off. However, the landing itself is completely uncomplicated, for a gorgeously soft undercarriage absorbs most of the loads that one may place upon it. Although the Tutor can bounce from a premature touchdown during the round-out, its general tolerance is most comforting. In normal conditions there is little tendency to swing during the landing run, although the tailwheel encourages a longer roll than might be anticipated; if needed, though, brakes provide solutions to both situations.

General reactions are very favourable. Everyone who has flown the Tutor likes it. It is a gentleman's aeroplane in its roominess and docility, while the powerful response from the ailerons at the high end of the speed scale helps to produce a positive feeling of being in control of the situation. Assessing it as an aeroplane to fly, it qualifies as excellent; judging it as a trainer on which to teach, it fails to object

CAN THE TUTOR TEACH?

sufficiently strongly to minor mishandling, so an instructor might not find his pupils' errors standing out as glaringly as they should.

Most aeroplanes in the Shuttleworth Collection retain their original military or civil identities; however, in 2006 the Tutor emerged from a major overhaul as K3241, in a startling fresh sunray colour scheme of the Central Flying School Aerobatic Team in the mid-1930s. This policy of recreating a 'new' historic aeroplane from time to time has a positive reaction among enthusiasts, especially photographers, whose interest in a specific machine is suddenly reactivated.

Colours apart, the world's only surviving Avro Tutor has a significant place in the Collection's range of Service trainers, all of which from the Avro 504 of 1914 to the Chipmunk and Provost of the early 1950s are represented. No other organisation can make this claim.

Chapter 15

The consolation prize
Hawker Tomtit

After extensive and surprisingly drawn-out trials, the Avro Tutor of the previous chapter won the day. However, the Tomtit was awarded a form of consolation prize and H.G. Hawker Engineering (predecessors of Hawker Aircraft) were granted a modest production order for twenty-five aircraft. Here we have an aeroplane that appeared at a transitional stage in the RAF's technical needs. Following a succession of wooden aircraft, the Tomtit broke new ground by having a virtually all-metal structure but retaining the traditional fabric covering of its predecessors. It was relatively light, with a loaded weight of only 1,750lb compared with the Tutor's empty figure of 1,800lb. So perhaps this generated greater benefits than such a small contract would appear to offer, for subsequently the company provided a very high percentage of the RAF's operational aircraft through the thirties, with names such as the Hart, Hind and Fury as the best known among the eight Hawker types concerned.

The first Tomtit flew in late 1928 and the early machines off the line entered service with No. 3 Flying Training School at Grantham. Subsequently, they served on a few other units including No. 24 Squadron at Northolt, where HRH the Prince of Wales flew one regularly. Most of these machines were released in 1936/7 and ten found their way onto the British civil register. Among these was K1786 – the last to have been built – which became G-AFTA in its new life. In addition to the Tomtits built for the RAF, five were constructed as civil aircraft for private owners, with four more for the Royal New Zealand Air Force and two for Canada, making a total production of thirty-six machines. Six earned their fuel and oil during the Second World War, camouflaged but still carrying their civil registrations, operating as test pilots' hacks for companies in the aircraft industry.

One such Tomtit was the personal 'hack' of Alex Henshaw, known for his Spitfire test-flying as well as record-breaking flights in the Percival Mew Gull. Post-war it became the private property of Neville Duke, chief test pilot of Hawker Aircraft, who later passed it back to the company, where it joined the firm's historic Hart G-ABMR and Hurricane G-AMAU. The three were resplendent in the company colours of dark blue and gold and in 1952-55 they appeared at several events organised by the Vintage Aeroplane Club, of which I was the young and inexperienced honorary secretary.

My next meeting with G-AFTA was in 1966 when I joined the Shuttleworth Collection at Old Warden, and it became the first machine on that historic fleet that I had the pleasure and privilege to fly. There is much that I could write about this interesting aeroplane's past life, but here we must concentrate on the main purpose: flying it. After conducting a thorough pre-flight external inspection, entry to the cockpit is easier than on many biplanes. Engine starting, though, is foreign to the modern mind. In addition to the two normal magnetos, a third 'starter mag' is energised by rapid winding of a small crank handle; this is placed inconveniently, to virtually guarantee scraping the skin off one's knuckles, so gloves are a protective necessity. This is the only dubious feature of an otherwise good cockpit layout with all main controls easily accessible.

To bring the Mongoose to life, correct internal priming is essential; with all three magnetos on, the pilot calls '3, 2, 1 now' to the propeller swingers, two of whom, with linked hands, are advisable to overcome the powerful compressions. Occasionally, the engine kicks back and revolves in the wrong direction, but assuming that all is well and it is running correctly, the third magneto is switched off and the mind concentrates on ensuring a rapid build-up of oil pressure. This is essential to avoid the risk of an internal structural catastrophe for, as a radial with just one hard-worked big end, the Mongoose needs a lot of it quickly; the gauge should register 70-90lb within a minute of starting, when the rpm can be increased from 800 to 1,000. By this stage the strange popping sound of the five-cylinder exhaust beat is obvious to all – inside and out. It is a slow-running unit and, after a suitable warming period, a static full power check produces only about 1,650rpm. At this stage the absence of a throttle friction nut is noteworthy, yet the friction level seems adequate throughout.

Unlike most earlier biplanes, which have tailskids fixed to the sternpost, the Tomtit's skid moves with the rudder and makes the taxying task relatively easy. It is essential, though, to be very careful to keep the stick hard back, for the mainwheels are set further aft than on many types and a burst of throttle to negotiate a turn can cause the tail to lift, possibly with expensive consequences. Take-off is a satisfying operation with a sprightly acceleration, not much tendency to swing and a comfortable ride due to the soft long-travel undercarriage. Unstick happens without effort at a speed below the minimum ASI reading on the way to a recommended climb figure of 65mph. Here, references to two sources state that this should lead to an achievement of 1,000ft/min, but I cannot confirm the truth as I dislike belting an ageing engine on a sustained full-throttle climb. However, healthy though the real rate is, I suggest that the quoted figure is a slight overstatement of fact.

Once in the level cruise, for which there is a precisely recommended low figure of 1,620rpm, the Tomtit settles happily at an indicated 90mph. At this speed the windscreens, though small, provide a reasonably gale-free ride. Although the Frise ailerons are on the lower wings only they are unusually large, starting as close in as the third rib from the root. At low speeds the roll rate is modest and there is a noticeable measure of adverse yaw, but both conditions improve with speed. The elevators, though, are sportingly responsive throughout and, overall, the Tomtit is a pleasure to handle, although it is rather loose directionally and can be uncomfortable in turbulent conditions.

An early test on any aeroplane should be its manners near and at the stall. Here, the Tomtit is exemplary. Helped by the fixed Handley Page slats the breakaway occurs below the lowest ASI reading, (probably at about 40mph) and either wing may go down, but recovery is quick and easy. At the other end of the speed scale, it loops happily from about 120mph, and the sprightly elevators provide a usefully sensitive touch throughout. Again, through respect for the age of both the airframe and its power source, I tried no other aerobatic adventures.

What climbs must go down, so now we discover how the Tomtit behaves on the critical phase – the landing. In smooth air, the approach at an initial 65mph IAS is pleasant and easy; after shedding a few mph, this is followed by a comfortable touchdown and short ground run, helped by the Mongoose's slow tick-over which leaves very little residual thrust. So long as it all happens into wind, the tendency to swing is minimal, but without brakes the Tomtit follows the pattern of its contemporaries and dislikes anything more than the most modest of crosswinds.

So, what is the overall assessment? As an aeroplane to fly it is a very likeable steed, especially in calm conditions. As a trainer of its time, when pilots would soon need to face 'hotter' mounts, perhaps it was a shade too docile; a few built-in or unintentional vices would have been of benefit. This, though, is a mild weakness that is shared with its competitor, the Tutor, and as both produced the right results in the longer term, clearly any such fault was not serious.

Several times, over several years, I had the pleasure of flying K1786/G-AFTA as the only Tomtit to exist anywhere in the world since 1948. Certainly, it warrants a permanent place among the historic aeroplanes that should be preserved for future generations to see where it belongs – in the air.

Chapter 16

Why the Elf fell short
Parnall Elf

In the late 1920s the world of private and club flying was developing steadily, largely due to the introduction of the Cirrus Moth in 1925. The Air Ministry had subsidised the supply of these to six English flying clubs and this had encouraged other aircraft makers to enter the sales race – Avro Avian and Spartan Arrow are examples covered in other chapters. George Parnall & Co, originally shop fitters in Bristol, had produced Service aircraft during the 1914-18 war, including Avro 504s and their own (not very successful) Parnall Scout. Subsequently, they built an assortment of military and civil aircraft – again without great success.

From this assortment the Elf evolved. The first of the three to be built made its public debut at the Olympia exhibition in February 1929, later to fly from Yate as G-AAFH. Several improvements were incorporated into the Mark II, including a reduction from full to half-span ailerons and a change from a tailplane with a facility to adjust the angle on the ground only, to a unit with inflight variable incidence. A production run of just two, G-AAIN and G-AAIO, completed the Elf line. The prototype flew behind a Cirrus Hermes I of 105hp while the two later machines boasted the additional 15hp of the Hermes II. Only G-AAIN has survived, owned by the Shuttleworth Collection at Old Warden.

The absence of sales success was not through lack of effort. Parnall's advertisements in the *Aeroplane* listed various 'features of outstanding merit'. Although broadly conventional at first sight, the Elf has several novel features, some of which are good, but others of which are less bright. Among the former must be counted the wing bracing, for instead of the usual vertical interplane struts towards the tips, with landing and flying wires inboard of those struts, a system of Warren girders provides the necessary rigidity and even eliminates the need for a jury strut when the wings are folded. The makers' booklet claims that in this condition the Elf is 1ft 6in narrower than other existing machines, to facilitate transport through gateways when being retrieved after a forced landing. How they must have known what was to come!

The fuel system, however, caused problems; unlike the gravity-fed Moths and Avian with tanks in the top wing centre section, the Elf's main supply of 18 gallons is in the fuselage and therefore pump-dependent for its flow to the carburettor. A capacity of only 3 gallons in the top (gravity) tank leaves a very limited safe endurance for display flying, take-off, landing and circuit work. Both the other Elves ended their lives prematurely following pump failures.

A bonus feature is that almost all vibration is damped between the engine and airframe. Although the upright four-cylinder Hermes is itself a smooth-runner, it has a minor lumpy spot at the low end of the power scale, but even this is not transmitted to the occupants. Possibly it is the smoothest piston engine/airframe combination of any aeroplane that I have met. Another 'plus' is the tailskid's ability to caster for a few degrees, which is helpful for taxying compared with the early Moths and the Avian, which have firmly fixed skids.

The Elf is flown from the rear cockpit, which is further back than on most designs, for even the front seat is behind the centre of gravity. Clearly the distance between engine and occupant(s) contributes to the lack of vibration. The layout is pleasant, but a baffling feature is the duplicated fore-and-aft trimming facility. A large geared wooden handwheel on the right cockpit wall alters the tailplane incidence, while a small lever near the floor, just ahead of the control column, adjusts the stick pressure by a bungee. I have been unable to find anyone who could advise on the need or use for this unique combination, but as no Elf had flown for almost thirty-four years when we launched 'IN following restoration at Old Warden in 1980 this may not be surprising! By starting with each device in the neutral position and experimenting in the air, we learnt fairly quickly that even with all this help the Elf is not over-endowed with usable trim range.

The large slotted ailerons have no cables or tie rods, but are moved by external steel tubing; compared with the Moths and Avian the aileron travel is restricted, but this is a handicap only when manoeuvring at relatively slow speeds in lumpy conditions, when it is easy to be frustrated by hitting the stops with a solid clunk. The rudder and elevators have normal cable connections. The small wing gap brings the upper wing very close to the top of the fuselage at little above eye level and therefore offers a better view than on many biplanes, while the designer's aim was to eliminate all technical jargon, with ignition switches marked 'stop' and 'run' and the trim lever with its range limits marked 'top speed' and 'stall'!

It is always wise to check a type's stalling characteristics early in the test process, for often it is at the low end of the speed scale that any unwelcome characteristics reveal themselves. Here there is nothing unusual to discover, except that there is very little pre-stall buffet to serve as a warning of things to come. The break-away itself occurs at about 45mph, which is comparable with the Avian, for which my notes recorded 43mph IAS; it is very innocuous, with immediate recovery on moving the stick forward centrally.

Unlike the Moths and the Avian, both of which would loop smoothly, the Elf is not cleared for aerobatics. It is essentially a tourer, cruising at about 80mph using 6.5 gallons an hour at 1,900 rpm so, in respect of performance, all three types are broadly comparable. An additional check, though, is to ensure that adequate fuel pressure is maintained as, in the event of pump failure, the main tank will be unusable.

Prior to landing, primarily to retain adequate control on the ailerons with their limited displacement, it is wise to maintain 75mph until settled on the final straight approach; then the speed can be reduced progressively to cross the aerodrome boundary at 55. The long nose ahead calls for a more marked hold-off than either of the other two types to achieve a three-point touchdown. The general tendency to swing as the speed decreases is broadly similar on all three, although, with the weight of the pilot so far behind the centre of gravity, I imagine that once started, a ground loop would be unstoppable; it is important to remain alert, especially if not directly into the wind.

The Elf is an interesting product of an imaginative designer's mind and well worth preserving as a flying historic exhibit. While not a world prize-winner, it contains several unusual features. It came to light when the builders of Moths and Avians were well established in the aviation market and clearly it was not a competitor in terms of numbers. Apart from its reliance on a fuel pump that caused the loss of two out of three, it is a likeable little aeroplane that deserved a happier history. As a broad, overall assessment, though, I think the production numbers – Moth, Avian and Elf, in that order – reveal the truth.

Unfortunately, the Elf was not alone in failing to capture the market, and the Parnall name slipped away quietly from the aviation scene, known only to those who were close to the pulse of the time.

Chapter 17

A roof over your head
de Havilland DH80A Puss Moth

The need for cabin comfort among some private owners started to break through in the late 1920s; the de Havilland DH80 enclosed high-wing two-seat monoplane seemed to set that long-term ball rolling, at least into slow motion. Although only one was built, flying from Stag Lane in September 1929, the design quickly matured into the DH80A Puss Moth. This became the first of the DH light aeroplanes to depart from the traditional wooden construction, for it boasted a welded steel tube fuselage, although several later members of the Moth family reverted to the earlier wooden system.

The Puss Moth was primarily a two-seater, but the rear position was off-centre so that a third occupant could be carried alongside. Failure of the wing structure during combinations of high speed and turbulence led to nine accidents, most fatal. A modification incorporating a small strut running from the front wing strut to the rear wing root attachment soon cleared the name. From then on Pusses proved popular, many remaining in their original owners' hands until the outbreak of war in 1939; altogether, 260 were built at home between 1930 and 1933, with twenty-five more made in Canada.

As with most good aeroplanes of the thirties, the Puss and its pilots found some records to smash. The first non-stop flight from New York to Jamaica, the first aerial crossing of the Caribbean, the first aeroplane to land in Ceylon and the first serious air mail route of more than 1,300 miles (Karachi-Bombay-Madras) were among the dozens of achievements. Before the famous MacRobertson Race from England to Australia in 1934, a Puss Moth flew the route in reverse in 8 days 9 hours to get to England to compete in the event, in which it attained third place in the handicap section.

Puss Moths established the frequently-tackled Cape record three times, the last with Amy Mollison at the helm, when she managed to achieve the best ever times in both directions. The first east-west solo crossing of the Atlantic and the first solo flight from England to South America (making also the first east-west solo crossing of the South Atlantic) were added to the type's many achievements.

Apart from its obvious suitability for records, the comfort and pleasant handling qualities of the Puss made it an ideal machine for general flying. In 1939-40, forty-seven were impressed for war service with the RAF and the Air Transport Auxiliary. Fortunately, several survived to reappear on the civil register in 1946; among these was G-AAZP, which was built in 1930 and had spent four years of its pre-war life registered in Egypt. I met it at White Waltham in 1951, shortly after restoration by Doug Bianchi's Personal Plane Services.

Originally fitted with a Gipsy III, 'ZP followed traditional practice and exchanged this somewhere in its career for the more usual Gipsy Major 1, offering 130hp. Instrument layout seemed to have enjoyed some facelifts too, but remained basic with one ASI, sensitive altimeter (an obvious latecomer), turn and slip indicator, climb and descent meter, vertical level, rev counter, and the most important of all dials, an oil pressure gauge. The layout had a vintage haphazardness that could confuse in serious situations; as an example, the altimeter filled the top left-hand hole in which one would hope to read airspeed. However, here a choice was provided, for in addition to the main cockpit instrument, a strut-mounted graduated plate, worked by the airflow pressing against a spring-loaded pointer, offered an alternative source of airspeed information. Unfortunately, in most flight conditions the answers, too, offered a choice.

Although standardised instrument layouts had not been invented in the early thirties, many other features, some of which we consider to be modern, were there from the start; effective wheel brakes, a cabin heater, folding wings (what a boon these would be in today's cramped hangar conditions) and air brakes were included, while tankage (one tank in each wing) of 32 gallons could offer an endurance of five hours. Unusually accurate and reliable contents gauges protruded below each wing, using extensions of the floats as indicators. In-out fuel cocks were in the roof just aft of the main spar and gravity from a good head provided the flow.

For taxying, an unexpected amount of power was needed to get the Puss moving, but once under way the ride was pleasantly soft without feeling wallowy. Manoeuvring was quite easy with help from the differential brakes, which could be pre-set on the ratchet or left off until needed. The engine and propeller (of coarser pitch than I would have chosen) created far less vibration than on many later Gipsy Major installations. Because of the propeller, full throttle at the start of take-off offered little more than 1,800rpm, which played a part in the sluggish initial acceleration, but a noticeable need was to apply a very positive forward stick movement to raise the tail in order to gain the flying attitude. Although markedly accentuated with a rear seat occupant, this applied even when flying solo – from the front. Unstick, however, was a clean-breasted exercise that happened even below the lowest ASI graduation at 40mph.

A sustained climb at 65mph IAS and 1,900rpm (the lot) produced a result below the modest published figure of 630ft/min, but once on the level the previous coarse pitch problems converted to a bonus. At only 1,800rpm the Puss purred for hours at a genuine 105mph, compared with a book figure of 108mph for maximum continuous cruise which probably meant 2,000rpm. Clearly 'ZP was going faster than it was intended to do when fitted with a finer-pitch propeller, so I tried the top end of the scale. Against a maker's claim of 128mph, 'ZP in her twenty-second year of life settled happily at 132 and 2,150rpm.

I am not surprised that pre-war Puss owners clung to their possessions. As would be expected, handling was not crisp, but it was pleasant and effortless. The ailerons, though heavyish, were firm in feel and reasonably responsive. As with so many types, the rudder was light and the elevators somewhere between the two, providing an imbalance that did not spoil the total effect. The Puss Moth was essentially an A to B aeroplane and did not call for extremes of control displacement.

No aeroplane is foolproof (a point so sensibly stressed in Tiger Club machines which have notices stating 'all aeroplanes bite fools'), but the DH80a tolerates more liberties than most. A stall from level flight with the throttle closed proved almost impossible, for if the stick is brought progressively back as the speed slowly decreases (it is a clean aeroplane) the machine adopts a steady sink at probably 10mph below the minimum ASI graduation at 40. In this condition the ailerons are ineffective, but the rudder stays in business.

Of course, all aeroplanes (regardless of makers' claims) can stall. If the nose is raised while power is on and then the throttle is closed, or if the nose is lifted fairly actively in the early stage of the glide condition, then a normal stall will take place. In 'ZP's case it did the job properly, with the port wing going down at the same time, and at about the same rate, as the nose. I imagine that this would have led to a spin without further pilot provocation, but in view of the type's earlier structural troubles, its age and the normal category CofA, I did not wait to confirm. Instant recovery was trouble-free.

In level flight the Puss provides an excellent opportunity to see so much of the surrounding area beneath, but in a turn and especially in the circuit, there is a need for more care and caution than on some types with other wing positions. Once on the approach, however, a markedly efficient gadget comes to its own; a lever on the right of the cockpit turns the undercarriage strut fairings through ninety degrees to form air brakes and these convert a very flat glide to a sensibly steep descent but, unlike flap lowering, this does not cause chaos with the trim.

The Puss is very forgiving in the landing phase. It is possible to approach at any speed between about 50 and 70mph, and the take-what-it-is-given undercarriage absorbs everything very comfortably.

Fifty-five seems the best hedge crossing speed and even if one makes contact with the ground prematurely during the round-out stage, this absorption takes over and it is rare for the machine to bounce back in the air again. The ground ride is exceptionally comfortable and accentuates the other qualities that combine to make it what would have been called a gentleman's aeroplane.

Fortunately, this Puss Moth is still with us. 'ZP had passed its twenty-first birthday when I met it for the first time and at ninety-two years of age it remains active.

Chapter 18

Not a Moth
Spartan Arrow

I describe in the book a number of products from the late twenties and early thirties of outwardly very similar patterns. The reputation of the Moths lives on, but few will have heard of either the Simmonds Spartan or the Spartan Arrow. Spartans of one sort or another existed in worthwhile numbers until shortly before the outbreak of war, when the breed virtually disappeared from the flying scene.

The original Spartan came from the brain of O.E. Simmonds, previously a designer with Supermarine. His concept had one very specific claim to fame. Ease, speed and economy of repair were major design features and almost any damage could be rectified with the support of only a minimum spares holding. All four wings were exactly identical, so that one spare unit could be used in any position; this, of course, meant that the aerofoil was of symmetrical section. Each elevator was interchangeable and the rudder could be used as an elevator and, of course, vice versa. Likewise, the undercarriage components were identical on each side.

The first Simmonds Spartan, G-EBYU, flew in the summer of 1928 and competed in the King's Cup Air Race a few weeks later. Although not successful in gaining a place, this prototype flew non-stop from Croydon to Berlin in September of that year and returned in similar manner only three days afterwards. The interchangeability of parts proved a sales success at first, but a symmetrical-section wing is not ideal in practice and the performance failed to sparkle; also, the Spartan earned a reputation for unfriendly habits in the spin. This led to some rethinking, but by this time nearly fifty had been built at Weston near Southampton, and most of these flew successfully for several years.

By 1930 the company changed its name to Spartan Aircraft Ltd; but Mr Simmonds remained very much in charge of design and from his experiences with the earlier machine he produced the Spartan Arrow. As the symmetrical wing needed to give way to a more conventional section (the well-known high-lift Clark Y), some of the interchangeability became lost, though separate removable wing-tips and trailing edge portions made it possible still to benefit from a measure of 'swopability' and the elevators remained identical, added to which the spinning problems of the original Simmonds machine disappeared.

Arrows flew with a variety of sources of power, initially with the upright Gipsy I of 100hp and later with the additional 20hp of the Gipsy II. The prototype, G-AAWY, first flew in the Spring of 1930 and production continued until 1933, with examples powered also by the ADC Cirrus III, the Cirrus Hermes and, as a test bed, the 160hp Napier Javelin. Arrows were used by the Household Brigade Flying Club, the Bristol and Wessex Aeroplane Club, the Isle of Wight Flying Club and others, but most were privately owned; although a few ventured into the Second World War, mainly in storage, only G-ABWP saw aeronautical daylight again after the war.

G-ABWP was registered on 18 May 1932 and completed in July; it was bought four years later by Richard Shuttleworth at Old Warden. This Arrow spent all the war years in storage and eventually emerged, for static display only, for the famous Fifty Years of Flying Exhibition at Hendon in July 1951. This was the display of displays for people with a love of vintage aviation, for many machines that had not been seen in public for years re-appeared for the occasion. 'BWP retired behind the scenes again afterwards, but in 1953 I met it for the first and only time. Doug Bianchi of Personal Plane Services, then based at White Waltham, acquired it for £100 from the Shuttleworth Collection on behalf of a client and I had the pleasant task of ferrying it for him. It had been assembled again by the Old Warden engineers and this was my first-ever visit to the Collection; in more recent times I have wished that 'BWP could have remained where it should belong, among hangars full of fellow early-birds, but its long-term owner,

Raymond Blain, looked after it impeccably for many years. This was not the case, though, when I stepped aboard; a lot later I learned that it had been bolted together for the one flight and had not even been air-tested after probably fourteen years in bits. Despite that, as you will read, the subsequent flight revealed no significant failings.

This Arrow was powered by the upright Cirrus Hermes II of 105hp, but unlike this unit when installed in a Moth, which had the cylinder-heads, rockers and valve stems exposed, the Spartan machine had a fully cowled engine. Entry was made easy by the provision of unusually generous doors on the right, while the other side was effectively barred as a means of access by the high position of the long exhaust pipe, which ran along near the cockpit within easy hand-scorching reach – a feature common to the upright-engined biplanes of the time. An unusual facility for the sporting owner was a large luggage locker on the entry side that extended almost the full length of the rear fuselage to accommodate golf clubs.

Different Arrows varied not only in power, but in a number of fundamental features. They came off the line in a mixed bag with ailerons on upper and lower wings or on the lower set only; 'BWP was one of the latter. The tailskid was fixed to the fuselage sternpost and, therefore, of no help when taxying, but the undercarriage offered a softer and more forgiving ride than that provided by the earliest Moths. Take-off was unspectacular; with a high-lift wing section and an empty weight theoretically 20lb more than that of the Hermes powered Moth, the Arrow unstuck at virtually no readable IAS, but at an indicated 60mph would clock about 600ft/min with one light occupant and no luggage. In this attitude the forward view was typical of a machine with an upright engine – poor – and the ailerons were reluctant to produce energetic results, but naturally both these sins diminished on a settled cruise, even though this occurred at barely 80mph. A very short burst at full throttle (limited out of respect for the engine's age) produced 98mph indicated, but I have no position error corrections and the textbook figures, variously quoted as 103, 104 and 106mph, cannot be too far wrong. The stall – a very innocuous and rather indecisive affair – occurred at 38mph, which, allowing for corrections, makes sense of the book figure of 41mph. It seems safe to assume that the ASI was under reading by 3-5mph throughout the range.

Memory fades over many years and one flight, with only one take-off and one landing, is insufficient to assess any machine comprehensively. I intended to carry out a few circuits at the destination end, but an intermittently cutting magneto prevented that, so I can only comment on one approach. 55 IAS seemed right; the ailerons were unresponsive, and the forward view was expectedly lacking, but the big elevators proved effective in the round-out.

The Spartan Arrow's main features centred on practical rather than flying virtues. The interchangeability of parts, the roomy cockpit and the large locker were more redeeming than the type's pure handling qualities, which were definitely a poor second to those of the original Moth range. (But on a calm day a DH60 could make almost any light aeroplane – ancient or modern – seem a bit coarse). Nothing on the Arrow happened very crisply and a pilot with sporting intentions would find it rather short of fighting spirit, but it was a pleasant, docile, handsome mount and certainly worth saving for the young generation to see. It cannot claim to have been a world winner in any field, but it cannot be called a bad aeroplane, so I am glad to say that G-ABWP remains with us.

The Shuttleworth Collection's replica of Mr A.V. Roe's Triplane No. IV has 'a rooted objection to responding to normal management' and more wings than the accustomed ration.

Shuttleworth's Bristol F2B Fighter – the most effective fighting aeroplane of the First World War.

Shuttleworth's de Havilland DH51 'Miss Kenya', the first aeroplane to carry a Kenyan registration and precursor of the Moth series.

Also from the Shuttleworth Collection, de Havilland DH60 Cirrus Moth of 1925.

Go! – Avro Avian about to be flagged away in a handicap race.

Shuttleworth's Parnall Elf: some novel features, but failed to impact the market.

de Havilland's move to an enclosed cabin and welded steel fuselage – the DH80A Puss Moth of 1930, with cabin heater and folding wings.

The Spartan Arrow has a large locker with space for a set of golf clubs. This aircraft has been owned by the same family for the last fifty-eight years.

Shuttleworth's Avro Tutor: relatively large, comfortable, but perhaps too forgiving of errors for a training machine.

Shuttleworth's Hawker Tomtit: lost out to the heavier, less economical Tutor but gained a limited order for the RAF and perhaps led to success for future Hawker aircraft of the 1930s.

Taxying out in Comper Swift G-ABUS for the start of an air race, with my future wife providing outside help.

de Havilland DH82A Tiger Moth – the RAF's primary trainer for twenty years from the early 1930s.

Pleasure flying from Southport beach with the de Havilland DH83 Fox Moth, a familiar sight both before and after the Second World War.

The Vintage Aeroplane Club's Avro Club Cadet, which took me to 1st Place in the 1952 Grosvenor Trophy Race.

BA Swallow – 'the safest aeroplane in the world', a docile piece of vintage machinery.

de Havilland DH87A Hornet Moth, previously with the Shuttleworth Trust: an excellent, comfortable tourer.

de Havilland DH89A Dragon Rapide: the short-haul airliner pre and post the Second World War.

Miles M.3 Falcon – a sporting tourer of the 1930s.

Ron Paine's Miles M.2L Hawk Speed Six: usually one of the fastest on the start line, with relatively few vices.

Alex Henshaw's Percival E2H Mew Gull: a hot ship, but a cramped cockpit for record-breaking flights.

Shuttleworth's Gloster Gladiator: the RAF's last biplane fighter, a true pilot's aeroplane.

Another winner from the Miles stable, the M.11 Whitney Straight – one of the very best touring aeroplanes of the mid 1930s, but impacted by the threat of war.

Derby Aviation's Avro Anson 1 with magnetometer; later Elstree's twin trainer and eventually flown with the Skyfame Museum.

Airspeed Oxford: the most useful and successful twin military trainer of all time?

Avro Anson C.19: one of the safest aeroplanes ever to see RAF service and an uncomplaining load-lifter.

Miles M.14A Hawk Trainer 3: not without fault, but a useful trainer – until concerns over glue failure put paid to club and school use.

de Havilland's departure from biplanes: the DH94 Moth Minor. A pleasant tourer, with folding wings for storage – but another good design impacted by wartime priorities.

Percival P.44 Proctor 5: a capable, though not particularly popular tourer. Again, the fleet was hit by glue concerns.

An early de Havilland DH98 Mosquito: a pilot's delight – on two engines, but little scope for error on one!

The Mosquito PR34: virtually a different aircraft with a 50% increase in weight and a doubling in range.

Miles M.38 Messenger – excellent short field performance.

Gloster Meteor – the first jet to enter RAF service. Here the first two-seat trainer, the T7 – good handling, but very thirsty!

Miles M.65 Gemini – the Elstree School's twin trainer, a more economical successor to the Anson 1.

Miles M.57 Aerovan – a brief encounter with an interesting but commercially unsuccessful machine.

Auster J/1N Autocrat – technically simple and economical for club training, but always ready to provide a bounce on landing.

Auster J/5F Aiglet Trainer – a little more sophisticated than the J/1N, aerobatic and more willing to stay down on landing.

Percival P.40 Prentice: roomy, comfortable successor to the Tiger Moth, but poorly harmonised controls and a better tourer than a trainer.

de Havilland Canada DHC1 Chipmunk, a delight to fly – but faced by obstructions to conversion for civil use.

Percival P.56 Provost T1: with 550hp, a large departure from the past Service practice of a low-powered, simple basic trainer.

National Air Races 1950: Auster AOP.6 starting to round a pylon, pressed by a Tipsy Belfair.

Elstree Flying Club 1956: Jimmy Vernon, Audrey Windle my future wife, me, Bill Bailey – the Hawk Trainer formation team ending an era, the last time one would see four Magisters/Hawk Trainers airborne together. Or was it?

Chapter 19

Toy-like dimensions with life-sized performance
Comper CLA7 Swift

The Swift was the idea of Nick Comper, who served at RAF Cranwell in the twenties and was closely involved in the series of light types that emerged from there with the designation CLA – standing for Cranwell Light Aircraft. In 1929, Comper formed the Comper Aircraft Company at Hooton Park, near Liverpool, to build the Swift, which itself was developed from the CLA3 racer. In fact, the Cranwell designations continued and the prototype CLA7 Swift, G-AARX, emerged early in 1930 with a 35hp ABC Scorpion to provide the power; in this form the total loaded weight was only 600lb and the selling price £400 or about 66p per lb! Clearly, however, the design had considerable development potential and soon appeared with the 75hp Pobjoy R seven-cylinder radial. Forty-one Swifts were built before Comper Aircraft ceased to produce aeroplanes in 1934.

It is a very small aeroplane, all wood, with a girder-type fuselage built in three sections and with strut-braced wings that fold from their normal span of twenty-four feet to only 7ft 6in. The undercarriage uses a rubber-cord suspension that is neatly and totally enclosed within the fuselage.

In 1931, Nick Comper flew G-AAZF for 2,600 miles from Croydon to Italy and back in twenty-six hours, while G-ABNH flew 7,320 miles in seventy-three hours and just failed to beat the existing South Africa record. Also, C.A. Butler, in G-ABRE with extra tankage totalling a capacity of 42 gallons and giving a range of more than 1,000 miles, flew without incident from Lympne to Darwin – 10,425 miles in just over nine days. Only someone who has experienced the Swift's cramped cockpit and absence of space for personal luggage can begin to appreciate what feats these long hauls must have been. 1932 saw Swift G-AAZA as the first light aeroplane to cross the Andes, involving a climb – without oxygen – to 18,000 feet.

I have already mentioned in Chapter 7 my good fortune in 1953 in being given use of Swift G-ABUS, *'Black Magic'* for some four years. This particular Swift was a very regular performer on the post-war racing scene and in it, in 1950, Tony Cole had obtained the 100km closed-circuit record for Class C.1a at a speed of 126.22mph, by which time it had been fitted with a streamlined headrest and all the control surface gaps had been taped. It had another slightly non-standard bonus, a Pobjoy Niagara engine that boasted fifteen more horsepower than the seventy-five of the 'R'.

The pilot really attaches himself to the Swift and, as some would say, he wears it rather than sits in it. The cockpit is cramped, but the low sitting position with the seat almost on the fuselage floor is not uncomfortable. Starting on G-ABUS needed to be a mildly alarming process, for despite many people offering an equal number of technical solutions, no one at the time consistently managed to achieve success unless a thoroughly fuel-soaked rag was placed into the carburettor intake and pulled clear as soon as the engine fired. This unorthodox method, which in mature retrospect frightens me, never failed.

When the Pobjoy Niagara burst to life it did so with quite a roar and was accompanied by sounds similar to several sewing machines and mangles combined. At low revs the double helical reduction gearing, which caused the propeller to revolve at less than half engine speed, made more noise than the exhaust note, but with increased power the seven cylinders provided a smoothness that is almost unknown in such a small engine. With a rev range of 600 to about 3,200, power response was marked in relation to throttle movement and, from outside, normal engine handling tended to sound harsh as the smallest lever movement would produce a change of several hundreds of rpm. View for taxying was not particularly good and

TOY-LIKE DIMENSIONS WITH LIFE-SIZED PERFORMANCE

control on the ground was not a feature of merit. With a fixed tailskid attached to the rear of the fuselage and therefore not steerable with the rudder, outside help was useful in confined spaces, although with practice carefully timed applications of power and rudder produced some moderately snappy turns.

Take-off offered few problems, for acceleration was rapid and the ground roll was remarkably short, but sufficient to need just a few seconds of positive corrective rudder. The most important precaution was to prevent the tail lifting too high, for the large coarse propeller of 6ft 6ins diameter offered very little ground clearance, so a tail-down departure was a wise move. Although I have no written record of the climb rate, I seem to remember about 1,100ft/min being turned out by G-ABUS on a C of A renewal flight test at the surprisingly high recommended figure of 80mph.

In most flight conditions forward visibility was rather restricted by the wings, for pilot's eyelevel was only marginally below them. However, the ground ahead and beneath was well in the sight line. Cockpit draught was considerable and occasionally suction tended to pull the goggles forward from the eyes; they needed to be tight-fitting and with strong bands, for if the elastic should break, eyes would stand very few minutes of flight exposure. Unfortunately, the Niagara, especially when running hot and flat out in racing conditions, tended to spurt little beads of oil that built-up on the windscreen and goggles, so long-term view could be counted as something of a luxury.

At a cruise setting of 2,800rpm, 'BUS indicated about 118mph; at all normal speeds the Swift handled pleasantly but required active hands-on flying all the time. A high roll rate with very light quick-responding ailerons made it ideal for racing pylon turns, and these could be pulled to make the radius very small indeed without any marked g effects. Fore and aft load was remarkably light with virtually no trim changes through the full flight range, despite the need for fairly positive changes in stick attitude positions between fast and slow speeds. It was just directionally stable.

The stall on G-ABUS was innocuous with only an occasional wing drop; a positive effort with marked elevator deflection was needed to achieve the fully stalled state from normal level flight. At the opposite end of the speed scale, the Swift would fly smoothly round a loop from about 130mph, but it was not easy to keep straight on the way up, especially just before reaching the inverted attitude. On the other hand, the torque and slipstream problems tended to negate themselves on a roll-off-the-top and despite some embarrassingly crooked loops I found a straight roll-off a much more likely proposition, although aileron effectiveness declined sharply at the bottom end of the speed scale and at roll-out speed a very marked lateral stick movement was needed to complete the manoeuvre cleanly. I cannot vouch for the full slow roll, for I respected the machine's age and the thought of negative g on a strut-braced high-wing monoplane was my excuse for omitting this from my limited aerobatic scope.

At all times I hoped for an uncongested circuit for, to obtain a view ahead, the only solution was to weave, as on a climb. The approach, however, produced the critical time, for although it was easy to line up on the landing path by looking well over the side, on a straight run-in (initially at 70mph) any obstruction dead ahead was impossible to see. A curved traditional fighter-type approach would not provide the real answer either, for the wing could easily get into the sightline. At this stage the reduction gearing could cause concern for the unwary, for with the throttle closed the propeller appeared to be ready to stop at its idling figure of little more than 300rpm. With the higher engine speed, of course, the problem was more one of visual effect than reality.

After crossing the boundary at 55mph, the landing itself was easy enough so long as it was treated as a genuine attempt at a three-pointer. In practice, to avoid the possibility of a wheeler and the risk of propeller contact, I found the simplest solution was to hold off slightly on the high side, get the Swift established in the landing attitude and then let it sink gradually to the ground. It liked to be landed precisely into wind when possible and, with a skid and no brakes, naturally preferred grass, but I kept 'BUS at Elstree and frequently the single tarmac runway presented problems; there was no directional control at very low speeds and I must admit to a couple of fairly energetic

TOY-LIKE DIMENSIONS WITH LIFE-SIZED PERFORMANCE

ground-loops, resulting from landing slightly downwind which, on 27 (nowadays 26) offered the advantage of an uphill ground roll.

Certainly, the Swift deserved the success and popularity that it achieved, even though it earned its reputation in a role for which it was not designed. Comper's aim was to provide an inexpensive runabout for the newly-licensed pilot, which may have made sense with the original 35hp ABC Scorpion (if it could be kept running) but the type's potential as a sporting mount brought it far nearer to the hearts and hands of more experienced pilots who achieved some highly commendable feats – making it a great little aeroplane.

The Swift's appeal continues to attract and four have been, or are being built in the UK from plans. Despite the inevitable toll of ninety years, eight of the original forty-one Swifts exist today, of which G-ACTF is flying in the UK with the Shuttleworth fleet.

Chapter 20

The eternal trainer
de Havilland DH82A Tiger Moth

The final product in de Havilland's Moth line of open-cockpit two-seat biplanes was the DH82 (later DH82a) Tiger Moth, which became by far the most widely known member of the genre, on which perhaps more British pilots have trained than on any other type. Following a first flight in 1931, 4,200 were built in England, initially by de Havilland at Hatfield, but wartime pressure on production of the DH98 Mosquito caused a move for the majority to be made by Morris Motors at Cowley, near Oxford. Tiger Moths were also made in Canada (including a version with enclosed cockpit, tailwheel and brakes) and Australia, bringing the total to about 7,150. It was 'beefier' than the DH60s, with a metal fuselage frame and staggered wings to ease baling out by parachute. It used the ubiquitous and solidly reliable DH Gipsy Major engine.

Although Tigers (as they were usually known) have earned their fuel and oil in both civil and military roles, it is in the latter that they were numerically strongest. An RAF Elementary Flying Training School of the forties would be based on a relatively small all-grass aerodrome where sound airmanship and discipline were essential ingredients. There was no radio or air traffic control, usually with just a watch office with one person ready to press the crash button in the event of an accident or serious incident. Fifteen to twenty machines in the circuit were regular occurrences, especially just before NAAFI break!

Although most Service pilots who trained on Tigers – including the author – would progress immediately afterwards to monoplanes with flaps and retractable undercarriages, the 'biplane effect' provided many thousands of pilots with the experience of practical basic airmanship that was never wasted. The Tiger was not easy to fly accurately and quickly; it revealed any shortcomings in a person's coordination of eyes, hands and feet. For this reason it proved ideal for pilot grading, when a short course of twelve hours sorted sheep from goats before those who passed that stage would begin training in earnest.

As with almost all Service trainers, including the Magister, Chipmunk, Prentice, Provost et al, the Tiger could be reluctant to recover from a spin, so a modification incorporating strakes on the fuselage sides just ahead of the tailplane, was introduced to rectify this weakness. Whilst many years ago spinning was removed from the PPL syllabus, it has always been an essential component in a Service pilot's course.

The Tiger Moth has always been a much-loved aeroplane, with many devoted owners caring for their valuable machines. It is a delight to fly, with relatively little draught in the front cockpit (where it is possible, but unwise, to fly without goggles) and rather more for the occupant of the rear seat. With a cruise speed of about 85mph at 1,900rpm it can take a long time to reach an upwind destination, but that misses the main point: flying it for flying's sake. Balanced flight calls for active use of all controls, especially the rudder, and keeping the top needle of the turn-and-slip indicator anywhere near the centre can be an exercise in itself. For those who wish to indulge in the act of aerobatics, the Tiger is cleared for all normal manoeuvres; the genuine slow roll requires the full biplane treatment with, again, generous rations of rudder. However, for those who wish to remain relatively upright, there is no shortage of either pleasure or challenge.

Like its predecessor, the DH60, the Tiger Moth has played a key role in the world of club and private flying. Shortly after the Second World War, an 'as-is' machine in fly-away condition could be bought from the Air Ministry for £50, whilst any flying training organisation that was a member of the Association of British Aero Clubs and Centres (a predecessor of AOPA) could acquire one for the concession price of £25. Not surprisingly, therefore, there were a lot of them about. Fortunately, for anyone who wishes to master (or attempt to master) the intricacies of pure flight, Tigers remain available today at several locations. Try it. Give yourself a treat – and a challenge.

Chapter 21

A very different Moth
de Havilland DH83 Fox Moth

The Fox Moth was the immediate successor to the DH82 Tiger Moth and built mainly from Tiger components, but was a very different aeroplane. The new wider fuselage provides the main difference, accommodating five people – four in a neat but rather tightly enclosed cabin ahead of the pilot's open cockpit. This meant that, unlike its many siblings, it was largely commercial in intent, but it had a very varied and successful career.

The prototype, G-ABUO, with its hard-working but willing Gipsy Major 1 of 130hp, flew from Stag Lane early in 1932 and subsequently ninety-eight examples were built there. Surprisingly, the design, slightly modified, came to light again as late as 1946, when de Havilland of Canada produced a further fifty-two. In its heyday, the Fox became known to many members of the public as it was a key mover in the world of local pleasure flights, with one operating from Croydon for seven years with Surrey Flying Services and two at Southport providing a similar service from Birkdale Sands. Apart from a break in the war, one of the latter, G-ACEJ, performed this task from 1937 until 1967, when it retired from commercial activity to join the Tiger Club fleet.

This was not all. Perhaps unbelievably for the modern mind, single-engine aeroplanes were permitted on scheduled services. Scottish Air Ferries operated from Renfrew (Glasgow) to and from remote islands. Other Foxes flew between Croydon, Portsmouth, Christchurch, Exeter and Plymouth. Sadly, Exeter is the only one that remains in use. For six years in the 30s two Foxes operated the schedule between Portsmouth and Ryde. Over much the same period Hillman Airways

A VERY DIFFERENT MOTH

used three on the Clacton-Maylands-Ramsgate schedule. Again, only Clacton survives. What has happened to civil aviation?

There is more: contrasting roles are with Imperial Airways for air mail services, with the Brazilian navy as navigation trainers, and one, G-ACDD, was modified with wheel spats and a coupé top for the then Prince of Wales. There was also a floatplane version. The DH83 also achieved an outstanding success in its first year of life, when Wally Hope baffled the handicappers in the 1932 King's Cup Air Race. The much-modified machine, which had the standard drag-producing fuel tank removed from between the top wings, the petrol carried in the cabin, a sliding cockpit canopy and other refinements, romped around the course at an amazing 124mph.

I had the good fortune to fly the long-lived G-ACEJ on two occasions, when it was one of Tony Haig-Thomas' broad but short-lived collection of Mothery. My initial impression concerned the position of the pilot's cockpit, which seemed strange with such a substantial portion of the aeroplane in front. Clearly this made the view ahead for taxying very restricted, but once on the take-off run with the tail aloft, all was well. My first flight was a lightweight solo affair, but even then the acceleration seemed more laid back than that of the Tiger Moth; once in the air, though, the downward view was greatly enhanced; this might not have any great safety value, but could be helpful when looking at objects on the ground.

On the level, the DH83 performed well, cruising at 96mph, which beat the best examples of its immediate predecessor. General handling was unexceptional, but wholly appropriate to a machine with productive commercial intent. The stall was tame and easily recoverable with only a minimum of height loss. Although capable of carrying four passengers, the Fox could do this and remain within its permitted weight only with less than half fuel aboard. At this load the climb rate is quoted at only 490 feet per minute, which is almost 200ft/min below that for the Tiger, but as the maxima are 2,070 and 1,825lb respectively, this is far from surprising.

On my second flight I had two other people on board, but the cabin is so well placed in relation to the centre of gravity that, whether light or loaded, there is relatively little difference in the required trim settings. I refrained from flying at full throttle for long enough to record an unchallengeable top speed, but the book figure is 113mph (four more than the Tiger) which, considering the wider fuselage, is very creditable; however, this reveals the extent of the modifications that must have been needed for Mr Hope to attain 124mph in the 1932 King's Cup.

The Fox Moth, with six still on the UK register, was the result of a stroke of genius by its designer A.E. Hagg, who successfully created a very efficient five-seat machine of commercial significance, all behind the economy (and reliability) of an engine used mainly on elementary trainers. The DH83 deservedly became more widely known than its production numbers might suggest, for it had a varied working life that was unique in its field.

Chapter 22

Club class
Avro Club Cadet

We now look at another biplane from A.V. Roe & Co. From the RAF Tutor trainer that you met in Chapter 14 they offered the Cadet as a lower-powered civil successor, and went further with the Club Cadet in 1933, appropriately named with simplicity and economy as key features – for example folding wings to minimise hangarage or parking space. The subject of this report, G-ACHP, was fitted originally with an Armstrong-Siddeley Genet radial, but later replaced by the ubiquitous, reliable and more smooth-fronted 130hp Gipsy Major in-line four.

'HP was the only Club Cadet to survive the war in flyable condition. Operated for a while by Saunders-Roe, the famous designers and builders of flying boats based at Cowes on the Isle of Wight, it lay forlorn for about three years before being rescued in 1952 on behalf of the Vintage Aeroplane Club.

Some aeroplanes 'click' immediately and others fail (or take time) to make any personal impact. I liked the Cadet as soon as I saw it and fell for it as soon as I climbed aboard. A pair of very roomy cockpits and a range of facilities that are missing from many later designs were part of the deal, for a combination of 'mod cons' (effective brakes, adjustable seats and pedals and variable incidence tailplane) and traditional open cockpit characteristics provided the pilot with the best of everything.

Starting was standard for a hand-swung Gipsy Major. Taxying was easy, with excellent manoeuvrability, a good view and with no tendency for the tail to lift as a precursor to nosing over. The ride was soft and smooth.

Take-off proved an uneventful activity, with sluggish initial acceleration and relatively little tendency to swing, but with an immediately effective rudder that ironed out any problems almost before they began. Climb rate was not particularly brilliant at about 630ft/min, but even at relatively slow speeds all the controls were markedly effective, and the ailerons, in particular, were very pleasant. There were four of these (aided by the aerodynamic refinement of inset hinges) and they extended to, and formed part of, a smoothly rounded wing-tip. Perhaps, apart from overall size and weight, these formed the main improvement over the earlier Tutor, which had ailerons with no outside help and wings with blunt, square tips. Almost twelve years lapsed between my last flight in the Cadet and my first in the sole surviving Tutor in 1966, but I clearly remember the Cadet's snappier roll response at the bottom end of the speed scale.

Feel, like appearance, can deceive. On the ground in particular and to a smaller extent in the air, the Cadet felt a heavier aeroplane than the Tiger Moth. Although very marginally larger, the Club Cadet at 1,222lb showed a tare weight only 100lb more than that of the Tiger, while the all-up figure is slightly less.

I have never been very fond of long doses of turbulence and one of the Cadet's many endearing qualities was its ability to take relatively little notice of bumps; it tended, somehow, to ride straight through them. G-ACHP stalled cleanly and gently. It had a positive break between the fully controlled and stalled conditions, but nothing untoward happened beyond that. A wing would drop if provoked, but with care everything remained laterally level even if the 'stick back' pressure was not fully released. I have no written record of the break-away figure, but thirty-eight remains in my mind and this can hardly have related to anything else, except perhaps oil pressure!

In full flight the Club Cadet came into its own – and a very good 'own' it was. Roll-rate was crisp and this made it an excellent mount for air racing pylon turns. For normal cruising – at about 90mph and 1,900rpm – it was relatively untiring, with room to spread maps and other belongings and with not too much cockpit draught. The luggage locker, strangely missing on the earlier Cadet, was largish and ample for all normal needs.

On aerobatics, most traditional biplanes are better in pitch than in roll, but in a loop the Club Cadet again presented this strange quality of feeling heavier than a Tiger. It needed a higher entry speed and decelerated fairly rapidly on the way up but did nothing desperate at the top if the airspeed was too low. In fact, the ailerons again showed their low-speed colours, for with generous displacement a fairly crisp roll-out was possible with virtually no IAS.

On the approach, initially at 65mph, for 60 at the threshold, the smooth lines of the cowlings round the Gipsy Major made the forward view remarkably good for a single engine aeroplane. A marked and positive back pressure was needed on the round-out to hit on three points (the nose attitude for which was low) but 'HP would take a wheeler with gentle dignity so long as this did not occur at the peak of the elevator movement. If the wheels touched at this particular point it gave back some airspace in generous doses. Further along the run any swinging tendency was slight, but when 'HP boasted a tailwheel (Tutors, Cadets and Club Cadets had skids or wheels) it needed help from the handbrake in no-wind or out-of-wind conditions.

Unfortunately, G-ACHP is no longer with us. In January 1956 it lost a battle with the aerodrome fence at Denham and from there disappeared – presumably for scrap. It was a highly desirable light aeroplane that deserves a place in history.

Chapter 23

'The safest aeroplane in the world'
BA Swallow

Before the Second World War, several light aircraft types with origins in other countries were built in the UK. Among these were the BA Swallow, a direct descendant of the Klemm L25 which had first flown in Germany as early as 1927.

The popularity of the L25 as an import led to the formation of the British Klemm Aeroplane Co Ltd factory at Hanworth (London Air Park) in 1932. In those days the training for a Pilot's A Licence was minimal, calling for only three hours solo, a simple flying test observed from the ground and no requirement for any navigational experience. Not surprisingly, there were numerous accidents. One of the reasons for the Klemm's appeal was its ability to fly safely very slowly, and this quality was maintained on its British successor. Initially, the machines were known as British Klemm Swallow ls, the first few powered by 75hp Salmson radials. Then, with a name change to the British Aircraft Manufacturing Co Ltd, minor modifications were introduced to increase the overall strength of the airframe and to ease production. This BA Swallow 2 initially used the 90hp Pobjoy Cataract radial, later also offered with the 90hp Cirrus Minor 4-cylinder inline. Total UK production amounted to 135 aircraft, a few of which were impressed into active service on the outbreak of war. At least one flew throughout the war, camouflaged, yet retaining its civil registration of G-AEZM and used as a hack by Airspeed test pilot George Errington. Some thirty-seven examples survived the war of which seventeen flew again when civil flying was allowed to restart.

So, what was this intriguing aeroplane all about? Although light, it was not small, with an unusually large span of 42ft (more than a

'THE SAFEST AEROPLANE IN THE WORLD'

Hurricane!). Although the wings could fold, the extra space needed for short-term hangarage, parking, or ground manoeuvring, was an inconvenience that seemed to be little if any deterrent to sales. The slow flying qualities and relative cockpit comfort enabled the type to hold its head high. The makers claimed that it was the safest aeroplane in the world; the high aspect ratio wing and a loading of just under 7lb/ft^2 enabled one to be soared – engine off – for twenty minutes over Dunstable!

I had the good fortune to fly both versions of the Swallow 2. My first experience was on the Cirrus variant – G-AEMW – from Elstree in 1960 and, several years later, in Cataract-powered G-AFCL from the more appropriate grass of Old Warden. By the standards of their time, the tandem cockpits were relatively spacious, while the internal layout was pleasantly simple. In both cases the equipment was adequate for the intended purpose, which was essentially visual flight. The three most important dials – airspeed, oil pressure and height – were present on both machines. Predictably, the last of these was of the old non-sensitive type, with its single pointer moving less than an inch for each thousand feet of change.

The overall view is not at all bad. Taxying is an easier exercise than on many machines of the era and only the relatively large wingspan gives cause for extra caution. Although all aero engines of the time refuse to tolerate coarse handling, the Pobjoy calls for additional care as it is a high-revving unit with reduction gearing, so small throttle movement gives very big changes in engine rpm.

Take-off acceleration is not impressive, but the low wing loading carries the Swallow into the air quickly at an airspeed below the minimum reading on the dial. The well-proportioned rudder is effective throughout and the subsequent climb is recorded in textbooks as a very creditable 800ft/min, higher than most machines of the era. From respect for the ages of the engines, though, I followed customary practice of not putting them to unnecessary tests at full power.

The 'feel' of the Cataract and Cirrus engined Swallow is very different and, as one who enjoys the vintage aspects of any relevant aeroplane, I preferred the one with the exposed, uncowled radial, which helped to provide a seemingly unique quality of flight. Also, 'EMW was the only Swallow ever to have an enclosed cockpit, so again, for me, 'FCL had an advantage! Resulting performance, though, is broadly identical, with published cruise and maximum figures of 98 and 112mph respectively. In each case I found the first of these to be a slightly unjustified claim, but I had no figures for position error correction and, whatever the result should have been, the percentage shortfall was minimal. Very short bursts at full throttle (with almost 1,000rpm difference between the outputs of the two units) gave the impression that the published figure might be achieved.

When moving to the low end of the speed scale on a strange type one must be ready for almost anything. Perhaps I had been spoilt, though, by receiving prior advice that I would find this to be a very tame aeroplane. How true this was. Speed took its time to decay and the stall was reluctant to make itself felt. When eventually (below the minimum ASI reading) the nose went down, it did so in a genteel manner and the wings remained level, immediately bringing back to mind the maker's safety claim. The only feature that I remember specifically is the slightly unnerving feeling on Cataract-equipped G-AFCL: when fully throttled back and at very low airspeed, the reduction gearing between engine and propeller gives the impression that the latter is about to stop. Although this applies to all Pobjoy-powered aircraft, at no time have I felt fully relaxed at that critical moment.

Back in normal cruising flight, the Swallow is peaceful and pleasant, but with no outstanding characteristics. Not surprisingly, with its large span, the ailerons are relatively heavy and the response unsportingly slow (a setback in bumpy conditions) so, although all aeroplanes must be treated seriously, the general impression is that this machine is very unlikely to bite the unwary. That feeling extends to the approach and landing, where a very smooth three-pointer can be made with one of those satisfying clunks at the point of touchdown. Even with the tail on the floor, the rudder remains acceptably responsive and copes admirably on a normal (for its time) landing into wind. I would not be happy, though, to try a tail-downer in more than the most modest of crosswinds.

The Swallow is a likeable, docile piece of vintage machinery, of which five still remain on the UK register, together with two early Klemm L25s.

Chapter 24

Built for comfort
de Havilland DH87B Hornet Moth

Unfortunately, my introduction to the Hornet Moth was not one to give me a lifelong love for the type. In the spring of 1952, whilst still flying in the RAF, I did occasional instructing for the West London Aero Club at White Waltham. I had been called in at very short notice and, expecting to teach someone how to fly a Tiger Moth (which formed the bulk of the club fleet), as an oddball outsider I was allocated a far-from-young pupil who was training on the Hornet Moth. I was warned that he had no flying aptitude and I had not stepped inside a Hornet Moth before. Perhaps I should have aborted the flight, but I was anxious not to disrupt the programme. All I will add is that the required circuit session was a rather unproductive flight for both parties.

So, what was so different for me about this new type? Firstly, it had side-by-side cabin seating compared with the Tiger's tandem open cockpit layout; and it had a single control column between the seats, with a Y-piece sticking out to put it in reach of either occupant. Later I met something broadly similar on the Tipsy Trainer, but I was not happy with it.

Before going any further, I should explain what the machine was all about. The de Havilland DH87 Hornet Moth emerged in 1935, which was a time of change. It was the last of the biplane Moths, high in level of comfort, headroom and in the view from within. It was an early example of a mount for serious executive travel that offered an overall quality ahead of its time. My initial impression – which I retained during and after several subsequent flights – was that it was an excellent tourer but not such a good trainer.

Although the first DH87 had flown in May 1934 (participating in the King's Cup air race only two months later!) this was experimental in nature and the initial production version, the DH87A, took to the air after more than a year of prototype tests. Even this was subject to change in the light of experience, as the pointed wings (as on other DH designs of the time such as the DH86 four-engine airliner and the more familiar scaled-down DH89 Rapide) had marked wing dropping habits when attempting a three-point landing. I can confirm this! Whilst considered acceptable on the larger machines that were flown mainly by experienced pilots, it was a sales deterrent on a private (or training) aeroplane, so the 'clipped wing' 87B became standard. Altogether 165 were built.

Now to today, the type remains very much alive. The DH87 has a fuselage using wooden longerons with stringers to which the fabric is attached; the wings, too, are made of wood, each with two spruce spars, while steel tube was used for the streamlined interplane struts. Ailerons are fitted to the lower mainplanes only. To remove flying loads, there are trim tabs on the elevators (adjustable only from the left seat) and a spring bias for rudder balancing; to provide ease of movement on the ground, the tailwheel is fully castoring. The faired undercarriage legs revolve through ninety degrees to act as air brakes.

As was the case with most light aircraft of the era, the Hornet Moth uses the remarkably reliable 130hp DH Gipsy Major 1 inverted four-cylinder air-cooled power unit, which fires into life after hand priming with a toggle and lever accessible from inside the port cowling. Hand swinging is the normal procedure, but even from the beginning an optional electric starter was available. The fuel to the engine is supplied from a tank behind the pilots' seats, with a generous capacity of 35 Imperial gallons providing a very worthwhile range of more than 600 miles. Above the tank is a useful space that accommodates two large bags, conveniently accessible from within, avoiding the need to open an external hatch that had been a feature of the earlier, open Moths. The full range, though, is not possible within the 2,000lb maximum weight with two people and full luggage.

Unusually for a tail-dragger, the view whilst taxying is good, with only a narrow blind band directly ahead. Taking care to check that the air brakes are closed, with elevator trim set by guesswork, the take-off requires the use of more left rudder than one might expect, as directional control is marginal until the tail is well clear of the ground. After unsticking at about 50mph the ailerons are disappointingly woolly and even at about 65mph for the climb they lack any sporting spirit. With the clipped wings the climb and cruise figures have lost some performance from that of the earlier 87A, offering a fully laden rate of ascent at 690ft/min compared with the original 800. On the level, if prepared to use 2,050rpm, the 87B romps along happily at 105mph with the nose unexpectedly low on the horizon, and the published full-throttle maximum speed is 124mph, although out of respect I never put that to the full test. It is possible to trim to remove both elevator and rudder loads, while the very comfortable ride and forward view are well ahead of the standards that would have been expected in 1935. Even at relatively high speed the ailerons remain unimpressive in both feel and response, but on a long straight run this criticism becomes a secondary issue.

Experience on three different Hornet Moths revealed slightly differing indicated speeds for the stall, but this could be through instrument inaccuracy or possibly incorrect rigging. In each case, though, the wings remained level and following breakaways at 42-46mph, recovery was instant. There is no need to worry too much about carburettor icing problems on this or many other types powered by the ubiquitous Gipsy Major 1, for as the throttle is brought back, warm air is fed to the intake through a butterfly valve. At full throttle cold air is supplied, therefore ensuring availability of maximum power. I have wondered many times why this simple, almost foolproof solution to a persistent problem has not been adopted by more recent designers; except, perhaps that it leads to a small increase in fuel consumption. That I rate as a modest penalty to pay for the increased likelihood that the engine will keep purring.

At some time, though, what goes up must come down. On a glide, even at 70mph, fully aft trim fails to provide stick-free flight and a fairly firm backward pressure is needed when reducing to an over-the-fence figure of about 60mph. At this lower speed the ailerons are remarkably ineffective, calling for unexpectedly generous displacement in order to achieve results. On the credit side, though, the view ahead is excellent and the elevators remain responsive throughout. As on the take-off, with the tail on the floor the blanked rudder is not as helpful as it should be and, especially in a crosswind, the brakes play an important part in the process of keeping straight. The final result, though, remains comfortable, as the oleo undercarriage is pleasantly soft, even on rough ground.

If I have been mildly critical about some of the 87's handling features, I am not meaning to downgrade it in the primary task as a tourer for business or private use. In this role, it is excellent. The seats are comfortable, the view ahead is good, the long exhaust pipe keeps noise to a minimum, the range is well above average for a light aeroplane and folding wings are a benefit in terms of both space and economy.

In its heyday the Hornet Moth fulfilled useful roles at home and roughly half of the production run was built for export. Many were impressed into wartime military service on communications duties and on calibration of radar installations. At the end of hostilities twenty-four had survived in the UK and, as evidence that the 87 is well liked as a tourer, three-quarters of a century later thirteen of these remain on the British register. One is G-AHBM, the machine that I met first in 1952, a survivor of four that had originally been built in 1935-6 as military seaplane trainers.

Chapter 25

'A pair of Tiger Moths strapped together...'
de Havilland DH89A Dragon Rapide

A few aeroplanes fulfil roles that other types cannot begin to tackle; the de Havilland DH89A Dragon Rapide was one such machine, effectively bringing shorthaul air services to practical reality in the mid-1930s. Perhaps we could even give the Rapide some of the credit (or the blame?) for sowing the seed for today's traffic growth, as after a period in military camouflage it re-emerged as a simple, reliable light airliner in the years immediately after the Second World War. It was one of a line of de Havilland designs that took the lead in their respective fields, just as the original DH60 Moth had placed club and private flying on its feet from the mid-1920s.

Developed from the DH84 Dragon of 1932, which normally seated six passengers on the power of two Gipsy Majors (also products of the de Havilland empire) and the DH86 which accommodated ten to the power of four Gipsy Sixes, the DH89 was a compromise. Two Gipsy Sixes (later, Queen 3s) did the work and the cabin held up to eight passengers; here was the most successful light transport of its time, which saw service in almost every country.

Of wooden construction with fabric covering, with a fixed trousered undercarriage and pointed wings of equal span upper and lower, the first Rapide flew in April 1934, looked right, was right and worked well. Railway Air Services, Olley Air Service and Hillman Airways were among the leading British users, while airlines with names still known today, such as KLM and Aer Lingus, had Rapides on their pre-war fleets. At the start of the war in 1939 many were

'A PAIR OF TIGER MOTHS STRAPPED TOGETHER...'

impressed for service with the RAF and the Air Transport Auxiliary, while production continued until 1946 with a military version, known later as the Dominie. Many flew with the Fleet Air Arm.

After the war, considerable numbers were released for civil use and once again Rapides set the scene for many short-haul airline services; British European Airways used them on runs to Jersey and Guernsey, round the Scottish Isles and between Land's End and the Scillies.

Now let us concentrate on the Rapide (or Dominie) as a flying machine. Perhaps the first feature to strike a pilot on initial acquaintance is the single narrow cockpit that feels – and is – both high off the ground and a long way ahead of anything else. With no chance of a dual check, the occupant of this barely furnished rostrum, which boasts no frills or non-essential trim, is really on his or her own in every sense; sometimes guidance was provided by another pilot standing in the door hatch behind and just to the right of the sole seat, but more frequently any advice was limited to a pre-flight briefing and a hasty exit.

Everything in the cockpit is well-placed and logical, with the possible exception of the layout of the instrument panel, which has a typical vintage haphazardness not confined to the type. The port fuel cock, sensibly, is on the left wall and the starboard on the right wall; nothing is out of easy reach, with the throttles and mixture controls fairly high on the left side, the elevator trim-wheel beneath them, the brake lever on the left of the seat and the two position flap lever on the other side. A very desirable feature for use in hot weather or for de-misting purposes is a downward sliding clear-vision window on each side of and just behind the two angled front windscreens.

Starting is straightforward, and as the Rapide relies on electrical power from a wind-driven generator on the top wing, there is no engine-driven supply, so it matters little which is started first; however, habit makes a starboard start the normal practice. In the early stages the Rapide's structural flexibility is noticeable, but when both engines are settled into smooth operation the result is a comforting purr.

With fixed-pitch propellers (except on later mark IVs) and a non-retracting undercarriage, there are relatively few checks for a machine of its size (48ft span) and weight, which normally stops at 5,500lb, but which was permitted to nearly 6,000lb in wartime radio or communications service. Rudder trim is the only item to notice that is additional to the checks on, say, a Tiger Moth.

Take-off into wind and at light load (and all aeroplanes are at their nicest when nearly empty of everything except pilot and fuel) is a sprightly process. The tail comes up almost as soon as the throttles are opened and while one is wondering whether it will swing it flies off the ground at little over 60mph with hardly any help from within. Naturally, events are a little more protracted with a cabin full of bodies aboard, but even at maximum take-off weight the get-away is quite creditable. In-flight performance is not quite as lively as the take-off suggests, but a steady climb at 95mph produces something over 800ft/min.

I remember being told by a very experienced Rapide pilot that it is just like flying a pair of Tiger Moths strapped together. I could not quite determine what to expect from this, for either this could mean twice the pleasure of a Tiger or double the trouble of keeping in balanced flight. In fact, neither extreme was true, but there is an indefinable quality that attaches some truth to the statement. At all normal operating speeds the controls are pleasantly responsive without being too light for the job.

Stalling is straightforward, although there is not an excessive amount of warning. Empty, the Rapide falls away at just under 60mph, but almost invariably the port wing goes down with the nose; it does this in a fairly leisurely manner unless the column is given a slight backward tweak at the point of break-away. Then it shows a determined spirit. Normally, from a straight stall, release of back pressure produces full and immediately effective results.

Textbooks credit the Rapide with a cruising speed of 130mph, but no power setting is quoted. In practice, 1,900rpm produces about 115mph on the dial, and this provides a most pleasant flight condition; the slightest throb through lack of synchronisation, though, transmits itself through the machine with the result that panels pant and fabric flutters. In roughish conditions the wings flex noticeably, but this is a designed-in feature for structural safety.

The Rapide is a pleasure to fly. It is a steady, stable platform in all but the roughest of weathers and only laterally does it show a very slight tendency to a wandering instability. It asks to be 'flown' and rolls beautifully and precisely into steep turns, which can be sustained indefinitely so long as full power is maintained. It rolls out equally cleanly. It is, of course, non-aerobatic. On one engine there is no climb performance and at full load the path is slightly downhill, but at normal weights height can be held at about 85mph; rudder trim range is sufficient to remove all foot load in this condition.

Pre-landing check are few. The manual mixture controls must be placed fully rich in case of a missed approach and, apart from the usual fuel and allied checks, only flaps remain for action. The very earliest Dragon-Sixes had no flaps, but the remaining Rapides have them in a very basic up or down form. In effect they are airborne barn doors and they offer no intermediate positions for take-off (for which they are quite unnecessary, anyway), or flying at low airspeeds. They do their allotted job moderately well and allow a light-load fence-crossing speed of 70mph. The next stage, though, is when the Rapide shows some strange spirit. As I discovered to my embarrassment, any pilot who is doggedly determined to three-point anything that he handles may have a shock; a tail-down wheeler presents no problems, but in certain sets of conditions a precise all-wheels-on touchdown may lead to a marked wing drop that is not easy to put right. In this case no damage was done, as the down-going wing just escaped making contact with the hard runway beneath, but it provided a well-warranted dent in my personal pride; I was in my twenties, so I thought I knew how to fly. We all need physically harmless incidents such as this to learn the truths of human fallibility. Wing dropping is a well-established characteristic with certain aircraft that have pointed wingtips; the DH88 Comet of pre-war England-to-Australia fame suffered badly in this respect and the original DH87 Hornet Moth did likewise until it had its wings cropped.

728 civil Rapides were built, as were 521 military Dominies, but, as identical aeroplanes, many swapped roles during their active lives. Today, eight Rapides remain active on the UK register and four of these have certificates of airworthiness in the Transport category – a stronger position than fifty-five years ago! Clearly and understandably, the Rapide has an enthusiastic following, which should ensure that the unique sight and unmistakeable sound will be with us for many years to come.

Chapter 26

A serious tourer
Miles M.3 Falcon

The M.3 Falcon was the first in a series of Miles low-wing closed cockpit monoplanes that enabled private pilots and their passengers to travel in draught-free cabin comfort; it was developed from the open M.2 Hawk which was the company's first production machine. The prototype Falcon, G-ACTM, appeared in 1934, in time to compete in that year's famous MacRobertson Air Race from England to Australia.

The Falcon was a multi-purpose aeroplane, with a serious touring capacity and some appeal to the sporting brigade. In original form it got into the air behind the inevitable Gipsy Major four-cylinder inverted engine; about twenty-five were produced with this power. Four of these were used by Phillips and Powis Ltd at Woodley near Reading, who built the Miles aeroplanes and operated the aerodrome, flying club and air taxi business there. The Miles family, though, had thoughts of greater things and the design had been stressed to enable the later production machines to take Gipsy Sixes with a minimum of structural inconvenience.

Falcons (known as Majors or Sixes depending on the engines fitted) appeared in three or four-seat forms. The first of these provided the pilot with the most roomy cabin imaginable, for he sat in a centrally-positioned seat in luxurious isolation, with surrounding empty space that must have proved a welcome bonus on long-distance flights. The two passengers sat side-by-side behind. Falcons joined the starting lines at many air races and, shortly after the Falcon Six was introduced in 1937, G-ADLC was first home in the King's Cup race of that year – achieving a remarkably creditable average of 176.28mph in the process. As was standard practice at that time, when British light aeroplanes were in demand all over the world, Falcons were ordered by customers as far afield as South Africa, Hong Kong and New Zealand.

During the Second World War, a few examples remained on the register and were used for various civil communications duties, but the majority were impressed into the RAF for similar work wearing Service markings. By 1945 most were tired; some were scrapped before reverting to C of A standard, but a couple were regular competitors again in the air races of the fifties.

This report is based on several flights carried out in 1949 and 1950 in G-ADFH, thanks to owner and restorer Doug Bianchi as explained in an earlier chapter. Entry to the Falcon to the front or rear was via a wing walkway and a centrally hinged upward opening door. The single pilot's seat in a cabin wide enough for two ensured that nothing was cramped or crowded. The centrally placed instruments, of which there were no more than necessary, created a well-spaced panel with ample room for map pockets and other paraphernalia. Everything within was manual and easy to reach and 'FH had an unusually large throttle lever on the left wall. Split trailing edge flaps were manually moved and could be positioned for various needs.

When the engine was started, by hand swinging the Fairey Reed metal propeller, the airframe suffered more than a fair measure of what can be described best as transverse vibration. At low revs, when the engine ran chunkily, there was a feeling that the main fuselage and top decking were aiming to move in opposing directions, but at that time the disease of suspecting all glue joints had not started and we assumed that all was well. When power was increased the airframe shuddering reduced, until at flight settings everything seemed solid.

The usual Miles-type ratchet-and-cable brakes operated differentially on the wheels as rudder was applied and they gave no serious trouble, but when set on the harsh side they could snatch and cause the tail to lift if the rear seats were empty.

In the early stages of take-off the rudder was noticeably ineffective and a fair measure of pressure was needed with the left foot. With

A SERIOUS TOURER

rear seats loaded the tail called for a physical effort to lift into flying altitude and the run was quite long. The rudder ineffectiveness at the start developed into a mild but definite snaking instability as the machine accelerated to the best climbing figure of 70mph.

Once settled into the climb, though, the Falcon Major plodded contentedly, but still required a more-than-expected pressure with the left foot. It could manage about 700ft/min which was about standard climb performance for the era.

In cruise conditions, with 2,000rpm giving 115mph (despite a published figure of 130) handling was effortless. Compared with the Hawk, extra dihedral had been designed in to make everything comfortable on long flights and, not surprisingly, this led to marked positive lateral stability. It was almost right, though, for after an initial resistance to roll even with plenty of aileron displacement, the rate improved once it started, and racing turns could be quite spirited. Most aeroplanes are at their best when nearly empty and 'FH liked to have its back seats unoccupied; with two people in the rear and a mild ration of luggage, it developed a minor dose of longitudinal instability and might have been a little unpleasant in certain flight conditions. Maximum permitted weight was 2,200lb, but no C of G figures were available at the time and, looking at it retrospectively in a load-conscious world, sometimes we may have operated slightly beyond limits.

At lighter loads, a straight stall from level flight with power-off (the revs seemed uncomfortably low towards the end, but the flywheel effect of the heavy metal propeller was reassuring) usually produced a marked left wing drop at a break away IAS of about 42mph. This was when clean; with more than partial flap lowered, the wings remained reasonably level but, as on take-off, the rudder seemed less powerful than its size indicated. Certainly, the thought of needing to rely on it to try to recover from a spin held no personal appeal.

The approach was unremarkable and 70mph for the early stages kept ample control in hand, 65mph over the fence seemed right, but some practice was needed for making consistent three-pointers. The glide-to-landing altitude change was considerable and, not unexpectedly, the elevators were far from crisp just before touchdown, so an initial backward pressure needed to be converted to a positive pull at the last second. This was when flying solo; with people in the back a more cautious sequence was advisable.

When landing in certain conditions, especially on smooth tarmac or concrete, the directional 'wooliness' appeared again. Lack of rudder effectiveness is one thing, but perhaps the trousered front legs, which provided a keel surface largely ahead of the C of G, had a part to play. To find out we should have removed the trousers and flown it with naked legs, but this we failed to do.

The Falcon Major, although undistinguished in character or handling, was one of the earlier touring monoplanes to offer real cabin comfort and a creditable performance on the 6 – 7 gallons per hour (gph) of a Gipsy Major. The Falcon Six of course, offered more sparkle but less economy. A forward sloping windscreen helped to offer a good view and kept away some of the rain; space was generous, the cruise effortless and noise level perfectly acceptable – so, for a design of which the first production machine flew eighty-eight years ago we can say that it offered as much as many others that came much later. A single Falcon remains on the UK register, and long may it do so!

Chapter 27

Ahead by Miles
Miles Hawk Speed Six

From the first production machine from the Miles stable at Woodley, the M.2 Hawk, the design was developed into a number of slightly more sophisticated products, many of which retained 'hawk' as part of the type name. The first to emerge was the Hawk Major, a more streamlined machine with a neat trousered undercarriage and powered by the ubiquitous 130hp Gipsy Major 1 four-cylinder in-line engine. Eighty-eight of these were built, but again the design formed the basis for several sporting successors, such as the Sparrowhawk and Hawk Speed Six, both of which were single-seaters that made their names in the field of air racing.

The Hawk Speed Six had the added 'puff' of the 200hp Gipsy Six. Three were built and fortunately one of these, G-ADGP, survives to this day. After a successful pre-war racing history, 'GP was acquired in the late forties by Ron Paine, then Technical (later Managing) Director of Derby Aviation who had the resources to make a number of modifications to the original design. The most noticeable changes were a large one-piece bubble canopy and comfortably upholstered seating. Whilst these may upset the purists among aviation historians, without doubt they transformed the type and, with the vastly improved forward view, made it a safer participant in the sometimes tightly packed racing environment; as the Speed Six lived up to its name and usually was one of the fastest machines on the starting line, it took off long after some aircraft had completed a race circuit and needed to overtake the slower machines (sometimes twice) on the way round a three lap course.

I explained in Chapter 7 how I eventually got to fly 'GP; as a purely personal assessment, I found it much more likeable than its racing counterpart the Percival Mew Gull (next chapter). In its modified form the view was very good, at the high cruising speeds the controls were crisp and it had relatively few vices. Capable of a climb rate of 1,400ft/min, in normal level flight it would penetrate the air at about 160mph, yet was perfectly docile on the approach down to an over-the-fence figure of 65mph. In racing (full throttle conditions) 'GP was fully capable of hitting 185mph. It was a very clean design and one feature that remains in my mind was its almost delightful reluctance to lose speed. Approaching the empty circuit at about 170mph, I throttled right back and needed to go once round the block before the speed reduced to a respectable figure for the downwind leg! During this time, the short stub exhausts of the high compression Gipsy Six emitted a healthy crackle of a kind that could be beaten only by a 'chopped' Merlin!

Like most aeroplanes of its era, although not as sensitive as machines with low wing loading, the Speed Six preferred to be landed into wind; in its heyday, this was possible at most aerodromes, but today caution is needed at many places. The large flaps could be lowered manually, at not more than 75mph and, at that relatively low speed, they were usefully effective although it would have been helpful to be able to use them at a higher figure. The subsequent transition to the three-point attitude – and in normal conditions it was customary to avoid a wheeler – seemed to occur very naturally. Deceleration was acceptably rapid.

As one who has had the good fortune to be involved for many years with historic aeroplanes, I have mixed feelings about late-life modifications to long-established designs. I understand the feelings of owners who go to great length to ensure that their mounts are restored to original configuration, yet equally I am aware that some changes can bring increased safety. Many years ago I flew a number of light types in handicap races but, as I was a relative pauper, these were all near the lower end of the speed scale: I was regularly overtaken by the back markers flown by the moneyed brigade and

AHEAD BY MILES

I found considerable comfort in the knowledge that the modified Hawk Speed Six, with its bubble canopy, offered its occupant a far better forward view than was possible with the original design. In normal circumstances, though, I support the aims of those who seek to build-in as much authenticity as is practicable.

Chapter 28

Too cramped for comfort
Percival Mew Gull

For a variety of reasons aeroplanes can become almost household names: they could have been built in considerable quantities, they could have earned fame in wartime, or they could be famous for one or two notable achievements, even though most people have never seen one. The subject of this report falls clearly into this last category.

From the early 1930s Captain Edgar Percival designed a host of light aeroplanes, many of which carried the name Gull, but we must not fall into the trap of thinking that they were all broadly similar. The Vega Gull, for example, was a full and comfortable four-seater, whereas the Mew Gull offered only minimum cockpit space for one. The first, G-ACND, with a span of only 24ft, started life briefly behind a Napier Javelin of 165hp, but soon this gave way to the ubiquitous 200hp inverted in-line Gipsy Six. With the latter engine it averaged 191mph in the 1934 King's Cup Air Race. Altogether six Mew Gulls were built, each undergoing various modifications during its life to make it suitable for a specific record-seeking task.

Very early in its career the rather ugly 'CND was extensively re-designed and rebuilt to the general shape of the subsequent Mews. A neater undercarriage, smarter fin and rudder and other alterations transformed it into a most appealing machine, albeit a 'hot' one. The second machine built, G-AEKL, looked broadly similar, but various refinements enabled it to achieve a flat-out level speed of 225mph and a cruise of 190. Unfortunately, in this machine, Tom Campbell-Black of Comet record-breaking fame was killed when the propeller of a taxying Hawker Hart went through the cockpit. The final Mew Gull, G-AFAA, with a Gipsy Six R and ram air intakes, proved itself capable of 245mph.

Mews did many things and had numerous claims to fame, but without doubt Alex Henshaw's achievements in G-AEXF hit headlines more than any of the others. After extensive modifications by Essex Aero Ltd at Gravesend, including fitting one of the special Gipsy Six Rs from the famous Comet G-ACSS, 'XF attained 247mph to finish second in the 1938 Isle of Man Air Race, but it was on a much longer and more strenuous flight that the real fame came. The top decking and canopy were lowered to give literally no true forward view; the tankage was increased to 87 gallons to provide a still-air range of nearly 2,000 miles and the Six R was replaced by a Six II with a constant speed propeller. Navigation lights and radio completed the requirements.

In this form the G-AEXF/Henshaw combination carried out a trial flight on which, with a tailwind, the pair made Marseilles from Gravesend in 2hrs 23mins. Then came the real thing, an attempt on the record to Cape Town. On 5 February 1939 man and machine set out and only 39hrs 25mins later they had completed 5,997 miles at an average – including stops – of 152mph. Not content with this, Alex Henshaw allowed only one day to pass in Cape Town before he set course for the trip home. He was, of course, a very worn man when he returned, but the cramped conditions in the cockpit, made smaller even than normal to make room for extra fuel, make one wonder how he coped at all. Much of the flight over Africa had been made at 18,000ft to avoid the worst of the weather.

I have already described in Chapter 5 how I came to fly 'XF at Hugh Scrope's invitation. We were at White Waltham, where the Mew and Doug Bianchi, who maintained it, were based. This was a fine familiarisation ground, for a large all-grass field with possible approaches in all directions removed many problems that might otherwise exist.

My immediate reaction was that the cockpit was too small. The Mew was in its low-canopy condition with the absence of forward view, so Hugh offered to come with me as a wing walker until I was well into the open field. The six-cylinder engine sounded slightly lumpy and caused a fair measure of airframe vibration; the hinged canopy, in particular, shook and flexed during ground roll. The throttle, however, was responsive and the small spade-grip, though lower than I would choose (as on a Proctor), was wholly adequate to the task. Apart from its occupant the enormous P-type compass was the largest item in the cockpit.

The only unusual pre-take-off action, other than to weave about energetically to check that a clear path lay ahead, concerned the propeller control, which was a large lever on the right-hand side of the cockpit just below the panel; it offered just two stops – fine or coarse – with a blade difference of 11° between the two extreme settings. With fine selected, we were ready to go.

I expected a marked swing to the right, but probably over-anticipated this as it has not stood out as something to remember. 'XF unstuck, clean, at about 90mph and I think the climb figure was about 140mph. In this condition a constantly curved flight path seemed sensible, with eyes firmly glued in the direction of turn. I recollect quite clearly that the ailerons were mildly disappointing, not only in lack of response but due to static friction, which no doubt could have been cured. But to criticise the response was unfair, for the Mew was not meant to be at its best at such a relatively low IAS.

Once on the level at about 1,500ft I tried the propeller control. I had been accustomed to fixed and variable pitch propellers, but this was my first taste of a two-pitch system. The lever was stiff, but went into its new home with a positive clunk, to the tune of a similarly abrupt drop of about 250rpm – it worked.

I am convinced that 'XF was not at its very best at that time. Flat-out on the level I could not do better than 192mph and even at that speed the ailerons were not as lively or positive as I had expected. Perhaps I had spoiled myself in anticipation of really great things, but more stick/aileron displacement was required to achieve a snappy roll rate than I had hoped to need.

Behaviour at and near the stall provides an acid test of an aeroplane's manners. I had no idea what to expect and had been unable to find out beforehand, so fearing a machine that might do fairly vicious things I satisfied myself with a gentle deceleration to what felt to be the lowest sensible figure for fully sustained flight. I cannot remember the precise reading but, power off, 85mph seems to remain in the mind. Control was quite sloppy, with a need for a strong backward stick force to prevent the nose from leaving me, but beyond that I can offer little. Lowish cloud prevented a more thorough investigation.

The descent was interesting. With fine pitch and a trickle of power, the engine burbled and spat through its short stub exhausts. I selected a long, clear, ground path into wind, but as I began to line up for an approach, a taxying Tipsy B disappeared under my nose, so I threw away everything and tried again. This time I was luckier. Hugh had advised me to retain 110mph on the way round to the final turn, so I did just that. The tiny trailing edge flaps were not particularly effective, but I had plenty of airfield ahead, so this was only a minor worry. I was advised to reduce to not less than 95mph over the hedge, but I cannot confirm or deny a precise figure. What I can remember, though, is the total lack of view for the last few hundred yards and throughout the hold-off and landing run. The tailskid dug quite well into the ground and no doubt helped to reduce any natural swinging tendency.

When I switched off after a walker-assisted taxy back to the West London Aero Club, I felt very contented but mildly dazed. I cannot imagine how anyone could have considered flying to Cape Town in G-AEXF, but one short local flight is unfair to use as a total yardstick. Clearly someone with plenty of experience on the type could provide a far more valuable assessment than I can muster, especially after so long a gap, but to fly a Mew Gull in 1950, or at any other time, was a rare experience and one that I shall never fully forget. I was twenty-one at the time and the Mew made its mark!

'XF has endured many knocks and escapes, including 'throwing' a con-rod during an air race, but fortunately it has survived to this day. For several years its proud owner was Desmond Penrose, who ensured that it was returned as nearly as possible to its original pre-war racing configuration. In 2002, though, he disposed of his justifiably proud possession to the Real Aeroplane Company at Breighton in Yorkshire, where it remains in appreciative ownership.

The Mew is a thoroughbred and fairly hot piece of aeronautical kit and is far from a daily fly-about. Fortunately, it has survived because there are people who understand its historical significance, based on past achievements.

Quite clearly the Mew Gull was a better and more spirited aeroplane than I have described, but when I flew it, it had recently returned from long storage in France in far from ideal conditions. Therefore, it is important to read this report as expressing how I found one specific Mew Gull, G-AEXF, on one specific flight, rather a long time ago; but it is an exotic aeroplane and still I remember the experience very clearly!

Chapter 29

Private Fighter
Gloster Gladiator

The Gladiator was the last biplane fighter to enter service with the Royal Air Force, first joining squadrons in 1937 – only two years before the Hurricane started to come into use. Although largely outdated in the early part of the Second World War, Gladiators served in many important operational roles, including defence of Plymouth dockyards in the Battle of Britain, operations from a frozen lake in Norway, action in the Western Desert and, as known most popularly, in the defence of Malta. 480 Gladiators were built for the RAF, and at peak, they served on thirty-one squadrons.

In contrast these days to the almost ubiquitous Spitfire, for more than fifty years there had been only one flyable example in the world, although a second was restored to flight some fifteen years ago. While we may not think of operational military aeroplanes as possessions for private owners, neither of these Gladiators would exist today without the efforts of just one such person – the late Vivian Bellamy. He had been a naval pilot in the war and later he managed to persuade the Disposals Board to release two rather battered examples into his ownership. Using the better parts from each, he created the first civil Gladiator, G-AMRK, which for just over two years he used as his personal fly-about. Both he and I were involved with the then active Vintage Aeroplane Club, and I had the youthful nerve to ask if I could fly it; not surprisingly, he refused.

Eventually, Viv Bellamy decided that his valuable reincarnation should go into the care of an organisation that would be able to ensure its long-term flying future so, for £50, he sold it back to its makers – the Gloster Aircraft Company – on condition that they would keep it flying. By 1960, though, Glosters were about to close and 'MRK was handed into the loving care of The Shuttleworth Collection – although another seven years passed before it came to its permanent home at Old Warden. This would not have happened without the determined effort by Wing Commander R.F. (Dicky) Martin, Gloster's Chief Test Pilot, who also was the Collection's Senior Pilot.

Following Viv Bellamy's perfectly justifiable refusal to let me fly it in 1952, twenty-five years later an unexpected opportunity arose. As most of the historic aeroplanes in the Shuttleworth are sole surviving specimens of their types, wear and tear on their component parts must be strictly contained, so in general they are flown only when necessary for an air test, ferry flight, or display – and normally a pilot is allowed only one type-familiarisation flight.

I had been involved in organising the Shuttleworth element of the Queen's Jubilee Air Pageant at White Waltham in May 1977 and the two-day event had drawn to a successful close. In the early evening, with duties done, I was walking along the flight line in relaxed mode, looking favourably at this rather special aeroplane, when Dicky Martin, who had flown it in the display, said, 'Don't just look at it; get in and go.' So, under his watching eye and with his very practical briefing, I did just that. There was a considerable amount of traffic, mainly departing visitors and light twins providing pleasure flights for the public, but the more human among pilots tend to forego some of their rights and privileges when such a special machine as the Gladiator taxies in their midst. They could not have known that the occupant had not done it all before and I was grateful for that touch of timeless courtesy.

I am not a believer in flying an aeroplane just once and then pretending to know enough about it to write an informative handling report. Sometimes this cannot be avoided, but during my subsequent involvement with The Shuttleworth Collection I had cause to fly the Gladiator on five more occasions – two air tests, two ferry flights and one demonstration – so that unexpected initiation was not wasted.

The cockpit is interesting and typical of the era. The pilot's seat is embedded among the exposed tubes of the fuselage structure and most knobs and levers are attached to these. There is no cockpit floor, so anything dropped remains out of reach and could possibly become entangled in the control runs. There are hinged doors on both sides and – unusually for the time – a sliding cockpit canopy, operated by a wheel moving along a groove on the port side. The large trim wheel is on the left, with its setting indicated by a rotating scale that revolves in the reverse direction. The Gladiator must be one of the earliest aircraft to have the subsequently long-established standard panel with its six flight instruments.

The 840hp Bristol Mercury nine-cylinder radial engine is primed by a Ki-Gass pump, excessive use of which can cause a fire in the air intake; I have seen this happen on several occasions, but fortunately with no serious consequence. To spring to life, both magnetos are used and the starter button must be given short jabs, for it operates a slipping clutch that readily lives up to its name, so long presses lead to a lot of noise and a flat battery. The engine can be hand-cranked if necessary.

Radial engines need plenty of oil pressure and, on starting from cold, the Mercury's needle leaps to the top of the capillary gauge to show $120lb/in^2$. Soon it lowers to about 90 and there, hopefully, it stays. While waiting for the engine to warm to an oil temperature of about 20°C, there is ample time to take stock of the surroundings and check that various items, such as the flaps, with just an up/down selector and a hand-operated hydraulic pump, are behaving as they should.

On moving forward, taxying is relatively easy, with only minimal need to use the pneumatic brakes, which work with use of the rudder and a hand lever on the spade-grip control column. Active weaving, though, is essential with a large radial obstructing the view ahead. Overall, even at this early stage, the Gladiator generates a sense of solidity and satisfaction for the lone occupant.

Before take-off, the normal 'vital actions' apply, with especial need to check that the fuel cock is set for the gravity tank, that the sliding hood and the side panels are locked, and that flaps are up – if not fully up or down, these tend to lower unevenly between one side and the other.

Although a fair ration of rudder is needed for a straight take-off, all the controls are responsive from the start, so it is easy to raise the tail too high, too quickly. With a (large) fixed pitch propeller, boost and rpm are directly related; full throttle gives +3lb boost, with an override to +5, but in the interest of engine life, high power settings are avoided whenever possible. The Gladiator unsticks cleanly at 60kt for a build-up to a climbing speed of 95kt. To reduce engine wear I have not attempted a full throttle rate of climb check, but according to handbooks this is a very inspiring 2,300ft/min – and it feels like it too!

As soon as the Gladiator is comfortably airborne and there is time to think about one's good fortune, it shows its merits as a true pilot's aeroplane. Handling qualities are perfect, with all three controls light and harmonised, with a really snappy rate of roll; it is statically stable throughout the speed range and trim changes are small. Perhaps the only weakness is the Mercury's extreme proneness to carburettor icing, sometimes leading to a sudden engine stoppage with no prior warning. Several pilots have experienced this and I was not exempt from the worrying situation. My immediate reaction was a fear of messing up a forced landing and breaking the only flyable specimen of a historically famous aeroplane. Fortunately, though, some energetic work with the carb heat control brought the engine back to life and blood pressure returned slowly to normal!

Cruising flight is very satisfying. The hood can be open or closed and as it is a rather tight fit I delighted in having it wound back, creating fresh air and a better view. Most people who are not pilots ask, 'How fast does it go?' This is not easily answered, as published performance is always given for a specific height, at which true and indicated airspeeds differ sufficiently for the real figure not to reveal itself. The books, though, quote a top speed of 220kt at 14,500 feet.

Although there is no pre-stall buffet or any other helpful warning, the breakaway itself is innocuous, occurring at about 45kt with no tendency for a wing drop. It all happens 2-3kt slower when the flaps are pumped fully down. On the descent to the aerodrome it is important to make a positive effort to keep the engine warm, prior to lowering the flaps at not more than 78kt, with a final approach at 65mph, reducing to 55mph over the fence. A three pointer – not advisable in a crosswind – calls for a moderate attitude change which leads to a definite loss of forward view, but if judged correctly the result is very rewarding. Except in a crosswind, keeping straight after touchdown is not difficult.

Although Gladiator G-AMRK has been in peaceful civilian ownership for more than half a century, it retains much of its Service ambiance. The gunsight is still in situ, as are the four – inoperative! – 0.303in Browning machine guns. It has all the feel of a military machine, with the delightfully crisp handling qualities that a fighter should have. What more could a pilot seek from the pure pleasure of flying for flying's sake?

Being airborne in such a valuable, sole surviving aeroplane imposes some measure of strain on any pilot who is aware of what he has in his hands, but after completing a flight safely and satisfactorily the feeling of elation can last quite a long time. Although responses vary, several very experienced pilots have said that the Gladiator is the nicest aeroplane that they have ever flown. Perhaps Dicky Martin's observation, 'There is only one thing I dislike when flying the Gladiator – getting out!' best sums up the truth about this unique machine.

Chapter 30

Annie the faithful
Avro Anson

Many aircraft have started life as military machines and, on retirement, have been cascaded into civil ownership; notable examples are the Tiger Moth and Chipmunk. However, the Avro Anson – knows as 'Faithful Annie' – initially went through this process in reverse. Although best known in its Service guise, in 1934 Annie first emerged as the Avro 652 light charter aeroplane for Imperial Airways, accommodating four passengers. This was well tailored to the needs of the Air Ministry as a new coastal reconnaissance aeroplane so, in July 1935, a first order was placed for 174 such machines, to be powered by two 350hp Armstrong-Siddeley Cheetah IX nine-cylinder air-cooled radial engines driving a pair of two-blade fixed-pitch propellers.

The specification called for a single forward-firing Browning machine gun in the nose, one or two machine guns in a dorsal turret and two 100lb bombs. Even for those days the scale of operational kit seems rather thin, but lack of complexity was the order of the day and there was not even a control for opening the bomb doors; on release the bomb's weight was sufficient to open the doors, which closed automatically by springs once the bomb had passed through. Reliable, rugged, and wholly lacking in sophistication, the Anson proved outstandingly successful and almost 7,000 were built in the UK. Although progressively withdrawn from front line duties between 1940 and 1942, Mark 1 Ansons more than earned their keep for training navigators, air gunners and wireless operators until shortly after the end of the war. By this time the design had evolved into the civil Avro XIX, which in turn became the Anson 19 for the RAF.

ANNIE THE FAITHFUL

Let us first look at the earliest Anson. After the war more than 100 found their ways on to the UK civil register and many organisations used these in a variety of roles. The last organisation to operate the Anson 1 commercially was Derby Aviation, which in 1954-55 used G-AMDA (formerly N4877) for geophysical survey work in Africa and in the English Midlands. It was this machine that I flew in several roles until well into the sixties.

Perhaps the first (and lasting) impression was that it had no frills. The airframe structure was exposed internally and many cockpit components were attached directly to it. At some stages of a flight the Mk 1 provided plenty of work for the pilot, but I have not heard of anyone who disliked it. The brakes were noticeably ineffective, and taxying seemed to call for three hands. Therefore, in practice, the control column had to be left to itself without any help from mankind, for the pawl-and-ratchet brake lever (fed from an air bottle which, on most machines, needed to be charged between flights) was on the central pedestal, and needed a lot of attention for minimal result. The left hand, of course, was fully occupied with the throttles.

The relatively low power and fixed-pitch propellers caused the take-off to be a protracted if straightforward exercise, with little tendency to swing. It was important not to use flaps to shorten the run, for they were pumped down by hand and were not interconnected, so they might lower to different angles. Safety speed, which is the target figure in order to attain full directional control should an engine fail, was a comfortably low 65kt, while the recommended figure for the climb was 78kt, using a maximum of 2,300rpm. This gave a text-book rate of 720ft/min (over-optimistic?). So far so good, but here the work began again. One feature of the early Anson that almost everyone seems to know is that it was necessary to complete 160 turns of the hand crank (to the right of the pilot's seat, so that it could be operated by either front-seat occupant) to raise the undercarriage. Often an Air Training Corps cadet would be given a flight in order (unwittingly) to perform this menial if lengthy and tiring task.

The author of the Pilot's Notes may have had a sense of humour, for among the advice offered is: 'at heavy loads, the undercarriage should be raised without delay, as this improves one-engine performance!' When eventually the wheels were up they protruded below the engine nacelles, and if a landing was made in this condition the brakes (such as they were) would work. The indicators to show when the wheels were locked down were probably unique for, instead of the usual green lights, two green knobs would pop out of tubes and move into view.

The Mk 1 gave a sense of reliability and confidence. The ailerons were moderately heavy and stiffened markedly with increase in speed, but those were not serious shortcomings in an aeroplane of this nature. The recommended cruising speed for best range was 104kt, and the maximum continuous power setting in weak mixture (manually controlled) was 2,100rpm. When fuel consumption was not critical, though, Annie would romp along 10-15kt faster. Like all radials, the Cheetah IXs needed a high oil pressure, with $70lb/in^2$ as the desired figure. Everything happened in a docile, unhurried manner, and the stall (at about 57kt 'clean') would lead to a gentle wing drop only if Annie was put to the test and the control column was held back determinedly. There was a fairly marked change of trim with changes of power, though, with a need to hold the nose down firmly when the throttles were opened.

The normal approach and landing were unremarkable, assuming, of course, that the undercarriage had been wound fully down, bringing the airspeed back to about 87kt before doing so, and reducing it to as little as 60kt for an engine-assisted flaps-down arrival, or 5kt more for a glide. While it seemed customary to make contact with the ground via a tail-down wheeler, with care a satisfying three-pointer could be achieved. There was remarkably little inclination to swing.

The Pilot's Notes contain little reference to flying on one engine, except to say that at 8,500lb weight (the maximum was 9,900lb) and with the undercarriage up, it should be possible to maintain height at 78kt. For an asymmetric landing, the Notes advise lowering the undercarriage while there is still plenty of height in hand. With the wheels dangling, flight 'on one' was definitely downhill, so not surprisingly there is no mention of a procedure for going round again.

I was fortunate to fly G-AMDA over a period of almost ten years, during which it was used and flown by several people for several purposes. After arrival at Derby 'DA was modified and equipped for geophysical survey work in West Africa, on which it was later engaged in the Midlands on behalf of the Geological Survey. Before all this happened, however, I air-tested the newly installed system and did the first flights with a magnetometer dangling 100ft behind and below the aircraft. Later 'DA was modified with dummy propeller pitch controls for twin conversion training with the London School of Flying at Elstree, where I flew it on several occasions. During this time 'DA was used for photographic surveys of the growing towns of Basingstoke and Swindon and some work for British Rail. Finally, after retirement from commercial work, G-AMDA completed its life cycle and reverted to camouflage, roundels and its original military serial, N4877, for the Skyfame Museum at Staverton (now Gloucestershire Airport), where I met it again. Although not airworthy now, 'DA remains intact and has been restored for static display by the Imperial War Museum at Duxford.

Just as the original Anson 1 of 1936 evolved from the civil Avro 652, so the post-war Anson 19 came about as the military successor to the civil Avro XIX. The latter was the result of the workings of the wartime Brabazon Committee, which in 1943 looked ahead to the likely needs of the post-war airlines and produced a specification XIX for a small feeder liner. In 1945, A.V. Roe and Co modified a military Mark 12 (a half-way house between the original and late variants) with nine passenger seats, oval windows and other trimmings to make it more 'civil'. This successfully fulfilled the committee's requirements, so the identity XIX (later 19) was born from unusual roots and not in the normal sequence of mark numbers.

Shortly after the Second World War, forty-eight new Avro 19s appeared on the British civil register, with Railway Air Services as the main operator having fourteen. Another six were used by the Ministry of Civil Aviation (a predecessor of today's CAA) for calibrating airport radio/navigation installations. These were based at a grass aerodrome called Gatwick (from which a few years later I did some part-time instructing for Surrey Flying Club on non-radio Piper Cubs!). Other Avro 19s were used as a demonstrator for the then emerging Decca navigation system, for aerial photography and as an airborne laboratory for Ekco radar trials. Hawker Aircraft and Armstrong-Whitworth Aircraft used them as company hacks and another earned its keep as a flying classroom with the College of Aeronautics at Cranfield. Overseas, three operated in Biafra for Save the Children Fund.

Alongside its various civil uses, the 19 filled a gap in the RAF's inventory and 263 were built, to be used mainly on communications work but also on air survey duties. The 'core' 19 was developed into the Marks 20, 21 and 22 as navigation and radio trainers. The last was delivered in May 1952, marking seventeen years of continuous Anson production, which had peaked at 130 a month and making a total of 11,020 of all marks – 2,882 of which were built in Canada. This gives an idea of the scale of flying activity and the industry's manufacturing capacity compared with today! The number of Ansons produced was beaten only by the Spitfire, Hurricane and, perhaps surprisingly, the Wellington.

So, with the Anson 19 we have an aeroplane that remained frill-less, but which was markedly less bare and basic than its predecessor, the Mark 1. The undercarriage and flaps were hydraulic and, unless things went wrong, the need for energetic hand pumping disappeared. A compressor on the port engine kept the pneumatic brakes in good shape; these were controlled in a conventional manner with a lever on the half-wheel control column. Power came from a pair of Armstrong-Siddeley Cheetah 17 nine-cylinder radials, each of which produced seventy more bhp than the Cheetah 9s on the Mark 1, with the added benefits of variable-pitch featherable propellers; the controls for these were among the type's few unfavourable features, as they were placed inconveniently at the base of the throttle box and worked almost vertically, with a need to push the levers almost into the floor to reach the feathering position. Strangely, the Cheetahs on all marks of Anson were not easy to synchronise and the familiar Annie throb became an unmistakeable aural identification before a machine came into view. The RAF's Mark 19 retained evidence of its civil origins, for the crew had cushioned seats; it was the only military type that I met with no provision for parachutes.

On take-off the 19 was a more sprightly performer than its lumbering forbear and the wheels retracted quickly, leading to a reasonably rapid acceleration to the comfortably modest safety speed of 80 knots; this was on the way to a recommended climb figure of 95, using $2¾lb/in^2$ boost and 2,300rpm. Early 19s, known as Series 1 machines, had the original slab-like wooden wings of the Mark 1, but early in the production stage these were changed to more aerodynamically clean metal units (changing the sub-title to Series 2) offering lighter and more responsive ailerons, providing a more balanced overall control package. It was more pleasant (but possibly less interesting!) to fly than the Mark 1; the 19 was a little more sensitive to weight distribution, although all versions of Annie were remarkably tolerant load lifters.

Cruising speed for maximum range was 105kt, but when neither range nor endurance was critical it was comfortable to romp along at about 120kt. The view was very good, Annie rode through moderately rough air very steadily and was a satisfying A to B vehicle. From wheels and flaps down to everything up, the stall occurred between 50 and 60 knots, before which a gentle warning buffet told the pilot what was about to happen, but when it did, all was very tame and a wing needed to be provoked to persuade it to drop. Not surprisingly, the wooden block was less likely to go down than its younger metal counterpart.

For a normal landing with flaps down the approach was started at 80kt, losing ten of these before crossing the fence, but retaining five or so for a glide approach or at heavy weight. The landing itself was straightforward, with only a minimal tendency to bounce or swing, but a missed glide or a heavyweight approach called for energetic nose-down trimming in the event of a go-around – or an overshoot as it was called then.

The ability to feather a propeller and to raise or lower the undercarriage quickly in the event of a power failure made asymmetric flight far less stressful than on the Mark 1, but, as with most twins of the time, the performance on one was far from sparkling. With the live engine operating at climbing power and at moderate weight, height could be held, but the rudder trim was unable to absorb all the foot load. When positioning for a single-engine landing, in order to retain directional control it was important not to allow the airspeed to fall below 85kt, delaying flap lowering until the airfield was within definite reach. An overshoot 'on one' was not a safe endeavour below 600ft, as about 400 of these could be lost in the initial cleaning-up process. In these circumstances accurate handling and a minimum of 80kt were essential for success.

The Anson was one of the safest aeroplanes ever to see service. Pilots pranged them, force-landed them, ditched them and even hit trees, often emerging unhurt. All variants shared well-earned reputations both as uncomplaining load lifters and for rugged reliability. At the start, many Anson 1 crews performed lengthy coastal reconnaissance missions, often in harsh conditions; however, it was on second-line wartime work that the type became more widely known. In the post-war period this work continued on later marks. After thirty-two years of continuous service, the breed was retired from active duties in June 1968, when the last six 19s on the Southern Communications Squadron made a final formation fly-past over their base at Bovingdon.

Many people consider the Anson and its contemporary twin the Airspeed Oxford to be broadly comparable, but except that each was powered by a pair of Cheetahs, they had little in common. The Oxford was spirited, knew how to drop a wing at the stall and could swing quite energetically on landing, so it was a good pilot trainer, but it objected to lifting a heavy load. The Anson, though, was exceptionally docile and, in my humble opinion, as a one-time flying instructor, too easy for the training role; but it was a virtual wonder in its ability to carry, without complaining, almost anything that could be squeezed into the cabin. Performance was never sparkling, but unlike most types, handling qualities changed only moderately between an empty and a loaded machine.

Fortunately, the breed remains alive and well. A genuine civil Avro 19 G-AHKX has been preserved and restored; it is operated by the Shuttleworth Collection at Old Warden. A former RAF T21, WD 413, is in private hands. Both fly on special occasions and, as time goes on, they will be increasingly significant reminders of our once prolific aviation industry.

Chapter 31

The Oxbox – outstanding twin trainer
Airspeed Oxford

In common with several second-line aircraft immediately before the Second World War, the Airspeed Oxford twin-engine trainer was a military development of a successful civil airliner/charter aeroplane, redesigned and produced hurriedly for the RAF's essential expansion scheme. It evolved from the Envoy, the prototype of which flew in June 1934. Envoys served on many internal air services varying in distance from Heston-Edinburgh to Portsmouth-Isle of Wight; but perhaps the best-known specimen was G-AEXX, delivered to the King's Flight in 1937, resplendent in the red and blue livery of the Brigade of Guards. Even before the Oxford materialised, though, six Envoys were equipped with dorsal gun turrets and bomb racks and supplied to the South African Air Force. Japan, too, acquired six and built ten more.

Not surprisingly, the Oxford (to Air Ministry specification T23/36) was beefed up a bit from the Envoy for its more arduous military duties. The prototype L4534 flew first in June 1937; even before this 136 had been ordered. Both the threat of war and the related demand for aircraft grew apace and by the outbreak in 1939 more than 400 had been delivered. Production continued without interruption until July 1945, by which time 8,586 had been built. Unlike most military designs, which developed progressively as they matured, the Oxford underwent very few changes throughout its life and the removal of the dorsal turret was the only noticeable change: as early as 1938 many were turret-less.

The Oxford, known throughout its working life as the Oxbox, was the RAF's first twin-engine monoplane trainer with a retractable undercarriage, so the first few were delivered to the Central Flying School, enabling flying instructors to gain experience before the type was delivered en masse to the growing number of Service flying schools. As a general rule at this time, pilots destined to fly multiengine aircraft started on Avro Tutors and graduated to Oxfords, while those targeted for singles would move on from Tutors to Hawker Hind trainers. Within a couple of years this sequence was changed to elementary training on de Havilland Tiger Moths or Miles Magisters followed by advanced work on Miles Masters or North American Harvards. The Oxford, though, outlived all these, into the era of de Havilland Chipmunks, for despite a short break in the late forties, Oxfords were reintroduced for training post-war National Service pilots until the type finally retired in 1954. I think it safe to say that the Oxford was the most useful and successful twin trainer of all time. Even the 370hp Armstrong-Siddeley Cheetah X 9-cylinder radial engines remained the source of power throughout the type's life at home, though the Canadian version had more oomph with 450hp Pratt and Whitney Wasp Juniors.

Now let us look at the Oxford – as this pilot saw it. Unfortunately, I trained during the type's temporary withdrawal from service, so I was required to progress in one stressful leap, from the Harvard to the Mosquito as my first twin, but later I had the opportunity to become familiar with the Oxbox and I held it in high regard. For an aeroplane designed in the mid-thirties, the cockpit layout and accessibility of all key items could not be faulted. Full dual controls were fitted and the central pedestal accommodated all the required kit: the two throttle levers, a single mixture control (with take-off, normal and weak settings), undercarriage, flap, and carburettor heat controls, fuel cocks, elevator trim wheel, rudder bias and even landing lights were all within easy reach of both front-seat occupants. Instruments were sensibly positioned, with not only the full standard panel and fuel gauge immediately ahead of the left-hand seat, but with boost, rpm (interestingly, reading vertically), oil pressure and oil temperature gauges paired just to the right of centre, with duplicate ASI, altimeter and turn-and-slip indicator immediately ahead of the instructor's position. Many later designers could have learnt from this early Airspeed initiative.

Fuel capacity was 156 gallons, and each engine was fed from its own two tanks, but with no crossfeed. The undercarriage and flaps were hydraulically operated. Early Oxfords had starting (third) magnetos, but by far the majority had booster coils, while some had conventional starter motors. Taxying was quite easy, especially on grass, and the column-operated pneumatic brakes were far more efficient than their cumbersome counterparts on early Ansons. They acted differentially with use of the rudder.

On take-off the Oxford showed its real worth as a pilot trainer; the pronounced tendency to swing to starboard called for positive corrective action by generous use of the rudder and by applying power gently, leading with the starboard throttle. This was a much more significant quality feature than is the case today, for trainees were destined to graduate onto more powerful tailwheel piston twins, some of which had very strong determination not to go straight ahead unless forcibly compelled to do so!

Here the Oxford could reveal one of its less charming characteristics. A high percentage of the lift was generated from the wing centre section between the fuselage and the engines. Dented or badly fitting fillets or panels could lead to stalling at the wing roots and there are several recorded cases of aircraft needing extended take-off runs or even failing to get airborne. I have met several people who had experience of this uncomfortable phenomenon and there was an appropriate warning in the Pilot's Notes, but I was fortunate to avoid it.

If all was well the Oxford would lift off cleanly at about 65mph and accelerate reasonably rapidly to the modest safety speed of 85mph – the figure at which directional control would be possible in the event of an engine failure – on the way to a recommended climb speed of 110mph, using a maximum of +2¼lb boost and 2,300rpm. Once settled into the cruise, with 2,100 and -1 generating about 120mph, the Oxbox revealed generally pleasant handling characteristics, with controls that were light, effective and rapid in

THE OXBOX – OUTSTANDING TWIN TRAINER

response to small displacements. At slightly less economical power settings leading to a modest increase in airspeed, the ailerons, in particular, were surprisingly crisp. All this, though, related to the load on board, for despite being laterally and directionally stable, any rearward movement of the centre of gravity brought with it some rather unpleasant longitudinal oscillations. With no more than three up, it was a delight to fly, but with more on board much of the appeal disappeared. It was not a good load lifter.

One of the many qualities sought on a handling trainer would be some life at and near the stall. Here no one should be disappointed, for there was extensive vibration before reaching the 'clean' breakaway figure of about 67mph; then either wing would go down, a bonus that prevented a pupil trying to anticipate the correct recovery action. With flaps and undercarriage dangling, the stall occurred at about 9mph slower, but then the wing drop tendency was less enthusiastic.

Very few early twins had sparkling asymmetric performance and the Oxford conformed to pattern. At light load, height could just be maintained, but the rudder bias required thirty-two turns and, even when fully applied, the remaining foot load would be quite heavy. The official Pilot's Notes, too, offered little help, with two seemingly contradictory statements: 'at full load the aircraft may climb away slowly at 85mph' and, a few sentences later: 'height can barely be maintained on one engine at full throttle.' Perhaps in fairness, though, the first would refer to performance from ground level while the other would relate to engine-out performance when cruising at several thousand feet. However, the true result would depend largely on the surface condition of the cowlings and wing root fillets on individual aircraft.

When 'on one', everything happened at 95mph IAS. It was the optimum for cruise performance and the recommended speed for manoeuvring in the circuit prior to an asymmetric landing. Speed should not be reduced to 85mph until the airfield was definitely within reach, but if it was not, there were few options, for there was no chance of a successful go-around from this state. This situation applied to all twins of the time, including early mark Ansons.

With everything working, the Oxford was a pleasant and well-mannered circuit aeroplane. The undercarriage could be lowered at up to 120mph and the final approach with full flap was 80mph. Pilot's Notes recommended an additional 15-20mph for a flapless glide, but I tried this and found the subsequent float too long for comfort. 90mph seemed to provide a happier solution if one wished to stay within the length of all but the longest runways. The Oxford would settle on three points with a comforting clunk, but this was an invitation to risk a smart swing that was more difficult to correct than from a tail-down wheeler. The active swinging tendency at both ends of a flight was a very useful bonus in the pilot training role – even if it was not intended at the design stage. After flight, the engines were stopped by pulling and holding out a slow running cut-out; the ignition switches were not put down until everything had stopped.

Just as the Oxford had evolved from the civil Airspeed Envoy, it completed the life cycle by reverting post-war to further civil use, mostly by conversion into Consuls which proved popular on the business and air charter market.

Unfortunately, unlike the Anson, no Oxford is likely to take to the air again. The last Oxford to fly anywhere in the world was V3388, which became civil registered as G-AHTW and operated for fourteen years as a company hack by Boulton Paul Aircraft Limited, based at the original Wolverhampton airfield. It was very well maintained throughout and four years after retirement it was acquired by the now defunct Skyfame Aircraft Museum at Staverton. It was repainted in its original RAF camouflage and flown for several years. I had the pleasure and privilege to fly this machine on several occasions and appreciated the good condition (no battered cowlings) in which it had been kept. When lightly loaded, it was a pleasant machine which responded well to spirited handling at displays. Now, in company with its former sister ship at Skyfame, Anson 1 G-AMDA/N4877, it is on static exhibition with the Imperial War Museum at Duxford.

Chapter 32

Casualty of war
Miles M.11A Whitney Straight

Not only was the Miles Whitney Straight one of many good British touring aeroplanes of the nineteen thirties; it was one of the very best. Yet its original concept came not from its designers and builders but because Whitney Straight, as the owner of five flying schools, sought something for his former students that would be more comfortable than the open-cockpit Miles Hawks on which they had learnt to fly. He put his requirements to the indefatigable Miles brothers, who burst into action and produced the right answer.

That answer was a roomy side-by-side cabin two-seater that emerged early in 1936. As a clean low-wing cantilever monoplane it led the field in appearance and performance compared with the biplanes to which many other manufacturers were clinging. An interesting comparison with the M.11A was de Havilland's competitor the DH87 Hornet Moth. Both were ahead of their time in comfort and very successful, but the sleek Miles machine was almost 20mph faster, which can be significant on the long hauls of which they were capable.

As with several other good light aeroplanes in the thirties, the Whitney Straight was well established in production when the threat of the Second World War caused several manufacturers to switch from the civil market to the urgent needs of the time. Only fifty M.11As were completed, but its popularity had led to orders from overseas as well as from home; it was not long before the factory facilities were turned over to the M.14 Magister, 1300 of which were built to help equip the RAF's rapidly growing number of elementary flying training schools. The Whitney Straight, though, earned its fuel and oil during the war, as twenty-one were impressed into military service as communications machines. Not surprisingly, their civil comfort levels made them very popular!

My introduction to the Whitney Straight was in the late nineteen fifties when G-AFGK (the last to be built) was based, in private hands, at Elstree. Visually attractive and not appearing old even today, the M.11A is entered via a single door on the port side, but perhaps the other side would have been preferable for changing passengers or for an instructor to step out after a dual check. The cockpit is wide and comfortable, fortunately with two individual stick-type control columns. The internal layout is pleasantly uncomplicated, with a basic instrument panel, below which is a control for the vacuum operated flaps. An electric fuel gauge with a left/right switch indicates the contents of the two generous 15-gallon tanks and a spring-loaded control for elevator trim is centrally mounted within easy reach of each occupant. Behind all this is a shelf to take 115lb of luggage.

The early stages of a flight reveal two old-fashioned features; starting calls for external hand priming and the brakes are typical of the time. They are cable operated via a large lever on the left and not very efficient. Apart from the need to weave while taxying – a feature of all tail-draggers – the qualities of the M.11A that followed were much more than just acceptable.

The makers' promotional publicity claimed that the take-off run into a 5mph wind was only 145 yards and I have no reason to dissent from this. By standards of the time there was little tendency to swing, with a subsequent climb rate that according to the makers again would be a creditable 850ft/min. I found this to be a very slight overstatement of fact, but it is the stage at which numerous variables, such as propeller type and pitch and age of engine have an impact. The get-away rate, though, was wholly satisfactory.

From the start the general handling on the climb proved to be pleasantly smooth and, as expected, even this improved with an increase in airspeed to the recommended 130mph and 2,100rpm, although I have tended to cruise a 130hp Gipsy Major 1 at a slightly lower power setting. Without doubt the Whitney Straight was and, if available today, would be a very practical (and comfortable) machine to choose for long-distance travel, with a more-than-useful published range of 570 miles.

Low-speed handling plays a key part in evaluation of any aeroplane and here the M.11A holds its own. The ailerons continue to work down to the stall, which in clear configuration occurs at just below 50mph, while having the flaps fully lowered delays the break-away by as much as 10mph. In all circumstances the behaviour is as benign as any among conventional aeroplanes.

After some time cruising contentedly on a calm day I felt no desire to return to base, but all good things must end sometime and most certainly I was not disappointed in the M.11A's qualities in the circuit. Although there was a blind area (more than a spot) behind, in other directions the view was good and the available range of flap settings made a variety of speeds practicable to suit the situation in the pattern. With a preferred initial approach at 70mph, if not dictated by other traffic the angle of descent can be a matter of choice, with a very steep full-flap line possible, but perhaps this would not be advisable in normal circumstances. Once more quoting from the makers' claims, the touchdown speed is 38mph (although not checkable from within the cockpit) leading to a stated run of just 100 yards. I have no reason to dispute these figures, but I can confirm that judging the landing itself is not difficult and there is not much tendency to swing, all of which is made more pleasant by the softness of the oleo undercarriage legs.

The Miles family designed and built more individual (and some extremely interesting) types of light aircraft than the de Havilland organisation, which most people consider as the main creators of the class. In the 1930s the British light aircraft industry was the world leader in the field and more than a dozen companies were active. While some of these failed through natural causes, the civil activities of several others were curtailed by the threat of war and the Whitney Straight was not the only type to suffer. Unhappily for GA the M.11A today is a rarity, with just two on the UK register. The type's virtual demise is sad, for here was a machine that deserved a numerically stronger and longer life than circumstances allowed.

Chapter 33

Monoplane trainer
Miles M.14 Magister/Hawk Trainer

When we think of a light, low wing cantilever monoplane with brakes, power operated flaps and an ability to cruise at 110-115mph, we would be forgiven if we assumed this to be a relatively modern piece of kit. Yet no; the aircraft concerned – the Miles Magister – entered service in September 1937 as the first mass-produced monoplane trainer in a world that was still geared mainly to the biplane era.

The Magister, known affectionately as Maggie, started life as a Service aeroplane, with about 1,300 built for the Royal Air Force, but the background was far from military. The all-wooden type was a logical development of a long line of Hawks that F.G. Miles had designed in the early thirties for the club and private flying market, as competitors to the many Moths produced by de Havilland. Although it failed to attract the aura that surrounded its Service counterpart, the Tiger Moth, it had many followers and there was much good-natured banter about the relative merits of the two types, which between them equipped the numerous Elementary Flying Training Schools (EFTS) of the Second World War. Aviation happened in massive doses then, when it was not unusual to have more than 100 hardworking Tigers or Maggies based on one relatively small grass airfield, with neither radio nor air traffic control. Aerodrome circuits were far busier than any today; it was all made a little less traumatic, though, by (usually) only one type, with all aircraft operating around the pattern at similar speeds.

But let us look at the Maggie in the flesh. With a Gipsy Major I to provide the power, the Magister had all controls fully duplicated, except that in the front cockpit the instructor had a master switch which could override the student's magneto switches in the rear. The control column was unusually thick, and handling seemed more pleasant when this was unofficially replaced by the slimmer stick from a Tiger Moth. The only unusual control was the small knob on the lower left of the cockpit for operating the pneumatic flaps. This worked horizontally forwards from up, through neutral, to the down position, with an arrowed gauge alongside, working in a similar sense. Unless exercised several times to exhaust the system, the flaps moved very rapidly and an intermediate setting for take-off needed practice to attain.

The Magister taxied well on grass or on a hard surface, but the cable brakes were difficult to set up with comparable effectiveness on both wheels. Constant circuit work, with all the ground manoeuvring that went with it, often produced brakes that were soggy by the end of the session or, even more frequently, with one biting and the other almost useless.

Take-off was rather protracted, for the Magister was more than a man's weight heavier than a Tiger Moth for the same available power, and the usual LA 596 propeller was coarser than the DH 5220 series used on the Tiger, for at the higher end of the Maggie's speed range the latter would bring over-revving too close for comfort. Hugging the ground, but with a hard ride from the oleos (which were difficult to balance evenly), it accelerated well once free; the recommended climb at 70mph gave 700ft/min, in which condition it needed a generous ration of left rudder to compensate for slipstream effect.

View and comfort level were markedly different between the two cockpits. In the front, visibility in most directions was excellent and the draught level was unexpectedly low for an open machine; flight without goggles was practicable for all conditions except for the relatively high speeds needed for aerobatic entries. The poor person in the rear, though, had lots of wind and not much view, but the latter was an excellent introduction to anyone destined to be a fighter pilot.

At the level cruise of about 1,950rpm and 110mph (very useful by comparison with the Tiger Moth's 85mph) the Maggie plodded on very happily, ignoring all but the worst bumps and with positive stability all round. At this and higher IAS figures, the ailerons were heavier than I would choose, but they were immediately responsive. At low speeds more bite would have been preferable. The stall was a real stall, occurring at 52mph in the clean state, but 7mph lower with the large all-through flaps in the fully extended position. Strangely, the right wing almost invariably dropped quite markedly at the flaps-up stall, but far less noticeably in the 'dirty' state. Spinning, which would occur without effort with sloppy or delayed stall recovery, was at a rapid rate and steep; in the early days Maggies presented recovery troubles, but before I met the type the customary fuselage strakes had been fitted and these made for happier times. Nevertheless, even when modified, the Magister tolerated no half measures. Only full rudder-pause-full forward stick would stop it from going downhill until there was no further to go.

Some aeroplanes invite aerobatics; the Maggie did not. Although cleared for all normal manoeuvres, it suffered from a rugged solidity that made it ideal for circuit work or cross-country exercises, but made it feel too heavy for energetic manoeuvres. Loops were uneventful from an entry of not less than 130mph, but ham hands or heavy feet coupled with low airspeed at the top could produce a flick-out not unlike that of the Harvard. Slow rolls were much more difficult; the first half produced few problems, but rolling out required a rare skill, for with much rudder applied the elevators were blanketed. Without top rudder the nose dropped hard; with rudder the nose dropped through elevator ineffectiveness. There were some who found answers to this, but I was one of many who failed.

The Maggie was very happy in the circuit, with really effective flaps and a marked trim change with each alteration in flight condition. A fairly flat clean glide at 70mph changed to a remarkably steep descent with full flap, the limiting speed for which was 75mph. Flapless approaches were interesting test cases of a pupil's accuracy, for 5mph excess airspeed at the threshold on a calmish day could use all but the largest airfield. These were important exercises, however, for they were advisable in crosswind conditions, especially on a paved runway (for which the type was not designed) where the reduced natural braking effect could produce pronounced swings coupled with a tendency for the into-wind wing to lift. This was because the flaps ran continuously, through the centre-section, and the air had no escape route. This problem was reduced when some operators disconnected the centre flaps and fixed them in the up position. Many a Maggie undercarriage, the tubes of which were intentionally weak (to prevent damage to the main spar to which the legs were attached) failed in the field, especially under heavy side-loads.

The low wing and large flaps created a strong cushion effect at the round-out stage and a slightly woolly touch down, but true ballooning was not as pronounced as might be expected. Contact was much crisper in the flapless condition, but a hard ride, sometimes accompanied by the clunking of legs reaching the limits of travel, was a feature of all ground operations.

Some pilots disliked the Magister. Certainly, it possessed its share of design shortcomings, but these tended to teach a person to exercise caution. The effect of the rudder blanketing the elevators (an interesting demonstration even in level flight) made sideslipping near the ground a recipe for short life, while the need for positive spin recovery put it in disfavour with some; but a trainer should call for care on a pupil's part and I had great respect for its ability to do its duty well.

After the war, many Magisters were demobbed and these were picked up avidly by flying clubs and private owners. In civilian guise the Magister was known as the Hawk Trainer III and in this capacity I was fortunate enough to do some instructing on the type. I enjoyed it. Unfortunately, though, in the late fifties the Air Registration Board decreed that Maggie's joints were creaking and refused to renew C of As in the Public Transport category. This put an end to the type for club or school use, but a few lingered on in private ownership. My last illustration shows the instructors of the Elstree Flying Club four-Magister formation display team – we thought we were ending an era but, overcoming glue problems, five Magisters were airborne together at Old Warden in 2022!

Chapter 34

The monoplane Moth
de Havilland DH94 Moth Minor

The appearance of the Moth Minor in 1937 heralded a major reappraisal by the de Havilland enterprise in relation to their future light aircraft. Until this time all production Moths had been biplanes or strut-braced high wingers. The new Minor, though, was a sleek aerodynamically clean cantilever low-wing monoplane, initially with an open cockpit but very soon available in enclosed form, with a very creditable performance on the new de Havilland Gipsy Minor of only 90hp and an attractive fuel economy to match. An early misfortune occurred during spinning trials with the centre of gravity at the aft limit. Despite attempts by two experienced pilots to recover, all efforts failed and two subsequently well-known names – Geoffrey de Havilland Junior and John Cunningham – baled out successfully. The problem was solved by fitting the seemingly inevitable fuselage strakes immediately ahead of the tailplane.

After this unfortunate setback, everything went well. By 1939, production was up to eight or nine aircraft a day, with a growing demand from purchasers at home and abroad. Although originally intended as a non-aerobatic tourer, its economy (100mph on about 4.5 gph) appealed strongly to flying clubs, so the Minor entered the training field. On the outbreak of the Second World War, production for the civil market ceased and the Hatfield factory's resources were concentrated initially on building the more rugged Tiger Moth for the RAF. The DH94's drawings, jigs and partly completed airframes were shipped to Australia where the type was built as a trainer for that nation's air force. Without doubt the DH94 would have been a great sales success and it was a leader among other light aircraft with fortunes broken by the war. By the time home production forcibly ceased, about 100 had been built and thirty-two of these were impressed into military service.

Now let us look at the physical characteristics of this interesting aeroplane. Although I am tempted to call it little, I could be taken to task as it has a span of 36ft 7ins, which is not surprising as the wing is of a high aspect ratio, easily foldable. There is a narrow fixed centre section to which the undercarriage is attached. The fuselage is a traditional plywood box structure, but the cantilever wing, with two spars, is ply covered from the leading edge to the rear spar, with fabric skinning behind. There are no flaps, but as it is such a clean design the gliding angle is very flat, so a very large and effective perforated air brake enables the machine to go down quite steeply, when required to do so. If fully extended this reduces the lift/drag ratio from 9.5 to 7.5:1. With wings folded, the packed width is only twelve feet.

Entry to the cockpits is via a wing walkway; the layout is reasonably spacious and more than usually comfortable with armrests on what are like small office chairs. Unlike previous tandem Moths, the Minor is flown from the front and instruments are fitted for that cockpit only. A very useful tray for maps and accessories is mounted below the panel and a large P-type compass sits beneath that. The lever for the cable-operated drum brakes is on the left, as are the throttle, mixture and trim controls; the last of these applies spring pressure to the sticks and there are no trim tabs. On the right is a long lever to operate the air brake.

My first contact with the DH94 was in 1949 with the Community Flying Club at Woodley aerodrome. When I booked it for the first time there it was, ready to go, but with no form of guidance, so I had the pleasure of discovering for myself what life was like aboard this sleek machine. It took very little time to find that it was good.

Whilst getting to know where things were within, I had time to digest the world outside and was favourably impressed by the shallow ground angle, which helped to provide the above-average view. I took a little time to grasp the fuel situation, but found that the port wing root held a tank of 13 gallons capacity, with a gauge immediately above it, while on the opposite side there was no tank, but space for small items. Apparently a second tank was available as an option. The main luggage holder, which I had failed to find, but then I had no need for it, came to light as being accessible from inside the rear cockpit.

The Minor has no starter and is hand-swung, as was the norm for the time. Before getting going, though, I found an engine data plate, which confirmed that the small Gipsy was a higher-revving unit than its older, bigger brother, the Gipsy Major. Once running, it offers its own relatively high-pitch exhaust note, with a slightly hollow ring to it, which together gives the DH94 its own unique aural identity.

I have heard comments about the Minor's brakes, both favourable and otherwise. I am convinced that everything depends on the cable adjustment and I found them to be more than adequate, making taxying a happy event, with less need for weaving than on most more nose-high taildraggers.

The little Gipsy builds up to 2,400rpm and take-off acceleration is good, but experience soon shows that to keep straight the tail should be held down for longer than on many types, as the rather undersize rudder fails to bite until there is a really worthwhile airflow. A subsequent climb at 65mph generates about 600ft/min and calls for a fair amount of pressure on the left rudder pedal. On the level, 2,200rpm provides about 95mph, which accords well with the maker's claim, for a slightly higher power setting – still within the cruising range – can produce a mile or two above their sales figure of 100mph.

The DH94 handles nicely and very little rudder is needed for balanced turns. The ailerons are light and more responsive than such long-span wings might suggest. Fore-and-aft damping checks indicate that stability is just positive, but the rudder, perhaps, is a touch too light for choice. Turning to the all-important slow-speed characteristics, there is no cause to complain. The straight stall occurs at about 45mph and one wing – usually the left – goes down in an unhurried manner. With the air brake fully extended, there is no difference, which is as one would expect as, unlike a flap, it is not a lift generator; recovery is quick and easy. I did not spin her as, at the time, I had no knowledge of her recovery behaviour.

The Minor has gone through various stages of flight limitation categories; when introduced it was intended as a non-aerobatic tourer and only later became cleared for basic manoeuvres. In recent years it has operated on a permit basis, so the original restrictions apply again. At the time of my flight, though, there were no such constraints and she went round a loop smoothly with remarkably light stick loads; rolling was a different story and with such high aspect ratio wings I found difficulty in maintaining a steady rate and keeping the nose on the horizon; perhaps practice would have improved things a bit!

Gliding at 65mph felt right, reducing over the hedge to 60mph; the subsequent round-out was a modest procedure due to the flat ground 'sit'. On an imperfect touchdown the undercarriage felt a bit hard, but this is a characteristic of the use of rubber blocks in compression, later used with such success on the Mosquito. As on take-off, the rudder was only marginally effective when the tail was down and ground loops were not unknown!

Several years later I flew the coupé version. Although the two variants are basically identical with similar performances, I found their effects on my attitude to be very different: not surprisingly the open machine had a sporting touch and invited investigation into various manoeuvres, while its hooded brother made a much more staid impact and asked to be treated as a tourer. I am biased, I admit, but in every way I preferred the one that offered the fresh air.

In a general assessment, I rate the Moth Minor very positively. I have heard it described as a lightweight Chipmunk and there are certain common characteristics. It is reasonably fast (top speed 118mph), very economical, pleasant to handle and can be housed in a small space. It is unfortunate that its potential could not be fulfilled, for I think it would have sold in big numbers over a considerable time span. Now the UK has a sole airworthy example.

Chapter 35

More glue please, Mr Percival

Percival Proctor

A common practice in the late thirties – when the Royal Air Force needed to expand rapidly prior to the Second World War – was for successful civil aircraft to be adapted for large scale military service. The Avro Anson and the Airspeed Oxford were well known in this context, while the much smaller Percival Proctor emerged from the Vega Gull, which was among the most 'developed' light aircraft of its time.

I mention in Chapter 28 that Captain Edgar Percival was a prolific designer of light aircraft in the 1930s, and the Percival Proctor is essentially a beefed-up version of his Vega Gull 4-seat tourer. It is not a type over which very many pilots enthused and some decidedly disliked it; however, it warrants a place here, for it served as a workhorse for a considerable period and has a distinctly sporting origin. As is usual with military requirements, to cope with the rough lives that Service aeroplanes tend to lead, the need was for more strength, and on 8 October that year the first Proctor 1 saw daylight under its wheels. Some 246 were built for communications purposes. However, due to the extra structure weight and various items of military equipment, including the then-cumbersome radio sets, the first Proctors reverted to three-seat status. The Proctor 2 was broadly similar to the 1, but the 3 became the standard radio trainer for the RAF – 436 Mark 3s were built.

From a pilot's viewpoint many aeroplanes – especially military ones – tend to go downhill as they are developed. The Proctor was no exception. Wider, deeper and longer, and therefore heavier than its predecessor, the Mark 4 was a very different aeroplane – 250 were built, serving on a mixture of radio training and, later, communications duties until the final specimens were declared redundant in 1955. Before this, however, the Mark 5 had appeared; essentially this was a civil 4, and 150 were built for the private and business market in 1946. These served with several large organisations such as Shell and Dunlop, while others operated with charter companies and flying clubs.

Unfortunately, the Proctor was a major sufferer in the saga of wooden aeroplanes and their alleged glue failures. In 1949, one specimen suffered structural failure in flight and others were found sick on subsequent inspection. The one major case, apparently, was not in any way due to a design shortcoming but was the result of using unseasoned timber in the main spar. It is indeed unfortunate that so many very sound aeroplanes of wood construction have been scrapped prematurely because of the ultra-stringent precautions and limitations that were imposed.

Briefly, the Proctor was a low-wing cantilever monoplane, with the 210hp Gipsy Queen II six-cylinder inverted in-line providing the power and a two-blade variable pitch propeller to absorb it. A walkway on each wing centre-section provided access to the cabin, which had forward-opening doors on each side. The two front seats were of the individual bucket-type to accept parachutes, but the later civil version had these replaced by upholstery. The general impression inside was quite businesslike, with plenty of space for maps and other odd items; the only point that I can remember with mild disfavour was the spade grip control column, which was too short.

Starting, with the centrally-mounted propeller control in full coarse, (which was foreign to my thinking, especially in relation to larger engines) was otherwise standard and the Queen uttered a comforting and fairly deep exhaust burble at low rpm. When the engine was running smoothly and the oil pressure had settled to about $50lb/in^2$, the propeller control could be moved to the full fine position, from which setting the pitch range was checked at 1,800rpm. If all was well, a full power check produced 2,400rpm and the boost gauge should normally show 0. Once on the move, adequate differential braking was available by setting the handbrake (the lever was between the front seats) two or three notches back.

At its maximum weight of 3,500lb, the Proctor 5 was quite a heavy aeroplane and certainly felt it on take-off. The book showed a run of only 250 yards at full load, but I would be prepared to challenge that claim. A crosswind from the left could be quite helpful, for one from the other side, coupled with rapid throttle-opening and delayed footwork, could produce a more man-size swing than one might expect. It was an aeroplane that was happier (or its occupants were) with a fair ration of forward speed and the recommended climbing figure was as high as 95mph using initially 2,400rpm and full throttle, reducing to 2,100 when economy was the order of the day. 85mph and full power produced nearly 700ft/min when everything was favourable. In calm weather the Proctor offered very comfortable cruise conditions with trim facilities for both elevators and rudder. 2,100/-3 produced a weak mixture consumption of 10gph and, with two tanks totalling 40 gallons, an endurance of more than three hours was very practicable. So, at 135mph, air distances of 500 miles were within scope, although in the main the Proctor was used for relatively short-range internal communications. In rough conditions it was not kind and at full load it suffered a slight longitudinal instability which could prove mildly aggravating.

Full throttle in level flight produced about 150mph (the book quotes 157) and at the other end of the scale the flaps-up stall occurred at 68mph. This was preceded by vibration on the control column (an early stick shaker?) and a series of up-and-down nose oscillations, while the port wing took the lead over its opposite number in frequency of dropping. Planned spinning was not permitted, but on the 4 and 5 the tailplane was set slightly higher than on the earlier marks in order to improve chances of recovery. Aerobatics, too, were off the menu.

The Proctor was not a happy aeroplane at slow speeds and flap lowering was permissible at a comfortable 100mph. The lever offered three positions, with an intermediate setting for take-off, but it was slightly strange in that it was up when flaps were down and, of course, vice versa. Over-the-fence speeds of 75 and 80mph were recommended for powered and glide approaches respectively, so by light aircraft yardsticks the Proctor was not a machine for the shortest of landing runs. On a mislanding, flaps were not to be raised below 400ft and 90mph.

The landing itself suffered from the cushioning of ground effect and was not really crisp in bumpy or crosswind conditions. The Proctor could swing quite markedly in suitable conditions and particularly when the tail came down on a 'wheeler.' I admit to one serious sin (fortunately with no VIP passenger on board) when I touched down on one runway, the tail came down at the conveniently placed intersection and I finished the run on the other runway! I was considerably more cautious after that.

Although some people disliked the Proctor and anyone seeking the type's vices would have little difficulty in finding them, especially in relation to safety at low speeds, I enjoyed several trips flying 4s on communications work. I did not meet an early-mark Proctor in the Service but flew a civil 3 some years later. Being slimmer and lighter, it was livelier and more pleasant to fly, with the recommended approach speeds (and the stall) more than 5mph slower. It was faster, too, with a cruise at 150mph and a climb rate genuinely touching 1,000ft/min, so altogether was more of a pilot's flying machine than its successor.

Over the years, wooden aeroplanes have suffered very seriously; in 1958 no fewer than ninety-eight Proctors graced the pages of the British civil register, but by 1973 a mere three had a current CoA. Today the situation is little different. Six Proctors remain on the register, only one with a current CoA.

Chapter 36

Speed, versatility and range
de Havilland DH98 Mosquito

Unusual with its largely wooden construction, in many ways the Mosquito stood alone. A private venture by the de Havilland enterprise (using the 1934 DH88 Comet racer as a design starting point), the prototype first flew from Hatfield on 25 November 1940 and became operational in squadron service less than ten months later. The type's first and last operational flights (in September 1941 – almost eight months before being used in its better-known role as a bomber – and December 1955 respectively) were on photo-reconnaissance work, but in between, the Mossie served in almost every conceivable role, including the essential wartime collection of ball bearings from Sweden and surreptitious carriage of special people in the immeasurable discomfort of the bomb bays. This dangerous and demanding work was carried out in civil registered Mossies by crews seconded to British Overseas Airways Corporation.

In earlier Chapters I have described my training on the Mosquito and my operational experiences; now let us look at it in more detail from the pilot's point of view. More than three times heavier than a Harvard and with almost six times the power, the thought of mastering this very sleek, streamlined wooden monster seemed out of reach. After a very thorough external pre-flight check came the art of entry, which was via a ladder and a rather small hole in the right-hand side of the fuselage, the size of which seemed very critical with a seat-type parachute attached to one's lower regions. Once inside, to reach the left-hand side it was necessary to juggle one's clumsy personal package past the right-hand control column between the instrument panel and the instructor's seat.

SPEED, VERSATILITY AND RANGE

Once settled in, the situation changed markedly for the better. The view in all directions was good and the lack of an engine 'up front' provided a very welcome clear space directly ahead. The cockpit layout must have been the subject of much thought, for with one exception everything required to make the kit work was clearly visible and within easy reach; the fuel cocks were the exception, for they were directly behind the left-hand high-backed seat, invisible and controlled by feel alone. Overall, the internal set-up did much to offer a much-needed feeling of confidence in the whole assembly.

Electrical power for engine starting was provided by an external plugged-in 24-volt trolley-accumulator, for the twelve large cylinders of a Merlin needed considerable persuasion to spring into action. This was an impressive exercise, for as soon as the first engine was running, even at low rpm, the feeling of purposeful power was noteworthy. The starboard Merlin was always the first to be fired into life for this had the only generator and, with electrically featherable propellers, healthily charged batteries were an important asset in case of need. With propellers in fine pitch (levers fully forward) the warm-up was at 1,200rpm until there were positive oil temperature readings, first checking that the oil pressure rose almost instantly to the top of the gauge at about 120lb/in^2, but subsequently lowering slightly. In addition to the customary 'mag drop' checks, it was necessary to exercise the propeller controls by setting zero boost and moving the pitch levers back and forth twice each way, checking the rpm changes between fine and coarse settings. Higher power checks were necessary only when some significant engine work had been carried out.

After becoming accustomed to considerable power changes for small throttle movements, taxying was not difficult, for the view ahead was good. It was necessary, though, to make constant checks on the coolant temperatures, especially in hot weather while awaiting take-off clearance. The usual checks included setting about ten per cent of flap before lining-up on and running directly ahead for a few yards to ensure that the tailwheel was straight, then increasing power gently, leading with the port throttle to absorb the strong torque and slipstream effect. As the tail rose, directional control became fully effective with rudder alone, so the throttles could be advanced together to the 'gate' position of (for early marks) +9lb/in^2 boost, before which time the Merlins were achieving their full output of 3,000rpm. Throughout this exercise, though, considerable concentration was required to keep the whole package heading in the desired direction. These lighter Mosquitos would fly off comfortably at about 100kt without much effort, immediately after which the wheels were braked and the undercarriage retracted. The lever for this was one of three in a row beneath the instrument panel, protected by a small shield that needed to be consciously depressed before the wheels could be pulled up. This must have prevented many ground accidents, as the flap lever was immediately adjacent and a wrong choice after landing would prove expensive, embarrassing and used as justification for disciplinary action.

After unstick, the aim was to accelerate as rapidly as possible for, if an engine failed at any stage before reaching the safety speed of 170kt, the drill was to cut the other engine immediately and crash-land ahead, regardless of the terrain. This was because it was the speed at which directional control could be maintained if one engine stopped when both were running at full chat. Several crews walked away unscathed from the resulting mess, while the alternative was far worse: a violent yaw towards the dead engine, followed almost as quickly by an unstoppable roll. It was not the custom to walk away from that.

Clearly it was sensible to reduce to a minimum the time between lift-off and safety speed, so the aeroplane was held low to build-up speed as quickly as possible; as soon as it was clean (wheels and flaps up) the power was reduced to +7lb/in^2 boost and 2,650rpm, at which settings the climb could be started safely at 155kt. Once in this fully controllable situation the early Mosquito was a delight to fly. A fighter-type broken-stick control column produced a quite snappy rate of roll, with a slightly heavier load in pitch.

At a cruise setting of +4lb/2,300rpm the Mark 3 would hammer along at 220kt at a fuel consumption of about 110gph. This may not make

SPEED, VERSATILITY AND RANGE

it the most economical machine on the market, but it was a weighty monster designed to tackle a serious job of work and was far from being intended as a personal fun flier. The fact that it was enjoyable and exhilarating to fly was just a bonus that we were more than happy to accept!

The Mosquito was an unusual mixture. Calling for skill and judgment on take-off and landing and especially critical on one engine, it was surprisingly docile at the stall. On throttling back, because of the clean aerodynamic design, the speed took time to decay and, as expected, the controls became progressively sloppy; shortly before the breakaway there was considerable airframe vibration and firm backward pressure was needed to prevent the nose from dropping and the speed rebuilding itself. All this provided ample warning of things to come. When the stall did occur, at about 95kt, the nose would go down quite determinedly, but the wings remained level and considerable provocation was needed to make one side drop. There was a spot of hidden deception, though, for although everything appeared to be very tame, a check on the altimeter revealed that it was unwinding more rapidly than external visual reference would reveal. So height was important!

All twins provide problems with asymmetric flight, but the Mosquito was determined to demand special respect. Height and particularly airspeed were essential. In normal level flight it was reasonably easy to maintain height at about 155kt, using +7lb and 2,650rpm on the live engine, but to achieve this it was essential for the propeller on the dead side to be fully feathered as quickly as possible. Difficulties would develop as soon as speed was allowed to decay, for with all power on one side, decreasing control effectiveness would call for progressively more rudder in order to maintain balanced flight. When full foot deflection was needed, any further speed reduction would lead to a yaw which, due to the increased speed of the outer wing, would cause a fairly rapid roll into the side of the dead engine. This could be controlled by the stark choice of either reducing power or lowering the nose and increasing speed, either of which would involve a loss of height.

Asymmetric flight formed a key part of a Mosquito conversion course. Although there were generally recognised speeds at which directional control could be maintained and these were published in Pilot's Notes, each individual aircraft would have a figure (if not a mind!) of its own, usually due to a slight warp in the wooden fin. Therefore, before practising a single-engine landing, we needed to carry out a test at a safe height; this involved shutting down the relevant engine, feathering the propeller to provide minimum drag, setting climbing power on the other side, progressively reducing airspeed and applying steadily increasing pressure on the rudder pedal until there was nothing left to use. Then the yaw into the dead side would start and, with very little delay, the worrying roll would begin. The idea was to check the IAS at which directional control began to disappear; usually at 2,650/+7, this was about 145kt. If it was more than this, the exercise would be abandoned, the other engine restarted and the aircraft would be declared temporarily unserviceable. Usually, a fin change rectified the situation.

With both engines operating, an early mark Mosquito was a very satisfying aeroplane, with the excellent forward view adding to its many virtues. In this condition, the only really critical flight phases were the take-off and landing, each of which could catch the unwary with marked tendencies to swing. The only other special task was to keep monitoring the pressures and temperatures – especially the coolant. The Merlin was an excellent power package and a smooth runner, but it disliked rapid throttle changes and could be put out of action with even a small leak in the glycol system. Fortunately, such a weakness was not common.

The downwind leg of the circuit was flown at 2,650/+4, providing about 155kt once the wheels were down. Although the usual green lights revealed that the mainwheels were locked where they should be, there was no indicator to show whether the little fellow at the back had come out of hiding. So it was necessary to push and, for a few seconds, hold down the undercarriage lever against the pressure.

Unlike propellers on most engines, the Mosquito's Merlins were never set in fully fine pitch except for take-off. So on the base leg the revs were set to 2,850, which provided the ultimate power output for an overshoot. Also, this helped to prevent propeller overspeeding in the event of a (hopefully avoidable) need for a rapid power increase on an approach or landing abandoned at a late stage.

After a final turn-in at 140kt, the straight approach would be started at 125kt, reducing to not less than 105kt over the fence. Three-pointers were very satisfying, but the general trend was for a tail-down wheeler, which allowed the rudder to remain effective and the main tendency to swing would come a little later. From this stage the throttles were a no-go area until the aircraft stopped at the end of the run. Today's late-stage rollers were not on the Mosquito's menu.

An asymmetric circuit and landing were more critical in terms of height, airspeed and use of power. With one propeller fully feathered, +7lb boost on the live engine would generate about 155kt, reducing to not less than 135kt for the final turn, leaving full flap to a later stage. From this point a go-around was neither safe nor permissible and, to prevent the yaw-roll sequence, great care was needed to avoid applying too much power in relation to the speed. Undershooting needed to be avoided at all cost, for if that happened the least dangerous decision would be to forget the airfield and hit the ground short of the runway.

All this may give the impression that the Mosquito was a vicious beast. This is not my aim, for when both Merlins were purring the lighter marks were a pilot's delight. When on one engine, so long as all procedures were adopted and followed, there was little cause for concern, but equally there was little scope for error in judgment, handling, or airmanship.

The Mosquito was virtually two aeroplanes. Unlike the lighter machines with their fighter-type control columns, versions that appeared in the later parts of the Second World War were distinctly more staid with bomber-style yokes. This difference alone gave the effect of being aboard a heavier machine, which was borne out by physical fact: the photo-reconnaissance PR34 had a maximum permitted weight of 25,500lb to the Mark 3's normal operating maximum of 16,600lb. Perhaps this was not surprising for, at 3,500 miles, the 34 had the longest range of any operational aircraft then in RAF service. It was almost double that of a loaded Lancaster with standard tankage, which compared broadly with the Mosquito FB6's published range of 1,770 miles.

Why was this? In the late stages of the war there was an urgent need for aerial photographs of hostile activities in the Far East. The 34 was created quickly and, although some of the results of the acceptance tests at Boscombe Down were not wholly favourable, the variant was cleared for squadron service. It differed from other variants in several ways. Because of camera equipment inside the rear part of the fuselage, and belly tanks in what otherwise would be the bomb bays, the c.g. was well aft, and this called for more effort to lift the tail on take-off. Although it is not mentioned in technical publications (and certainly not in Pilot's Notes), this mark (alone) had an additional section of elevator balance that protruded slightly ahead of the smooth curve of the tailplane. There were several other differences from the earlier variants. To keep the coolant temperature within limits on long climbs to operating heights, open/closed switches for the radiator shutters were replaced by manual hand-winders allowing any position to be selected. Two speed, two-stage superchargers enabled the 1,720hp Rolls-Royce Merlin 114s to have new leases of power at height.

Broadly similar to the PR34 was the B35 (bomber), although with a more forward centre of gravity, smaller tankage and shorter range its behaviour and performance were not so critical. Although the Mosquito underwent various changes during its active life, there was relatively little visual difference between the early and late marks. The most noticeable alteration was the bulge in the belly on the 34 and 35, to accommodate fuel or bombs respectively.

So, what was it like? The late-mark Merlins created deeper notes than the 25s on the lighter Mosquitos. In general, though, checks and procedures were broadly identical on all variants, and the main noticeable differences from a handling aspect related to the increased weight. At full load, which included more than 1,200gal of fuel, the take-off run could be fairly protracted. With the throttles opened to the gate and the hydromatic propellers in fully-fine pitch, the 114 delivered 3,000rpm and +12lb/in^2 boost (+9lb on the earlier marks), but if additional power was needed to ensure a clean get-away, the spring catches on the levers could be pulled back and the throttles fully opened to give +18lb (+12lb). At this setting (allowed as an 'operational necessity' for a maximum of five minutes) even a laden PR 34 would accelerate fairly quickly to 110kt, at which it would take to flight quite willingly. Under these conditions, though, safety was as high as 185kt, so power was reduced as soon as practicable to +12lb/2,850rpm for the best rate of climb at 160kt. For maximum range, though, the recommended settings for the climb were +7lb/2,650 and 175kt.

The exceptionally high safety speed and the possibility of needing to do a wheels-up landing onto a belly loaded with fuel were contributory reasons for Boscombe Down's reluctance to clear the mark for service. However, as late as 1951 several modifications were carried out by Marshalls at Cambridge, and these included a speed-up of the undercarriage retraction to improve acceleration.

As most PR flights involved climbing to considerable heights, the 114's two-stage two-speed superchargers were key players in the success story. By about 20,000ft the maximum available boost dropped to about +4lb, so the 'blowers' were switched from MOD (low gear) to AUTO (for high gear) and then the engines had new leases of life. The desired climb settings could be re-established, again calling for progressive throttle opening as further height was attained. Many of the tasks were carried out at 30,000ft, but full-throttle height was 37,000ft, which also was the height for maximum range.

This is where the PR Mosquito showed its spurs. For most of the time we were alone in the high sky. Few other aircraft went up there – or could get up there. One machine that could match us, though (on performance at height, but not on range or endurance), was the Spitfire 19, again proving its value as a specialised PR vehicle.

In general, the characteristics of the earlier variants applied to the later machines, but due to the extra weight and power, the 34 in particular was rather more critical – especially in asymmetric conditions – and called for an additional 10kt on approach and over-the-fence speeds. Continuation training formed an essential ingredient in the currency commitment and each pilot was required to carry out four feathered asymmetric landings each month. A large coloured wall chart revealed to all when this had been completed and it was wise to tackle it as early as possible to avoid the possibility of being compelled to do so later when the weather might be bad. This exercise led to several accidents and, on the basis that training for something that might not happen was a waste of human and material resources, a few years later all feathered flight at low level was discontinued. I have mixed feelings about that.

I may be guilty of bias (for which my earlier book* may be taken as evidence), so let us finish by stating the facts: for two and a half crucial years in the Second World War the Mosquito was the RAF's fastest aeroplane and it remained the fastest in Bomber Command until the introduction of the Canberra in 1951. Also, it developed into the longest-range of all aircraft in operational squadron service. No other type in the history of aviation can claim both these usually incompatible extremes of performance. It was a truly remarkable aeroplane.

---

* Ogilvy, David: *The de Havilland Mosquito Through The Eyes Of A Pilot,* Amberley Publishing 2017

Chapter 37

The end of a long line
Miles M.38 Messenger

The last of the single-engine low wing monoplanes created by the Miles family, the M.38 Messenger, was intended as an Air Observation Post, but entered service as a communications machine. Following a first flight on 12 September 1942, only three months from the start of the idea, just twenty-one were produced for the RAF. Messengers earned their keep by providing 'field' transport for Service chiefs, including Marshal of the RAF Lord Tedder and Field Marshal Lord Montgomery. It was claimed that with a fine pitch propeller the short take-off and landing performance was as good as that of the famous German Fieseler Storch. For its military role, the Messenger was built to be robust, requiring only casual maintenance from relatively unskilled labour, with a single strut undercarriage to withstand heavy landings; more recent civil experience has shown that access to some critical parts of the airframe is difficult. As with all Miles designs of the time, the structure was all wood, but with plastic bonded ply skin.

At the war's end its suitability as a tourer for the private market became very clear; some seventy-one airframes were built at Newtownards in Northern Ireland, but flown to Woodley for final painting, with the last to leave the line in January 1948. In addition, many of the Service batch survived and were converted to civil use. The military Messenger was powered by the 140hp Gipsy Major 1D, but for its civilian role used the 155hp Blackburn Cirrus Major. With 18 gallons in each wing root, it can carry four average people and provide a range of 450 miles. If luggage is carried, though, either fuel must be reduced, or a seat left empty. The maximum weight for service and civil versions is identical at 2,400lb.

I had the good fortune to carry out a few hours of twin-conversion instructing on the Messenger's younger sibling the M65 Gemini, so when I had the opportunity to climb aboard the earlier machine I was pleased to do so. The specimen concerned was an ex-military example, known in its civilian form as the Mark 4A, powered by a Gipsy Major 10 of 145hp instead of the original Major 1D. The Messenger has typical Miles auxiliary aerofoil flaps protruding behind the wing trailing edge; access to the cockpit is by a step on each side, then up to a walkway on each wing root, with essential handholds on both sides of the fuselage. As with many light aircraft of the era, getting in is not the easiest of tasks.

Once aboard, I found the cockpit to be comfortably spacious and the only adverse comment that I have heard is that the leg room is insufficient for a very tall person. The kit includes a Ki-Gass primer, a large low-geared trim wheel on the left and an equally low-geared wheel between the seats to work the flaps; these can be drooped to 30°, with a position marker protruding through the top of the port wing. The Bendix cable-operated brakes are mastered by a fly-off lever on the left, with the rudder pedals providing helpful differential action. There is a large and very useful cubby hole for maps etc to the right of the instrument panel, which on both military and civil variants is of the standard RAF layout.

For a taildragger the view for taxying is good, helped by a large wrap-around windscreen, but the rudder has less effect than I would choose and there is a strong weathercock tendency: this must be due largely to the machine's triple fin design, which becomes more beneficial in the air. On take-off there is relatively little swing except where affected by a crosswind, when the weathercock tendency comes back into play. The get-away is quite good, but the 4A has a Hoffman propeller of coarser design than when in Service use, as the very short-field ability of the military machine has given way to a more usefully improved cruise performance. The resulting rate of climb remains very acceptable at about 740ft/min.

In level flight the M38 has light – but not very effective – ailerons and this quality is retained even at higher speeds. Using a comfortable

1,950rpm for the cruise generates about 103mph and an increase in power to 2,050 adds about 10. The three rudders remain relatively ineffective and accurate flying in all but the calmest conditions requires full-time control inputs. Today many pilots would not like this, but as an old fogey who puts flying the machine at the head of the list I have no criticism!

Although I have not needed to operate the Messenger in conditions of poor visibility, it can potter along happily at about 65mph with 10 degrees of flap and 1,800rpm. Taking it further down the scale, slight buffet begins at just over 50mph and the published clean stall occurs at a reduction of a further 12. The breakaway behaviour is benign. The flaps can be extended to 30° and when these are lowered the ailerons droop in useful sympathy. Even in this condition the angle of descent is not as steep as might be expected, but the rudders are not sufficiently powerful to provide effective side-slipping in compensation. An initial approach at 65 reducing to 55 over the fence makes realistic sense, but those with expertise on the type claim that the final figure can be reduced to 40 for getting into a really short field, which was essential in the machine's days on military service. However, out of respect for someone else's aeroplane and my lack of time on the type, I avoided putting this to the test.

The hold-off angle to achieve a three-point touchdown is quite large, but this is to be expected with a machine intended for short-field operation. There is no problem in keeping straight when able to land into wind, but the weather-cocking tendency calls for active use of the differential braking when not so fortunate. However, it remains fully controllable in all reasonable conditions and I finished the flight with a general feeling of satisfaction.

Today ten Messengers remain on the home register and four are airworthy. Of these, G-AKIN warrants a special mention, as it has been based at Sywell almost since new in 1947 and is owned by a Trust that exists solely and deservedly to protect its future as a living flying machine. I hope that this is not the only example of the type that will be with us in the years ahead.

Chapter 38

A taste of the jet age
Gloster Meteor

Some may feel that inclusion of a jet fighter in a book devoted to veteran and vintage aeroplanes is out of order, but the Gloster Meteor – the first jet to enter squadron service with the Royal Air Force and the only one to see operational use in the Second World War – first flew as long ago as March 1943. This was only seven years later than the date on which the first Spitfire flew; yet the Spitfire has been considered an historic aeroplane for several decades. The Meteor has many claims to fame. In its earliest form it was grossly underpowered, for the first to be completed failed to get airborne, as each of its Rover turbojets produced little over 1,000lb thrust. Despite this the type gained ground without delay, for by August 1944 the first V-1 flying bomb had fallen victim – not to the Meteor's guns, but by being formated on and rolled-over with the Meteor's wingtip. This fortuitous success, which was the result of enterprise by one pilot whose guns had jammed, caused wing-tipping to become a standard procedure for dealing with the V-1 menace – preferably over the sea before the intruder reached England.

Qualified piston pilots had converted quite readily after extensive briefing, one of the most important points of which was to stress the turbine's slow response to throttle movement. With a reciprocating engine, a pilot could check a tendency to undershoot by an application of an appropriate ration of power, with immediate result, but with a jet things were different. A noticeable time-lag occurred between throttle movement and anything useful happening; this caught several pilots unaware. From a general handling angle, however, the jet was simpler than its piston predecessor; with a tricycle undercarriage and no tendency to swing or roll as power was applied, the take-off and landing procedures presented no problems.

The Meteor developed quickly; production Mark 3s, which were the first to enter large-scale squadron use, were powered by Rolls-Royce Derwents, which became standard equipment on all subsequent variants. The Derwent progressed from 2,000lb thrust in the 3 to 3,600 in the later marks, and performance increased in sparkle accordingly. Inevitably the need for a dual trainer arose, and the first Mark T7, with two seats in tandem, full dual and no armament, joined the RAF late in 1948. More than 500 were built. This useful mark of Meteor found its way to many tasks and units; examples were added to strengths of fighter squadrons for continuation training, Instrument Rating renewals and comparable duties. It was in one of its off-beat roles that I met the Meteor, among the few to serve, strangely perhaps, with Bomber Command. I explained in Chapter 5 how I managed to acquire some Meteor time.

Not only were there many marks of Meteor, but various versions of the T7. All had the clipped wings introduced on the 4, but early production versions possessed ailerons of only modest power, whereas WL 366 was one of the first to appear with spring-tab ailerons; these were really delightful. I had one flight in an earlier 7 without this luxury and the difference was quite marked. Later 7s, sometimes known as 7/8s, had the rectangular fins and rudders that were fitted to the ultimate day fighter version, the F8. Later still, some marks, including the photo-reconnaissance and night fighter versions, reverted to the large-span rounded wing tips.

Let us look now at the Meteor as then seen by one who had met a modest range of piston types, but who had thought that only gliders could fly without propellers. Entry to the tandem (in the case of the T7) cockpits is via retractable footsteps and fixed handgrips on the port side. There are separate external and internal handles for opening and closing the hinged hood. Once inside, the seats can be adapted for height by levers on their starboard sides, and the rudders can be set for distance by pulling out a release knob on each of the panels.

Engine handling, of course, differs in technique between piston and turbine types. At the base of each of the two compartments of the main tank (325 gallons) is a low-pressure fuel pump that feeds fuel via the low-pressure (LP) cock to the high-pressure pump. From each HP pump, fuel flows under pressure to the throttle valve and to the barometric pressure control; the latter automatically maintains the correct fuel/air mixture for all operating conditions. Fuel passes from the throttle valve via the HP cock to the burners. The LP and HP cocks relating to their respective engines are on each side of the pilot's seat and, as are all other controls, duplicated in each cockpit.

The starting procedure is through an automatic cycle. There are many checks to complete before going through this process, but then the sequence for getting the Derwent engines going is first to have LP cocks on, the HP cocks off and the throttles (slotted into the port cockpit wall) fully closed, with the LP pumps on it. It matters little which engine is started first. Press the selected starter button for two seconds, release it and wait. A clue to the cycle sequencing comes when the green undercarriage lights go dim (stressing the electrical load) at which time the HP cock should be opened, initially to the half-way position and then gently to the fully open limit as the rpm increase. Mishandling at this stage can cause mild chaos including resonance, overheating and flooding. In this case, the HP cock must be switched off, excess fuel must be drained and then the engine can be dried out by carrying out a false start with the HP cock off. Then the proper process can be repeated.

With a turbine engine a pilot must retune his mind to operating figures that are strange to the piston world. For example, the Meteor's Derwents must maintain a minimum oil pressure of only $5lb/in^2$ and on the ground not exceed a maximum jet pipe temperature (JPT) of 500°C. Taxying is easy and smooth but, not surprisingly, a considerable amount of power is needed to persuade the Meteor to move forward from a standing start. Except in confined spaces, turns can be made by differential engine usage alone, but care must be taken not to indulge in coarse throttle opening as the ever-present bogeys of engine flooding and excessive temperatures present themselves again.

Pre take-off checks include a few points of special significance, such as air brakes closed, fuel cocks and pumps on and oxygen on. After building up some power against the brakes, the take-off itself is straightforward and there is neither cause nor tendency to swing. The nosewheel lifts happily at about 85kt and the machine must be flown off (rather than left to come off) at about 120kt. The unstick is an unclean, waffly affair and is one of the very few unfavourable features of the type.

With wheels braked and retracted, the machine should pass through the safety speed of 160 at a shallow angle until the required climbing figure is reached. If in a hurry, full power and 300kt combine to give the best performance, but in the normal unhurried atmosphere of type familiarisation or continuation training, 280kt and 14,100rpm (a small reduction from a governed maximum of 14,550) provide a more-than-acceptable climb rate of about 7,000ft/min. This, perhaps, is a characteristic that hits the average piston pilot more than any other; the Meteor is delightfully smooth and, when both engines are running, easy to handle, but to the uninitiated it consumes fuel, sky and countryside in quantities that are mildly alarming.

Unlike a piston-powered aeroplane on which the operating height is not very critical, the turbine machine consumes fuel at low levels at rates that leave little scope for error. At sea level, at a best range speed of 275kt IAS, the rate of burning on a clean aircraft with neither ventral nor drop tanks is 6.4 gallons per minute; never before had I met consumption measured in anything other than gallons per hour! With an internal capacity of 325 gallons, such a clean machine could soon run dry, but for most training operations a belly tank of 175 gallons helped in a small way to ease the time burden.

In normal flight the Meteor has a smooth but solid feel; the controls are pleasant but not harmonised in relation to each other. The ailerons, especially if fitted with spring as opposed to geared tabs, are ideal at most normal speeds, although at low figures they need to be moved generously in order to obtain much response. The elevators are responsive throughout, but the rudder foot-loads can be very heavy, not only at high speeds, but at circuit speed when in the asymmetric condition, a very large deflection is needed. However, in normal flight, little rudder use is required, and the light elevator/aileron loads make everything very satisfactory.

It is advisable to climb to a worthwhile height for any training exercise, both for fuel conservation and reserve in the event of subsequent height loss. Stalling and recovery cause no problems, the break-away figures varying between 90 and 115kt according to load and clean/dirty configuration. Elevator buffeting fairly well before and airframe vibration just before the stall give reasonable evidence of things to come; an unhurried nose drop and a tendency for either wing to go down can precede easy recovery. Spinning is not such a friendly affair. Pilot's Notes warn that the minimum entry height should be 25,000ft and recovery should be started before two turns have been completed. Various characteristics such as pitching, lateral snatching of the control column and changes in rotation rate combine to make the exercise mildly unpleasant, but in my very limited experience the Meteor recovered reasonably quickly. Again, however, the Notes issue a warning that if in need at the recovery stage the inbound engine should be opened – a situation that I am glad to say I was not faced with. The spin seems to be one condition in which the Meteor presents a new face, for at most other times it seems to be quite amicable.

In the main, the smaller and lighter an aeroplane is, the easier it is to loop and the harder to roll; with larger and faster types the reverse applies. The clipped-wing Meteor with spring-tab ailerons is very easy to roll and it seems to do so happily from a reasonable range of entry speeds, with 260-280 IAS laid down on the recommended list. The loop, on the other hand, from a textbook 370-380, can be quite a test. It consumes thousands of feet and takes some time, each of which allows scope for mistake – a good feature for a trainer.

When meeting his first jet, a pilot may come face-to-face with the Machmeter, which sits in the panel just to the left of the ASI. At height, this instrument takes over from airspeed readings as the guideline to critical figures. For the uninitiated it is marked from 0.5 to 1.0, the latter being the speed of sound. In later times the Meteor 7 has had a warning band from Mach 0.78, but to attain the earlier permitted limit of 0.84 the nose needs to be held firmly down to fight the machine's way through the early stages of compressibility. Again, to the newcomer, it is quite an experience.

The whole concept of flying a jet aeroplane calls for a change of outlook and attitude for the piston pilot. In the main, a powerful propeller-driven machine requires careful handling and both take-off and landing may present problems, whereas the turbine type is generally simple to fly. Operating, by contrast, reverses the coin, for the enormous thirst of the jet engine, especially at low levels, calls for very careful flight planning with special reference to heights to fly for optimum range or endurance. Thirty minutes of energetic circuit work can drain a full Meteor dry.

Circuit handling is easy and pleasant. It is essential to start the downwind leg with at least 60 gallons aboard, using 10,500rpm, with one third flap, and a resulting IAS of about 170kt, reducing to 8,500/150 for the base leg. Checks, of course, are important on any aeroplane, but an essential safety factor on the Meteor is to ensure that the airbrakes (which protrude from the wing inboard of each engine) are in. If the brakes remain extended on the final turn-in, the nose tends to drop, sometimes quite violently, and no amount of backpressure on the control column will rectify the situation. Very quick thinking and rapid retraction of the offending air brakes will provide the only solution.

On a final approach with full flap and 130kt, power should be maintained at not less than 7,500rpm as, below this setting, engine response is very sluggish. Airspeed should be progressively disposed of to 110kt at the threshold. A gentle easing of the column leads to the easiest landing imaginable, but after touchdown the nose should continue to be held well clear of the ground to achieve effective aerodynamic braking. There are some who insisted on a reverse process by placing the nosewheel on the runway and immediately applying the wheel brakes. This was both pointless and wasteful in normal conditions. A go-around from ground level calls for another 60 gallons of fuel.

So far I have made no mention of asymmetric handling. The performance 'on one' is excellent and in this condition a level speed of more than 300kt can be attained, but at low speeds the rudder load is almost intolerable. The rudder trim control is a small knurled wheel on the left of the pilot's seat and it is neither sufficiently easy to turn quickly nor adequate in effect; it is one of the Meteor's very few weak features. It shows its shortcomings to the full on an asymmetric overshoot, when really only a locked leg can withstand the load, but this problem is partially offset by the machine's remarkable willingness to climb away happily and rapidly, with ample reserve of power. Never before had I met a machine that offered more than a marginal climb performance in this configuration. The Meteor's other characteristics include many interesting features, such as the maximum rate descent; at 0.7 Mach this offers a height loss of more than 15,000ft/min, helped by the effectiveness of the air brakes when extended at high speed.

Although the early and sadly underpowered Meteors saw only limited service in the later stages of the Second World War, without doubt the type matured quickly into a highly successful and very workmanlike machine. By 1948 the ultimate day fighter variant, the F8, had flown, and this equipped twenty-nine squadrons. There were night fighter variants from Marks 11 to 14 and a specialised photo-reconnaissance version, the PR10, which was the last variant to be retired from front line service in July 1961. However, two modified Mark 7s remain in active use by Martin Baker Aircraft at Chalgrove for ejection seat testing. So, fortunately, despite an active birth as long ago as 1943, the Meteor is far from dead. It is a very good, strong and reliable aeroplane that formed the backbone of the RAF's fighter force in the late forties/early fifties and it warrants a key place in aviation history.

Chapter 39

A practical twin
Miles M.65 Gemini

Immediately following the Second World War, very few private or club pilots flew twin-engine aircraft; the only type that those who did could afford, either to buy or fly, was the Gemini. Business aviation in today's sense barely existed and although for taxation and other purposes several machines were registered to companies, by far the majority were used for purely personal purposes.

The Gemini was British throughout. The all-wooden airframe, of bonded ply construction, was built by Miles Aircraft Ltd. at Woodley and was the last type to be produced in quantity before that company fell to the Receiver's axe. With the exception of two odd examples, every Gemini was powered by British engines. The main problem, causing the Miles collapse, was that the design and building ability were at their peak after wartime experience of large-scale production, but the business side fell short in that every machine produced was sold at considerably less than a properly calculated cost price.

The prototype Gemini flew within a few months of the end of the war and production started immediately, with 130 being built in the first year. Considerably more than half the number built found their ways to other countries.

In the private field the Gemini came to its own both commercially and in renown. Steeply-banked Gemini were part of the racing scene of the 50s and three, in particular, were on the starting line of almost every event. Of these G-AKDC, fitted with 145hp high-compression Gipsy Majors instead of the usual 100hp Cirrus Minors, crossed the finishing line first in the 1949 King's Cup and repeated the performance in at least three other races during the next six years.

After the demise of the main Miles activities at Reading a development known as the Aries, offering the further-increased power of 155hp Cirrus Majors, appeared from Redhill, where F.G. Miles had established a small aircraft engineering concern from the ashes of the old. Only two specimens were completed as such, but a few existing Gemini were converted almost to Aries standard, including a pair for Shell-Mex and BP.

Now let us look at the Gemini as a flying machine. A low wing with walkways just outboard of each side of the fuselage made access easy without the need for a high step up, but as the flaps extended behind the wing trailing edge and clearly were not intended for human feet, each would-be occupant needed to bypass these on the way up. The large upward-opening door, hinged at the fuselage top centre line, enabled easy entry to front and rear seats of the four-seat layout. Because of the large area of Perspex (helping to give an excellent view out) and minimal structural area in these doors, they were very flexible and one of the most important of all checks on the Messenger/Gemini family was to ensure that both doors were securely home and locked. Many doors were allowed to open on take-off and in at least three cases (probably considerably more) tail units were badly damaged when doors came right off.

The cockpit was roomy and comfortable, offering a really excellent view, especially forward. The seats were not adjustable and for some they were too low, but a personal ration of cushions soon brought the view line and the controls to the right position for the dimensions and whims of the individual pilot. The inside was of essentially 'civil' trim, with light (blue or grey) colouring and with glove and map pockets alongside the main flight panel. Throttles were on the port wall (with a dual set on a central pedestal on machines equipped for training purposes) and a large elevator trim wheel enabled accurate fore-and-aft adjustments to be made easily. Flaps were wound up and down by plastic hand-wheel and the guideline was a pointer protruding up through the wing. For anyone accustomed to large solid undercarriage selection levers, the little electric switch below the instrument panel was not quite as satisfying as it might have been, but it did its job admirably and at least one well-worked school Gemini, G-AJTL, which spent most of its time on the circuit, suffered no failure in this respect.

With the lone generator on the starboard side, this engine was started first; usually on the machine's own internal batteries, which coped remarkably well. The rpm indicators, on the cockpit side of each engine on the top of the nacelle, were typical of those fitted to the Cirrus family and tended to read in erratic steps, sometimes indicating a rev. increase when one magneto was switched off at the 1,600rpm power check! However, the true situation could be assessed audibly, so it was nothing more than a nuisance when trying to explain the checks (and the reasons for them) to a trainee.

The excellent forward view could encourage people to taxi too enthusiastically, and some did. The brakes, though, were not always able to cope with the Gemini's (relative) mass, especially when manoeuvring on a hard surface. Turning response to the use of each engine individually was good once the machine was on the move, but as this was the first twin to be met by most private pilots, unscheduled ground gyrations formed an occasional part of the training scene. Pre-take-off checks called for nothing unusual except a final clunk on the door handles.

The take-off itself could be interesting. Into a light wind on grass (or preferably with the wind blowing from port) there were no problems and the throttles could be treated almost as one. On a runway, though, and with the wind from the other side, the Gemini was as good as any twin for a useful exercise in differential throttle usage. With engines of low power the levers needed to be moved moderately well forward before very much happened and there were extreme cases in which the starboard throttle was half-way open before its opposite number had any productive part to play. Most people who had trouble created it for themselves beforehand, by failing to run-on to straighten the tail wheel before going into action in earnest.

With only the front seats occupied the tail lifted easily, but even then a positive forward pressure on the stick-type column was advisable if an inefficient three-point unstick was to be avoided.

At full load a definite effort was needed to achieve the same aim. Loading was critical, for with full tanks the Cirrus-Gemini was a marginal three-seater, and before weight and loading started to receive serious attention in the private flying field, many pilots in their blissful ignorance filled everything (tanks and seats) and staggered sluggishly into the air.

At light loads, unstick was not a very positive affair and one just found oneself airborne without being very aware of a clean break-away. At high weight, however, an attempt at a premature unstick merely resulted in the tail going down again. Either way, the undercarriage retraction was a comfortably quick operation and this helped very considerably towards achieving a full-flight condition. With any twin, rapid acceleration to a speed that will give reasonable asymmetric control is one of the first essentials.

The Cirrus Minor 2 (or, in some cases, the hard-top 2a) was best when fitted with the Fairey-Reed metal propeller. 2,300rpm was essential for the 600ft/min climb to prevent crankshaft 'whip' and this same figure was permitted for the cruise, although in training/local flying conditions most users settled for about 2,150. In normal level flight with both engines operating and well synchronised, the Gemini was very pleasant. A fair amount of control displacement was needed to achieve a healthy roll-rate, but the ailerons were light even at relatively high speeds; at a normal pottering speed of about 120mph they were just right.

A four-seater of 3,000lb maximum weight could not be expected to perform very well on only one of its 100hp engines with the other creating a generous ration of windmill drag. Nevertheless, some machines were known to cover useful distances 'on one' and the poor performance provided an ideal recipe for a training exercise. With two up and moderate fuel aboard, height could be maintained at low altitudes at about 85mph and with a heavyish footload, so a standard practice on a twin-conversion course was for the instructor to chop one (usually, but not always, the port, in order to maintain power to the generator) at 1,000 feet a few miles from the airfield and call for a rejoin, circuit and landing. Crossed controls would produce a steady downhill slide, but with accurate handling a maximum of 100 feet should have been lost before the undercarriage was lowered at the end of the downwind leg. An asymmetric overshoot was impracticable, if possible, so realistic judgement was needed all the way in; the last stage of the exercise was invariably a glide approach, which made the landing phase roughly identical whether one or both engines were in active business.

Many pilots tended to 'wheel' the Gemini, but it provided a satisfying mount for three-pointing, which was entirely practical when arriving into wind. However, on a hard surface and with no helping wind, and particularly if for any reason it was advisable to land slightly downwind, many a pilot suffered the indignities of a ground loop.

In the past wooden aeroplanes suffered mercilessly at the hands of the authorities, although the fears propounded by the pundits in the late fifties have proved largely unjustified. At a time when the Air Registration Board was pressurised to impose severe restrictions on the lives and uses of such machines, many were abandoned by their owners as being uneconomic to maintain. Often extensive glue-joint inspections cost as much as the value of the aeroplane, so the Gemini, alongside its single-engine counterpart the Messenger, declined fast.

No Gipsy Gemini has survived, but a couple of Cirrus-engined specimens remain in active use. They have been around for more than seventy-five years so, in their present caring hands, we hope that they will be with us for many more.

Chapter 40

Van ordinaire
Miles M.57 Aerovan

At the end of the Second World War, Britain had a vast aircraft manufacturing industry, with at least twelve independent companies geared for large-scale production of military machines of all shapes, sizes and roles. Before hostilities ceased, though, many directors and designers put their minds into planning for the time when the demand for Service aircraft would cease, creating a need to find civil markets. Some companies modified existing types to minimise delay, while others created entirely new designs in remarkably short time. Among the latter was George Miles, who overstepped the mark by designing and building a new machine, the Aerovan, without Ministry permission, flying it as early as January 1945. He was taken to task and ordered not to build another until the war was over.

What was this Aerovan? A high-wing monoplane with a single-spar wing of 50ft span and a pair of 150hp Cirrus Major 3s to provide the power, it was of typically-Miles wooden construction with a large freight (or passenger) pod of plastic-bonded material, the rear end of which opened for loading bulky goods onto the cabin floor which conveniently was only two feet from the ground. Motor cars were carried on several occasions, while a quick-change-act to passenger seating made it potentially attractive for mixed operations. Several variants appeared, from the sole Mark I with four rectangular windows each side, the Mark II with five circular windows and a longer fuselage and the III which was almost identical. The main production run went to the Mark IV, with four circular windows each side, a tare weight of 3,000lb (400lb lighter than the Mark I) and an all-up weight of 5,400lb for passenger use or 5,800lb when functioning as a freighter. When used as a people carrier it could have seating arrangements for 6-10 passengers.

My opportunity to come face to face with this interesting machine was by a combination of chance and inexcusable nerve. In 1954 I was the relatively youthful CFI at Elstree and an Aerovan IV arrived to be refuelled. I approached the owner pilot with proverbial tongue in cheek and asked, 'When can I fly your Aerovan?' To my surprise and delight he replied, 'I'm going in for a coffee. Take it now.' I did.

Access to the operating end was through a largish door on the starboard side. The immediate effect was one of a glasshouse, for from the pilot's seat when facing forward it was possible to see literally in all directions through what seemed a welcome acreage of Perspex. The cockpit was light, roomy and with an essentially civil flavour, which was unusual for a medium-sized twin at that time. The overall feeling, though, was of a relatively lightweight structure and a lot of the airframe rattled and physically seemed to change shape when the first engine was started. However, when power was in business on both sides the situation seemed more comfortable.

The Aerovan was a tricycle machine in a largely tailwheel world. Nosewheel steering was possible by coupling to the rudder bar, or the front leg could be left free to castor with the use of differential throttle and brakes, which were connected to the pilot's pedals. Taxying was easy and the view excellent, though the absence of much structure in the front of the cockpit was a mild discomfort to an imaginative mind. The Aerovan was empty when I flew it and, with a small ration of the Miles-type electrically-actuated flap for take-off, it was airborne long before I was ready. I cannot remember consciously correcting a swing tendency, so it must have been virtually absent, but I can recollect the machine's marked willingness at such light load to clear the ground quickly and climb quite smartly. At commercial working weight it must have been very different, but in this condition it clocked more than 800ft/min in an attitude and with a view that made it feel like a sky-lift rather than a flying aeroplane. The noise, however, which was quite aggressive, left no doubt about the truth.

At a sensible height I tried two of the things that one should try with an unfamiliar twin. Chopping an engine from normal cruise at about 110mph produced a more noticeable yaw than might be expected, but it was easily corrected and well controllable. I tried critical speed checks at this and full power settings, but I cannot remember the break-away figures; however, on the full throttle/engine out check I remember clearly the high nose attitude or, to be more precise, the absence of a fixed datum ahead to use as a guideline, which created the feeling of hanging in the air. In this unloaded condition the Aerovan climbed at about 150ft/min at 80mph with the port engine 'out', but clearly when loaded to the gills it would be much more miserable in asymmetric performance.

I remember the stall most clearly by the amount of vibration that originated at the back of the machine, presumably through flexing of the tailboom, which made the three fins and rudders engage in a little war dance. With the throttles closed, the bulbous fuselage and the various trimmings made the surrounding airflow quite audible and even with moderate power on, a gentle descent produced a marked whistle within. For normal and even mildly ambitious manoeuvres the empty Aerovan was pleasantly light and lively. The landing was straightforward and the nosewheel could be held-off to provide very effective aerodynamic braking, which surely is preferable to the modern nosewheel on/brakes on tendency.

Here was a type that could offer a remarkable range of uses. My brief and very limited assessment, however, concerns it solely as a pilot's flying machine and it is one of my many weaknesses to view aeroplanes in this way. First and foremost I like to think that any type should be pleasant, but not necessarily easy, for the person in the front. Commercial considerations, I realise, must call for an entirely different yardstick, but if a pilot is flying for pleasure (s)he should be able to derive some and, if flying professionally, (s)he needs to sit there for a long time. Either way, therefore, an aeroplane should be designed and built with the pilot's needs and wishes in mind; these seem to be entirely absent from some machines produced 'by the yard.'

VAN ORDINAIRE

Unfortunately, although pleasant to fly, the Aerovan was not a great commercial success and its life was short. Relatively few survived to earn honourable retirement; at least six were destroyed by strong winds, six came to grief following engine failures in flight and no fewer than seventeen were written off in a variety of other situations, including two on take-off. The bulky fuselage pod with a capacity of 530 cubic feet could easily be – and apparently frequently was – overloaded and almost certainly many of the casualties were due to some operators' commercial greed. No example seems to have survived later than 1960.

Chapter 41

A brace of Austers
J/1 Autocrat and J/5F Aiglet Trainer

When private and club flying restarted in 1945 following a total ban during the Second World War, very few practicable touring aeroplanes were available. The then Air Ministry released hundreds of surplus RAF Tiger Moths and Magisters which, with their open cockpits in tandem, played key roles in the subsequent training scene, but clearly something with at least the basics of cabin comfort was essential if people were to 'go places', whether for pleasure or, in a modest way, for business.

One aircraft immediately filled that vacancy: the Auster J/1 Autocrat. Auster Aircraft Limited (formerly Taylorcraft Aeroplanes (England) had developed the original Taylorcraft Cub design into a series of Auster marks for military service such as artillery spotting and light communications. During the late stage of the war they had wasted no time in foreseeing the future and made plans for a civil successor to their military machines.

What, then, emerged? A three-seat trainer/tourer powered by a 100hp Blackburn Cirrus Minor 2 that caught on quickly with flying clubs and private owners, while qualifying also for business and light charter use. Perhaps surprisingly, an Autocrat conducted the UK's first post-war commercial charter flight on 1 January 1946, the day on which civil operations were allowed to restart. While two other aircraft – the Percival Proctor 5 and Miles Messenger – were in competition, the Auster product was lower powered, less expensive to buy and operate and therefore more friendly for the limited purchasing power of the average flying club. By the end of 1947 more than 400 had been built, making it the only purely civil light aeroplane to be mass-produced in Britain since 1939. In addition to its normal private/club role, the Autocrat was used for crop spraying, glider towing and even fitted with loudspeakers for public address messages. One flew on skis and another had an experimental castoring undercarriage for easing crosswind landings. Yet another, owned by the publishers of *The Aeroplane* magazine, was the first civil machine to land post-war on an aircraft carrier – HMS *Illustrious* – in October 1946.

Now to the Autocrat as a flying machine which, I am pleased to say, remains alive today. For economy the standard panel fitted to the military Mark 5 was dropped, so the few dials were spread rather widely. Essentials such as ASI, altimeter, turn-and-slip and oil pressure gauge are standard, while some owners have amended the layout to take any extras that their roles or fads may dictate. Normally the cockpit contains dual flying controls, with one central throttle while longitudinal trimming is controlled by a rotatable handle in the roof. Most machines have heel brakes for the left-hand occupant only and this created some problem in training use. This was overcome in practice by the instructor initially occupying the left seat, transferring the student gingerly into that position only when (s)he had shown some signs of mastering the art of keeping straight. Although this fairly fundamental position change at an impressionable stage in the newcomer's course could have caused serious setbacks, it did nothing of the sort; a cross-cockpit seat transfer proved to present bigger obstacles when a pilot had more experience and had become more hard-set in familiarisation with the surroundings and the external view. A fuel tank of 15 gallons capacity lives just ahead of the instrument panel, immediately behind the engine bulkhead, with a circular-type gauge mounted on its top just inside the cockpit; some machines also have external belly tanks holding 13.5 gallons.

Generally, the Autocrat must be hand-swung, but the attitude and low height of the propeller make it one of the easier machines to master in this respect. Most were built with rather coarse wooden propellers, but for improved performance many changed these for finer-pitch metal Fairey Reed units. Internal post-starting checks call for relatively little work, but some practice on the ground in working the flaps could prove useful later. A lever above the port door has a handgrip that must be moved forward (with the help of some upward pressure if obstinate) to clear the notched ratchet and which can then be moved into any one of four positions, with full flap offering as much as 53° deflection. The right-seat occupant cannot operate the flaps.

Taxying is easy enough after some familiarisation, but the heel brakes can prove difficult to engage and, apart from a tendency to snatch or, in wet weather, fail to function at all, they need careful equalisation. The need to depress one pedal into the floor and fear nosing-over with a touch on the other could make progress hazardous and a nosewheel-trained pilot is likely to have serious difficulties. A parking brake lever below the instrument panel on the extreme left add to the limitations of flying from the right-hand seat.

Take-off includes a modest tendency to swing to the right, but this is easy to keep under control. Solo or with two aboard the run is reasonable and the break-away is quite clean at about 40mph, but with the rear seat occupied the performance picture deteriorates sadly. In the latter case some flap, a positive forward push and an extra 5mph at unstick are advisable. The normal clean climb is best at 65 when the maker's book claims a precise 568ft/min. However, I have noted variations in excess of 100ft/min between different approved propellers, which themselves created an interesting tale.

In the late fifties several Cirrus Minor II engines broke their crankshafts in flight. Apparently, crankshaft whip when under climbing load with lowish rpm caused an untenable strain and two factors emerged; one was a recommendation to twist the metal propellers to a finer setting and climb at not less than 2,300rpm and the other was a major modification to the engine itself which involved a solid-looking hard top bolted on to the crankcase to increase rigidity. The result was known as the Cirrus Minor IIa. There were relatively few failures after this. In normal flight the Autocrat and others in the series earned themselves reputations for not the crispest of handling. High wings with their unavoidable pendular stability are resistant to roll and the Auster has done little to disprove that theory. With the control column emerging on a curved passage from under the panel, movement is not always as directionally logical as it would be for a stick that comes straight from the floor. This is most noticeable at the extreme ends of the fore-and-aft movement range. Laterally, behaviour is logical enough from neutral elevator positions, but aileron displacement and therefore lateral stick movement need to be markedly generous for positive results.

The stall is innocuous with no built-in tendency to drop a wing; clean and light, breakaway occurs at 35mph but with full flap the Autocrat remains in marginally full flight to a figure 10mph lower than this. Recovery is without problem, but in the latter condition, with a person in the third seat (not usual, of course, for training) the marked degree of forward push and the small power response from the engine are notable.

The Autocrat can be cleared in the semi-aerobatic category if strengthened seats and full harness are fitted. Perhaps surprisingly, it goes round a loop cleanly and easily, with the elevators responding quite crisply at the higher end of the speed scale, and still behaving well round the top. With strut-braced wings stressed for tension loads only, any tendency to falter on the top should be avoided.

Cruising airspeed varies between propellers and between individual aircraft, but on average 2,100rpm can offer 85mph and this makes economic sense at 4.5gph. In calm air straight flight is untiring, but the Auster family feels the bumps and it is easy to work too hard over-correcting situations which, with time and practice, tend to resolve themselves. The noise level is bad, but headphones create a wholly acceptable set of flight conditions. The only problem on the approach is the possible obstinacy of the flap lever. The split flaps are fully effective and pilots tend to avoid the lowest notch, but many a pilot unfamiliar with the type struggled with the lever until he was too high to use the field and then needed to throw away that circuit. Hence the earlier remarks about the wisdom of practice on the ground.

The Autocrat climbs back to circuit height reasonably rapidly at light load and from a minimum flap setting, but a full-flap go-around from ground level can be very hard work, especially with three up, a hot day and a coarse propeller. In fact, I think certain combinations of conditions could make the operation impossible, but the landing itself offers the most worthwhile challenge. The Autocrat is wholly unforgiving to the careless; even the most painstaking pilot can find himself (or herself) poised in an embarrassing, nose-up, almost speedless situation following an unexpected bounce. I know no one who could manage consistently to make a smooth arrival with this basic bouncing Auster, but one secret is to hold-off slightly too high and leave it in the three-point position until it lowers itself to the ground. Even then, though, the error can be heard if not seen, for on a hard runway the clatter of a firm arrival echoes well beyond the boundary of the smaller aerodrome; but the most important thing to avoid is a slightly premature touchdown during the round-out stage. It gives back far more than is given.

The Autocrat was followed by a range of different civil Austers, almost all broadly similar in appearance – strut-braced high-wing cabin monoplanes – but they varied more in performance and utility than their shared shape might suggest. So let us turn to the J/5F Aiglet Trainer, which came to light in 1951 derived from the four-seat J/5B Autocar which in turn had a Gipsy Major 1 of 130hp in place of the earlier design's 100hp Cirrus Minor II. The wings were shortened by four feet, the fin was enlarged and the bracing struts were strengthened. The result was a semi-aerobatic machine stressed to between 3.5 and 4.5g depending on the loaded weight. In common with other Austers, despite doors on each side, the J/5F is not particularly easy to enter, but once inside the simplicity of the generous cabin has its own appeal, with a large dose of clear Perspex ahead. Many features were unaltered from the earlier Autocrat, but with a four-point harness in place of the original lap-strap. The compass remains suspended from on high viewed through a mirror and a high-speed winder in the roof dictates the elevator trim. Straps are fitted to the rudder pedals and the smallest imaginable heel brakes emerge from the floor. The functionally simple cockpit reveals all cables in the open for all to see. Unlike its predecessor, though, which had a fuselage-mounted fuel tank ahead of the cockpit, the J/5F has tanks in each wing root accommodating a total of 32 gallons.

On the move, the Trainer with its free-castoring tailwheel behaves quite well, and once the heel brakes are mastered taxying presents no problems. Compared with many tail-draggers, the view ahead and around is good. There are pros and cons to most things and despite increased power and a Fairey-Reed metal propeller the get-away performance is less impressive than one might expect. No doubt this is due to the reduced span and heavier wing loading, leading to a comfortable lift-off speed of almost 60mph. The subsequent climb rate is about 650ft/min.

On the level, a fairly generous 2,100rpm produces a cruise of almost 110mph, using 6.5gph. A noticeable bonus at this stage is the improved performance by the J/5F's Frise ailerons compared with the relative slop of those on the Autocrat. Here, unlike on take-off, the reduced span reveals its positive qualities. The stall is innocuous at all flap settings, but with the lot lowered the rate of nose drop is very marked.

Not surprisingly the Aiglet Trainer feels generally more manoeuvrable than its predecessor, but the high-wing strut-braced configuration does not put one into an aerobatic mind frame. Although a loop from only 10mph above cruising speed goes round very happily, the rolling plane is a bit more cumbersome. Again, the fault may well be mine, for I am being comparative and when I tried it I had established an amicable relationship with the user-friendly Chipmunk! Perhaps my comments become fruitless, though, when I remind readers that the famous Avalanche – basically a half loop with more than a flick roll on the top – created by Ranald Porteous and made public at the Farnborough display in 1951, was performed on the prototype J/5F.

Back on the circuit, the initial approach at 70 leads to selective use of flaps, which are controlled by a handle, three feet in length, beside the left-wing root rib, with a sleeve that is pulled forward to lower 10, 20, or 30 degree settings. This is not particularly easy to operate and can be reached only by the left seat occupant, which is a marked disadvantage on a trainer. This, like many other of the type's features, is a leftover from the Autocrat and its forebears.

After a final line-up at 60, the J/5F touches down on three points more readily than its forerunner, which had a reluctance to stay down and would bounce energetically on a premature contact during rather than after completing the round-out. Despite the extent of the flat side area, with differential use of the heel brakes, Austers in general are relatively easy to keep straight on the landing run, although some care is needed to avoid a nose-over. Overall, the bungee suspension seems more tolerant than on earlier machines.

Unfortunately, Austers in general tend to reveal their failings before they show their virtues, but of the latter they have a very creditable supply. Technical simplicity heads the list; a fuselage of simple steel-tube, and not much of it at that, with a straightforward slab-side fabric covering and a solid wooden main spar with no glue joints inside to cause concern, all combine to offer a minimum of scope for the corrosion bug. There are no frills and the only failures on regular training work were tailwheel attachment bolts, which disliked hard ground, and undercarriage bungees which literally let the side down from time to time.

Almost certainly from the handling aspect, the Aiglet Trainer was the most pleasant of the many Auster products and without competition from the used market more would have been sold. Long may these products of Leicester live, for although they are easy to criticise, they have many qualities based on a correct concept and among these favourable features is one undeniable fact: it is almost impossible to wear them out.

Chapter 42

Missed the mark
Percival Prentice

Shortly before the Second World War, throughout the war, and for three years or so afterwards, the British Services used the well-respected de Havilland Tiger Moth as the standard elementary trainer. More than 7,000 were built and without doubt it proved one of the greatest successes of all time. The Royal Air Force made a bold if unfortunate step when planning the Tiger Moth replacement. Clearly the time was right for an open-cockpit biplane to give way to something more in keeping with current trends, and the Percival P.40 Prentice heralded a complete break from tradition. As a low-wing all-metal cantilever monoplane with a variable pitch propeller, side-by-side seating for two and provision for an extra pupil to act as an observer behind (a philosophy that failed before it began), the Prentice resembled a transport aeroplane more than an ab-initio machine on which to introduce young men to the art of aviation.

The prototype Prentice first flew in March 1946, but there were many trials before the type was accepted for unrestricted Service use. Early tests revealed an unacceptable level of lateral instability and the rudder became blanketed at most times when it was really needed, both in spin recovery and in emerging from a slow roll. Neither cure was wholly successful, but ugly upturned wing-tips reduced the lateral troubles and slices removed from the inboard ends of the elevators permitted greater rudder travel and encouraged it to play a more useful part in a day's events.

Altogether 353 Prentices joined the RAF, arriving first at No. 3 FTS at Feltwell, in Norfolk, where the type was frequently referred to as 'the abortion'.

Perhaps crew comfort and convenience were the most praiseworthy features of the Prentice – a strange quality for an ab-initio trainer, as later in their lives many pilots were forced to squeeze themselves into very cramped quarters in the cockpits of some operational types. Nevertheless, the all-round spaciousness, with ample room for maps and navigational paraphernalia, made the start of a flight a pleasant process. Although roomy, the interior had that nice stark military blackness that I find so much more palatable than the pseudo-plush trim of later types. Everything was well within reach, from the spade-grip control columns, with brake levers and transmit buttons attached, to elevator and rudder trimmers (the latter a luxury for a single) on the lower left wall. These and other essentials such as throttle and rpm levers were duplicated, with an instructor's set on and around a central pedestal. This area housed also the single gated flap lever and fuel cock, a single port/off/starboard affair controlling two wing tanks each of 20 gallons and worked by a tank-mounted booster pump. The electrics were on the then-newish 24-volt system.

The Prentice offered no special procedural tricks and starting the 240hp Gipsy Queen 32 from fine pitch was straightforward. I have never liked the practice on some engines of stopping/starting in coarse. Pitch-changing checks were made at 2,000rpm, with a governed range of 1,900-2,500. The pneumatic brakes were fully effective, and I have not met or heard of any nosing-over tendencies.

The take-off was too tame for a basic trainer. The tail lifted without the help of the human hand and, so long as the tail wheel was straight at the start of the roll, the tendency to swing was both negligible and constant. It was possible to prejudge a ration of rudder, use that and then follow a straight path without needing to work hard. The only significant problem concerned propeller over-speeding, which was quite a serious matter if the throttle should be opened harshly.

The Prentice, although not ready to hurry itself in acceleration, was ready to fly itself off the ground with little backward pressure once it attained 60kt, with a subsequent IAS increase of only 10kt to find the recommended climb figure. This, together with full throttle and 2,400rpm produced a bare 650ft/min (marginally lower than that of the Tiger Moth!), with obvious time penalties for aerobatic, stalling and – particularly – spinning sorties.

I dislike unbalanced control forces or heavy ailerons, and the Prentice had both. The rudder and elevators were light, but laterally there were several shortcomings. Not only were the ailerons heavy (although, in fairness, they were reasonably responsive) but the machine was neutrally stable. For those who may have forgotten their theory (which in far too many instances includes this writer!) this means that when a wing went down, it remained in that position, neither continuing to drop further nor returning to the level position of its own accord.

Stalling held no secrets, with pre-stall warning in the form of elevator buffet and unstable pitching. Break-away speeds were just either side of 50kt for flap-up and flap-down stalls; the engine overspeeding tendency was the only handicap. Spinning, however, was less innocuous, for the attitude was steep, rotation rate rapid and the whole exercise was accompanied by vibration; but with patience and several turns (and considerable height loss, which was given grudgingly in view of the time taken to gain it) the spin smoothed out. Recovery was instant in the early stage, but was more protracted and demanded a very heavy push force if the machine was allowed to settle steadily in the fully-established spin.

Aerobatics presented difficulties. Firstly, the climb to a respectable height was a long-drawn-out event, and on arrival the machine's characteristics were far from spirited. A loop from 145kt lacked both problems and interest, while a slow roll (recommended entry 130+ kt) was a very hit-and-miss affair with a decidedly barrelled exit. Usually there are specialist experts who manage to overcome the tricks of specific types, just as the late C.A. Nepean Bishop managed to perform consistently elegant slow rolls in a Magister while most of us made a mess of them, but on the Prentice there seemed to be no way of stopping the nose from falling fairly violently on the way out. Not surprisingly, aerobatics and spinning were forbidden with anyone in the third seat.

No aeroplane is wholly black or entirely white. Even the best machines have their faults and although most of my comments about the Prentice have been critical, there were times and circumstances in which it came into its own. The cockpit roominess, a good forward view and the comfortable spade grip column made cross-country trips (at 2,100/-2 and 12gph for weak mixture cruise) very pleasant pastimes. The cruising speed of 115kt was a positive improvement on its predecessor's 75.

Full flap (the lever offered only three positions, the centre gate providing a take-off setting) offered a steep descent path at 65-70kt, calling for a healthy heave for the round-out from a glide approach; but the tail down attitude was quite shallow and from a flapless approach there was very little attitude change to gain the three-point condition. There was no real tendency to swing and, once down, both wings remained level with no likelihood of one lifting on a crosswind landing.

Perhaps the Prentice was better as an aeroplane than as a trainer. It lacked the surprise element that any good trainer needs to keep a trainee pilot fully awake. The finesse needed to fly its predecessor completely disappeared; ham hands and feet were almost a virtue when handling the Prentice. The period during which pupils graduated to Harvards produced an increased ground looping trend in the Prentice-Harvard era compared with the immediately preceding Tiger Moth-Harvard period. I think it must be the only pilot trainer to lack decent control harmony to have entered full-scale RAF service; the Tutor, Tiger Moth, Magister (although a little heavy), Chipmunk and Provost have all had pleasantly responsive ailerons which must have made substantial contributions to the enjoyment of flying, which is an important feature in any pilot's training.

The Prentice's Service career was unusually but understandably short-lived and by 1955 (by which time the Chipmunk and the Provost were firmly established) 248 survivors had been sold – mainly to Aviation Traders at Southend, whose directors had several ingenious plans to modify them for extensive civil use as five-seaters. One, G-APJE, emerged with seats for seven and trials were carried out with the Gipsy Queen 70 of 340hp as a replacement for the standard 240hp Queen 32. Although a few five-seaters were sold, the majority fell to the breaker's axe.

Although the Prentice cannot claim fame in its intended role, it served a purpose training signallers and on communications duties in the Middle East; a few filtered into civil use. That a three-seat Service machine was sufficiently capacious to convert to a five-seat private aircraft, with room that warranted experimental modification to a seven-seater, puts it into a unique category in its class. Despite my critical comments, which are aimed at viewing the Prentice as a trainer, I do not really dislike it. I met the type briefly when new in 1948 and managed to 'borrow' one for a long weekend a year later, but I have not touched one since then, so with such a long time passage at least a slight element of nostalgic vintage appeal has crept in.

Chapter 43

Classic fighter-like handling
de Havilland Canada DHC1 Chipmunk

The Chipmunk started its flying life in May 1946 as the first type to emerge from de Havilland Canada. By 1949 it was in production in the UK to become the RAF's standard trainer to replace the ageing Tiger Moth; subsequently it had a remarkably long and successful career in all three Services. Today, more than seventy years after the first machines were delivered to Oxford University Air Squadron, two Chipmunks remain in active military use with the RAF Battle of Britain Memorial Flight, for converting jet jockeys to the use of piston engines and, perhaps more significantly, to the art of taildragging.

For any reader who seeks the pleasure of flying for flying's sake, I fully recommend the Chipmunk. Fortunately, there are well over 100 on the current UK Register, many ex-RAF (and I have described in Chapter 8 the problems associated with that transition) including some operated by flying clubs. So let us begin where we should be, in the cockpit. In original, unmodified military form, this is neat and sensible, with that stark all-black environment which some of us find more acceptable than the modern greys and other more nauseating colour schemes. Entry is via walkways on either wing, with a rearward-sliding canopy that covers the twin tandem seating positions. On the left are the ratchet-type brake lever, throttle and mixture controls, trim wheel, ignition switches, ground/flight switch and generator warning light. The standard panel of six flight instruments is augmented only by the rpm indicator and oil pressure and temperature gauges. The P-type compass and an on/off fuel cock are centrally mounted just ahead of the control column. On or near the right wall the only controls in regular use are the three-position flap lever, radio-frequency selector, the carburettor air control, and the pull-to-fire starting ring. It all adds up to a completely unconfused (and unconfusing) layout.

A pilot seems to fit into the Chipmunk rather than just in it. Certainly, the bearers for the 145hp Gipsy Major 10/2 engine have very little in the way of damping qualities and, on start-up, engine roughness is transmitted right through the airframe causing the instrument panel and canopy to shake uncomfortably. Also, the standard 18 gallon tankage for military models (9 gallons in each wing, with a possible increase to 12 gallons each) is a little mean and the ridiculous little luggage hatch is meaner, but remembering how the Chipmunk earned its living, only the first of these is a justifiable cause for complaint.

Although the brake lever offers little positive feel, the results of applying it are good. Each wheel has a hydraulic brake unit and a master cylinder, fed from a reservoir mounted on the firewall. Braking is differential if applied in conjunction with the rudder pedals. The clearly marked elevator trim wheel (positions forward of neutral being black and those behind being white) is set two divisions forward, and the take-off is straightforward, with a slight right-hand swing if power is applied coarsely. Little physical effort is needed for a clean unstick at 45kt, and even at this low speed the controls are pleasant. A comfortable climbing speed for the Chippie is 70kt, giving a reasonably adequate cooling and ease of handling, but not the best rate of ascent, which can be improved to 800ft/min with a slight airspeed reduction.

I think the Chipmunk has the most pleasant and best-harmonised controls of any standard production light aeroplane; the ailerons work effectively and actively right through the speed range. Trim changes are minimal with variations in speed, power setting or flap position, but sufficient to remind a student to use the facilities that are available.

In a slowish light aeroplane, wind plays havoc with performance over the ground, but at 2,000 feet, 2,050rpm should produce 95kt at just 6.5gph – nearly 14mpg. This is not strikingly economical, but the

Chipmunk has so much more to offer than a mere A to B capability that something must suffer slightly.

Stalling is straightforward, accompanied by a varying amount of elevator buffet and, sometimes, hood vibration. The clean, power-off breakaway occurs at 45kt: the dirty, approach-power stall about 10kt later. Recovery is quick and easy. Spinning, now that the various earlier troubles have melted into history, seems a happy enough event so long as both rudder and strake modifications have been carried out.

To guarantee entry into a genuine spin a spot of cheating is advisable. For if full into-spin rudder is applied about 5kt before the stall, a real spin occurs. If rudder application is delayed until the point of stall, the Chipmunk may choose to indulge in a spiral dive. From a true spin the proper procedure of full opposite rudder – pause – stick forward produces the right results, but an unusually high forward stick pressure may be needed.

The Chipmunk begs to be rolled. The low-set wing, effective ailerons and generally precise qualities of the whole machine give it a fighter-like feel. The book recommends 120kt as entry speed, but in practice it will find its way round contentedly from 105 to 110kt. With the long-chord rudder a fairly slow roll can be achieved, due to its extra effectiveness at the roll-out stage. Unfortunately, though, the fuel system tolerates nothing in the way of inverted flight and the engine coughs or fades as soon as any negative loading is applied. A loop calls for 130kt, but some caution is called for to avoid over-speeding the engine, which is allowed to go briefly (but not comfortably for my peace of mind) to 2,675rpm – I think 2,500 should be enough for anyone.

For the circuit and initial approach, one-third flap may be lowered below 93kt. This improves low speed handling, but by generally accepted standards no improvement is needed. Full flap – only 30 degrees – is permissible from 71kt but is not as effective as it might be, so even on a glide the descent angle is shallow. Over-the-fence speed, though not critical on a fair-size airfield, needs to be reasonably precise at 55kt if a long and embarrassing float is to be avoided. A sizeable attitude change is required in order to achieve a

CLASSIC FIGHTER-LIKE HANDLING

three-point arrival, but a satisfyingly solid clunk (the legs are hard, using very effective and trouble-free rubber blocks that proved so successful on the Mosquito) accompanies the operation. The brakes can be used safely as soon as they are needed and they are creditably effective in both stopping and acting differentially. The ground view from the front (solo) cockpit is good for a tail-down aeroplane, but the occupant in the rear (instructor's) seat has restricted vision, calling for energetic weaving when taxying.

The Chipmunk has had a unique career; it is tough and, as a Service trainer, lasted longer than both the First World War Avro 504 and the Second World War Tiger Moth added together; in the whole of UK military aviation history only the Canberra has outlived it. The 'Chippie' was extremely popular as a pilot's aeroplane among all who flew it and continues to be equally appreciated by those fortunate enough to do so in its current general aviation role. Whilst today GA is primarily a mode of transport – misunderstood and not properly recognised by many at central or local government level – flying the right aeroplane adds a special touch. The Chipmunk is one of those 'right aeroplanes' and there are enough about for most readers to find examples within reasonable reach of their homes. However, as a former flying instructor, I must add these two points: although the Chipmunk is not difficult to fly, it is a taildragger, so for safety's sake be sure to have an appropriate conversion and, before attempting to indulge in aerobatics, do undergo relevant training. With those provisos, I repeat my opening recommendation: find an available Chipmunk and fly it. If you are disappointed, I will be very surprised.

Chapter 44

A turn in the training tide
Percival Provost

In 1953 the introduction of the Percival Provost into RAF service as the basic trainer brought about an entirely new concept in pilot courses. Ever since organised training had begun, British practice had supported the idea of a low-powered simple trainer with a minimum of frills. The Avro 504 and Tiger Moth between them symbolised the instructional role for more than thirty years, but the Provost was quite different. In 1915 the 504K offered 110hp and the Tiger Moth followed with only twenty more, but this new machine from Luton confronted a pupil (who might never have touched an aeroplane before) with no fewer than 550 horses to be harnessed and tamed. Certainly in between came the Prentice, but its career was brief and its performance far from sparkling.

The first station to offer basic tuition on the type was Ternhill, where No. 6 Flying Training School operated these machines until after the other schools had exchanged them for Jet Provosts in 1961. This was largely because the relatively short runways at Ternhill were unsuitable for the later type. Unlike the Prentice, which, with its three seats, retired from the training role to serve a useful purpose on communications duties, the Provost offered space for only two occupants; nevertheless, a few specimens remained active for a further eight years serving as 'targets' for trainee controllers at the RAF's Central Air Traffic Control School at Shawbury.

At full weight the Provost registers 4,400lb, making a sharp contrast with the 1,770lb of the Tiger Moth. Weight, power, bulk and layout offered an awesome presence to a student, but this accorded well with the current military theme; the design and comparative complexity of the cockpit set the mind to work on the right lines and eased the later transition to more advanced machinery. Clearly though, it put paid to the earlier concept of just flying rather than operating an aeroplane.

Adjustable seats and pedals, a lean-forward type harness, a handle for winding the canopy open or closed, a 24-volt electrical system, variable-pitch propeller, pneumatic brakes and flaps, windscreen wipers, cockpit heating and ventilation (the latter very necessary), an accelerometer, trimming facilities for rudder as well as elevators, ailerons with servo-tabs, oil cooler control, three-position air-intake lever and so on combined to create an 'advanced' atmosphere for the beginner. After carrying out external and internal checks that occupy nearly six pages in the Pilot's Notes, the main points for starting are to set the propeller at maximum rpm (fully forward), unlock the controls (lever down) and, as a personal preference, direct some air into the cockpit. After turning on the master switch, the fuel can be selected and checked audibly, for when the lever (on the central pedestal) is moved forward for 'on', the electric pump makes welcome sounds. With the oil cooler closed (lever out) and air intake at filter (up) we are ready to prime for 2-4 seconds. This is carried out by a pushbutton on the end of the starter lever which is pulled upwards to select and fire a cartridge. The lever, which incorporates a booster coil control, should be held up until the engine is running steadily.

Warming at about 1,200rpm may be a fairly lengthy business, for if the pneumatic pressure is low it is necessary to wait for a build-up to at least $220 lb/in^2$ for taxying, while below this figure the flaps will not operate. With the three-position lever in the up position, the flaps will raise themselves very smartly as soon as, but not before, the correct pressure is reached.

By this time the oil temperature should have reached the prescribed minimum of 20°C for the engine check. After the usual dead-cut procedure, the throttle should be opened to static boost, for exercising the rpm fully twice and for checking the magnetos and plugs. The engine idles pleasantly at 600-800rpm, but obviously this condition should be maintained only momentarily.

Unlike many closed-cockpit military machines, the Provost has its hood closed for take-off. This, apparently, is because of the width of the cabin which could cause considerable air flow difficulties. The swinging tendency is far less noticeable than might be expected with 550 horses aboard and from the start the rudder very effectively cures any inclination to wander from the straight and narrow path. However, a positive forward movement is needed to prevent a three-point unstick, and then the Provost needs lifting off at 60-65kt which it does very cleanly.

The climb is sustained at 100kt with 2,900rpm and + 31/2lb boost, which produces a very creditable ascent rate despite an enforced power reduction in the type's early life. Originally, the Alvis Leonides nine-cylinder radial operated to +9lb, but problems – mainly blown cylinder heads – caused the authorities to introduce a lower limit almost as soon as the type entered service. Before that the rate was considerably more than 2,000ft/min. I had the one-off pleasure of experiencing this temporary but very enjoyable supply of surplus power, for whilst doing my then annual RAF Reserve fortnight with 187 (Ferry) Squadron at Aston Down, I collected the eighth production Provost from the factory and delivered it to Ternhill. There were no Pilot's Notes and, apart from help from a fitter on starting procedure, there was no one to tell me anything about it. Fortunately, it was an almost perfect day weather-wise so, by trial and error, I had the chance to discover a few things before I stepped out at the other end. Such opportunities, alas, disappeared many years ago. Before my next contact with the type, the power reduction had been introduced.

As soon as the Provost is on the move, its delightful handling characteristics show themselves. All three controls are remarkably light and, to add to the pleasure, very effective at all normal operating speeds right down to the stall, which occurs at 60kt with flaps at the slope, or 65 clean. The ailerons work efficiently even down to the break-away condition, which is preceded by about 5kt with very mild buffeting on the elevators.

Normal cruise can be set up over a range of speeds and settings, with 2,000rpm as the recommended minimum. This, with zero boost, consumes about 17gph and produces an IAS at the lower end of about 110kt; endurance speed is 85 and it is possible to cruise as fast as 140 and remain within the advised power combination limits. Even at the lowest speeds handling is easy and comfortable, especially as partial flap may be used at anything below 125kt.

One experienced industry test pilot, who had instructed extensively on Provosts, described the type as the most pleasant machine to handle that he had ever flown. Whether on the circuit, in the cruise, or on aerobatics, the well-balanced controls leave no cause for criticism; a strange personal memory is that the Provost's servo-tab ailerons feel uncannily similar to those of the later Meteors fitted with spring tabs.

For those who specialise in the aerobatic art the Provost offers a host of opportunities, but even for the rest of us it behaves encouragingly. It is possible to roll straight from a fast cruise of about 140kt, but preferably with 2,600/+3½ established on the engine dials. Not much rudder is needed and an excusable tendency is to apply more than is required, especially at the exit/roll-out stage, which then accentuates any proneness to a barrel effect. Power should remain constant throughout the aerobatic regime, for the fuel system provides a supply for brief periods of inverted flight, which eases the problem of effecting a genuine slow roll. Recommended entry speed for a loop is 165kt, with an additional 10 at the start for a roll-off; the radius is sufficiently large to allow time for a trainee – or an experienced pilot – to commit directional errors on the way up.

In the circuit, filtered air should be selected and rpm set at 2,600, when half flap and 3lb boost will offer just over 100kt; about 90 is right for the final turn and, with full flap, about 75 over the fence for a powered approach. The Provost sinks rapidly as speed decays, especially from a slow run-in, and the touchdown is solid. Keeping straight presents no problems, while for an overshoot a climbaway IAS of 90 presents a healthy start on the rapid return journey to circuit height.

There are several peculiarities to remember and these accentuate the difference between the Provost and its predecessors; the throttle and rpm levers must be fully back before the control locks can be engaged, (intended, of course, as a safety device at the start of a flight when it becomes impracticable to start the engine with the locks in position) and, before leaving the machine, the flaps should be selected and left down.

No doubt the introduction of this relatively complex machine made trainee pilots learn to establish completely new sets of values; on the Tiger Moth, balanced flight was impossible without generous use of the rudder, slight crosswinds created problems and called for handling skills, and the weather-related 'feel of flight' was a key feature. The Provost, on the other hand, would keep straight on take-off and landing with little help from the pilot, the rudder came into full play only on the ground or in spin recovery, while wind conditions, within reasonable limits, presented few problems. However, the knobs, levers and checks associated with them made the later pupil activate his mental processes from the very beginning.

Today, this pleasantly powerful and sprightly machine remains alive and active with XF603/G-KAPW airworthy with the Shuttleworth Trust; a very few others are in restoration.

Chapter 45

Air racing in the 1950s

Air racing can hold a strong appeal to pilots who enjoy challenges, who wish to test their skills in handling and judgement and, for those who seek it, can offer much more than just travelling from A to B. Unlike other speed contests, though, air races hold relatively little appeal to the viewing public, despite the fact that flying displays are the UK's second most popular spectator attraction. This general lack of interest may seem strange, but it enables a winner to avoid the indignity of being branded a celebrity!

I concentrate here first on the pre-Second World War air racing scene of the 1920s and 1930s. There were many variations on the competitive scene, for example, the local authorities of Manchester and Liverpool challenged each other in an Inter-city race, which was won by a Gipsy Moth at 98mph. I doubt if anyone suggesting this idea to today's councils would receive an acceptable welcome! The activities of the 1920s and 1930s included some intense challenges, including the famous Schneider Trophy races when, in 1931, a Supermarine S.6B seaplane set up a world speed record of 379.05mph; the constant struggle for improved performance played a key part in Britain's success in the Second World War. Perhaps the oddest of all was the Vertical Interception Race at Brooklands in May 1933 where the 'finishing line' was an autogyro circling at 3,000ft and, on a handicap basis, the winner was the first pilot to climb up and pass the machine!

Also, at that time, surprisingly, there were more women racing pilots than there have been since the war and as early as 1931 the Ladies' Handicap, flown from Woodley aerodrome near Reading, drew nine participants.

This was the time when the British aircraft industry (comprising a wide range of large and some very small firms) was the unchallenged world leader in design and construction; many of the products had strong sporting potential and a few companies created world record breakers.

Entries for the 1933 event for the King's Cup included seven Comper Swifts and by the following year the overall scene was dominated by the famous de Havilland DH88 Comet designed, built and flown within nine months, and three of which were entered for the MacRobertson Air Race from Mildenhall in England to Melbourne in Australia. Initially, this attracted no fewer than sixty-four entrants, but as the complexity of the commitment became clearer most withdrew and, well before the start, the hopefuls were reduced to twenty. The overall winner was Comet G-ACSS, Grosvenor House, which covered the 11,333 miles in 70 hours, 54 minutes, and 18 seconds, averaging 158.9mph.

By the latter half of the 1930s the scene had settled down to a relatively steady and even predictable pattern; the types that had been designed previously for racing and records were competing alongside aeroplanes of more general intent. Among the well-known specialist performers of the day were the diminutive Comper Swift, Miles Sparrowhawk, Hawk Speed Six, and Percival Mew Gull. Fortunately, examples of all these reappeared to enliven the race circuits of the 50s.

I turn now to the post Second World War air racing scene. The war had put a halt to all private and sporting flying, and considerable numbers of light aircraft had been impressed into temporary military use. Many succumbed, but some survived and reappeared on the civil register to restart the leisure flying movement. Added to these were substantial numbers of Tiger Moths, Magisters, Proctors and others that had been built as Service aircraft and were released as war-surplus equipment at peanut prices; a fly-away Tiger Moth cost £50, or to a recognised flying club, £25. To complete the line-up at the start of the new peacetime era were several pre-war types that had either escaped the call-up or had been considered unsuitable for the needs of the

Service. Combined, these groups formed the basis of the entries for the air races of the late 40s and the 50s, but sometimes spice was added with examples of former military operational aeroplanes.

Although, shortly after the Second World War, there were fewer civil light aircraft and fewer private pilots than there are now, there were many more small aerodromes (the seemingly incurable closure disease had not been invented) and many of the aeroplanes that competed then were those that had achieved successes around the pylons of the 30s.

Air races take several forms, but the majority are handicap events around a laid-out course, with large conspicuous pylons as the turning points. In most cases entries are open to all types, but sometimes they are restricted to aircraft within specific weight, power, or speed ranges. Occasionally there are one-type scratch races, with (for safety reasons) a strictly restricted number launched at the same time, usually flown around several laps of a short closed-circuit pattern, often all in sight of the base aerodrome. Although generally unappreciated by the public, these can be quite spectacular events!

For the more conventional races open to a variety of aircraft, the handicappers have the difficult task of assessing each individual machine, based on the type's known performance, on the information given on the entry form and on a visual inspection. If there are several machines of the same type, there can be many easily recognised differences, one of the most noticeable being whether the aileron gaps have been taped-up, but more crafty modifications, if not declared, can have significant effects on performance and can lead to investigation and disqualification after the race.

All this has remained standard through many years and, as far as I am aware, only two significant changes have occurred in the post-war period. One is the need to hold a Competitor's Licence, which is not difficult to obtain, calling for a minimum of 100 hours as first pilot, although more and appropriate handling experience would be preferable. The other is the introduction of the British Air Racing Championship, awarded to the pilot who gains the highest number of points in a season. On this sensible basis, the recipient may not have won any race, but would have had consistently good results over several events.

Many race entrants are well-heeled and can improve their chances of success by titivating their mounts, but others just go along with what they have or can obtain. In 1950, as explained in an earlier chapter, I was given the opportunity to race 1935 Miles Falcon G-ADFH in the Daily Express Air Race along the south coast from Hurn (Bournemouth) to Herne Bay. It was a large-scale event that attracted seventy-five entries of all sizes and probably was not the most suitable idea for a novice. The most impressive participant was a civilianised Handley Page Halifax four-engine heavy bomber, and the thought of being pursued by 25 tons of metal projected through the air by almost 7,000 rampant horses would keep me on the alert. My little mount offered 130hp. Although the Halifax was the largest, it was not the only former military aircraft to join the fray. The back marker was the Hawker Hurricane G-AMAU, 'Last of the Many', which would cover the route at almost three times the speed of my best hopes. However, all my aims or fears were thrust aside and replaced by frustration when, within ten minutes of being flagged off, the oil pressure chose to back away at an alarming rate and I made a hurried landing at Portsmouth airport. As soon as I had switched off, out came a man who announced himself as the Chief Engineer of the local flying club and who instantly set about sorting the problem. An ageing oil pipe had split and almost the whole tankful was spread over the blackened underside of the attractive cream aeroplane. He completed the task and refused to take a penny for his efforts, saying that he was keen to help to keep the pre-war machines flying. There were some very good people about.

At around this time several pilots felt a need for an organisation that would look after the needs and interests of owners and operators of the older aeroplanes. As one of the instigators of the idea I became caught as honorary secretary of the Vintage Aeroplane Club. Although this involved a reasonable ration of voluntary work, it provided one positive benefit: we found a slightly unairworthy Avro Club Cadet of 1933 brew, G-ACHP, bought it for £75 and, thanks again to Doug Bianchi, paid a similar sum for a new C of A, giving an inexpensive fly-about for members who lacked their own machines. This was a delightful roomy old biplane with good brakes and even adjustable seats; ailerons on upper and lower wings provided just the required manoeuvrability for pylon turns. In exchange for being the new organisation's chore-horse I was given the privilege of entering the newcomer in any air races of my choice. I saw no reason for delay.

The early post-war pattern for air races differed little from the system used in the 1930s, but there was a short-term increase in the range of power and speed produced by the aircraft used. This created more problems for the handicappers who (most people agreed) did the difficult job very well. A prospective entrant needed to submit an application showing relevant details of the aeroplane and of his/her flying experience, including information on participation in any previous events. Assuming that this and the competitor's licence were in order, the next move would be to be present at the start site by a laid-down date and time. Usually, though, competitors would arrive well before this to allow opportunities for race practice, to become thoroughly acquainted with the route and its turning points.

After a comprehensive briefing for pilots, the aircraft would be positioned on or near the starting line with the machines assessed to be the slowest in pole positions as the first to be flagged away. Once the spirit of the race was active, the time waiting to be unleashed was the most stressful (but not the most exhilarating) part of the day. The course to be flown could be a very long haul, often with no other competitors in sight for much of the time, or it could be a very short circuit with all or most of the route within view of the start and with all participants closely bunched. As a general rule there would be a permitted entry limit of one aircraft per mile of the route.

The rules were simple but strictly checked. The most common fault was to cut over or inside a pylon and sometimes this occurred because of misjudged wind, but to avoid time loss it was essential to make the turn as closely around the marker as was practicable. Some aircraft could be manoeuvred very tightly and these would provide quite spectacular sights, but some pilots preferred gentler turns to avoid the loss of air speed.

As wind is effective over time and not distance, the slower machines always suffered when it was strong; straight legs would be flown at heights that provide maximum help or minimum hindrance, as appropriate.

Usually, the route would be flown over several laps, and the more of these there were, the more difficult it could be for a spectator to try to pre-judge a result. As a late starter, a very fast machine would need to overtake others more than once, so all participants could be well scattered or bunched at any time, with meaningful bunching occurring only close to the finishing line at the end of the last lap. If the handicappers had done their jobs well, all the machines would reach the line within a very short time interval.

The winner is not necessarily the pilot who flies best, and that honour may not always be awarded to the first across the line. An aeroplane that has not raced for a long time (or even never) may beat or be beaten by the handicappers and as the sole surviving Avro Club Cadet had not competed since before the war, no one could know precisely what its performance would be. So to fly it in the 1952 Grosvenor Trophy Race at Woolsington Aerodrome was an interesting venture. I had not finished very close to the front in any earlier race and I was pleased to find that my ageing steed was giving me a new experience; unexpectedly I seemed to be in the lead, but was pipped just before the post. Although I was second to cross the line I was surprised to be told later that I was the winner: the pilot who beat me had performed so unexpectedly well that he was ordered to have his engine stripped down and this revealed undeclared high compression pistons, so he was disqualified. In the King's Cup race on the following day I achieved ninth place.

The handicappers needed to calculate the likely performance of an untried aeroplane and compare this with a mixture of well-known entries; most of these had remained unaltered since previous races, and others may have undergone various modifications – declared or not. Almost always, although sometimes disappointed, competitors accepted the judges' decisions and a formal challenge was very rare. Although all pilots would like to win, most flew to enjoy the sheer sporting nature of the day.

Unlike motor racing, the system ensured that no pilot could become an unchallenged winner over a long string of events. When an aeroplane had achieved a very clear win, on the next occasion it would be re-handicapped.

The main differences between events of the 1950s and those held today would be the scale of the overall activity, the variety of the aircraft and the wide range of pilot experience. The Halifax that competed in the Daily Express race of 1950 – finishing twenty-fourth out of sixty-one that completed the course – was the only really heavy aeroplane to participate. For the following year the organisers imposed a limit of 12,000lb, which still left the field open to some fast and potent machinery. The uniquely smooth sound of a Rolls-Royce Merlin was not uncommon on the race circuit and in one King's Cup event national records were achieved by two Spitfires.

High-powered participants were very much in the minority, but the overall field was far from dull. Regular scenes on the start line included many machines that had gained pre-war fame such as the Percival Mew Gull G-AEXF in which Alex Henshaw had established the South African Cape record in 1938 and Ron Paine's Miles Hawk Speed Six G-ADGP which participated in more UK races than any other entrant, usually averaging speeds just short of 190mph. Other vintage types that reappeared on the racecourses of the 1950s included the Comper Swift, Miles Sparrowhawk, Hawk Major and Falcon, de Havilland Moths of many kinds, the two Mosscraft and several others that were more occasional participants.

Air racing at the time appealed to a very broad spread of pilots, some of whom had only limited experience, while others were well known in their professional fields: Group Captain G.F.K. Donaldson, who had attained the world air speed record of 616mph in a Gloster Meteor, purred around the circuits at little more than 100mph in his 90hp Taylorcraft D (the earliest form of Auster), while Squadron Leader Neville Duke, chief test pilot of Hawker Aircraft and a keen member of the Vintage Aeroplane Club, was a regular participant in his favourite mount – the last surviving Hawker Tomtit of 1928. This attractive two-seater, powered by an uncowled Armstrong-Siddeley Mongoose five-cylinder radial, remains airworthy today with the Shuttleworth Collection at Old Warden.

Whilst most air races were open to all, others were more specific in their entry requirements, with some restricted to very high-speed aeroplanes. In the early post-war years when Britain retained a competitive aircraft industry, there were several events in which companies could exhibit their products. One of the first of these, flown from the long-lost aerodrome at Lympne, had a field of six: two Fairey Fireflies, a Spitfire, a Blackburn Firebrand, a Hawker Fury and a Vampire; the last of these was first to pass the post, flown by Group Captain John Cunningham, de Havilland's chief test pilot.

In those more enlightened times, the flying Services made intermittent inroads to the civil racing scene; a Chipmunk or military brand of Auster would appear on an entry list. However, it was the now-long-gone Royal Auxiliary Air Force that took the lead with its own events for the Cooper Trophy, flying Merlin-powered Spitfire 16s, Griffon engined Spitfire 22s and Vampires from the various squadrons located around the UK.

Back to the civil field, there were several privately sponsored races, including one in which each flying club that was a member of the Association of British Aero Clubs and Centres (a forerunner of AOPA UK) could enter one machine. Then there was an event held each year at Burnaston, open only to instructors employed by the Derby Aviation/Air Schools Group, flying Miles Hawk Trainer 3s. In 1956, Norman Jones formed the Tiger Club, which in September of that year held its first race meeting, at Elstree, with six Tiger Moths. I was fortunate to be able to compete in both these one-type scratch events.

In 1954 the Vintage Aeroplane Club organised one very restricted event at Denham, creating the most nostalgic of post-war races. Participating aircraft included de Havilland's own 1925 Cirrus Moth, DH Leopard Moth, Blackburn B2, Avro Club Cadet, Spartan Arrow,

Miles Hawk Major, Falcon Six and Hawk Speed Six, all but one of which was the sole surviving airworthy example of its type. Nothing like it has been or ever could be held again.

Considerable numbers of less specialised but very appropriate types took part regularly and those entered for the 1951 National Air Races included no fewer than eleven Hawk Trainers, nine Proctors and five Gemini. Unfortunately, due largely to an unrealistic demand by Customs and Excise (forty-two per cent of the income from ticket sales) the Nationals for that year were abandoned.

As mentioned in Chapter 7 I was privileged to race Comper Swift G-ABUS, which gave me enormous pleasure and some 'experiences', including a very hurried forced landing when the main oil pipe split open in the middle of the 1955 King's Cup air race. The aeroplane and I were covered in oil so I could see nothing, but on closing the throttle and just landing ahead I was pleasantly surprised to stop in the centre of the then all-grass Baginton Aerodrome (now Coventry Airport). Fortunately, the little Swift was kinder to me in the following year and made amends by bringing me home into third place. Sometime later Doug Bianchi was heard to say, 'don't lend an aeroplane to Ogilvy – he leaves his oil pressure scattered all over the countryside!'

Air racing in the UK has a very creditable safety record, but an especially unfortunate loss was HRH Prince William of Gloucester, then the active President of AOPA UK and a very enthusiastic private pilot, with his own airstrip in Northamptonshire. In 1973 he was killed when things went wrong on a pylon turn, although the formal accident report failed to find the precise cause.

The scope and atmosphere of the scene today may not be quite what it was seventy or so years ago, but I am assured by current participants that it remains very enjoyable and I recommend any pilot with a sporting competitive instinct to look into it.

Chapter 46

In Closing

My working life ran from the age of eighteen until I withdrew from remunerated work at eighty-two to care for my wife Audrey who was suffering from Alzheimer's disease. Since then I have been involved in honorary capacities with several national and regional aviation organisations. In these years I discovered that, with determination, it is possible to get some unreasonable rules or regulations cancelled, or at least modified. I hope that this information will be helpful to readers who face irrational actions by the relevant authorities. I am not suggesting that you break the law, for we must have it and it must be obeyed; only when it is clearly unjustifiable, try to get it changed and remain determined to achieve your aim.

In Chapter 2 I described my first brush with the powers of the time when I attended the RAF Aircrew Selection Board and failed the medical examination because I was unable to stand on one leg with my eyes shut. My youthful persistence persuaded the Chief Medical Officer of the unit to turn a blind eye to the situation. I will remain very grateful to him, for this decision enabled me to continue with my plans. It gave me added confidence for the future.

Perhaps the biggest situation that I needed to tackle was the case of the military Chipmunk T10 that was considered to be unsuitable for civil use. Until we had bought five for the London School of Flying, we were unaware of the need to carry out modifications that would cost more than we had paid for the fully serviceable aircraft. The whole tale was worsened by the fact that the Chipmunk had started life and had been cleared as a civil machine before it was adopted for the RAF. It was just that the basically identical variants had been

IN CLOSING

cleared by two different authorities, which at the time refused to accept each other's standards.

I may be accused of repetition as this and several other examples of unacceptable situations have appeared earlier in the book, but I see a need to bring a few of these together to tell of the problems that we faced in the early post-war years. Today's difficulties are very different, but they still exist, and I hope that those people adversely affected will have the confidence to fight forcefully. In the meantime, though, take care to obey the rules in the hope that the worst can be changed. If we could do this seventy years ago it can be done again now, but it needs confidence and determination.

Amongst the worst that must be simplified is pilot licensing, which has become more muddled within the last few years. Perhaps the biggest single problem facing general aviation, though, is the continuing loss of aerodromes to building developers, with many threats ahead. At long last the CAA has realised that action is necessary, but they should have taken this aboard several years ago. Unless facilities are available within easy reach of all centres of population or industry, the use of an aeroplane for business and/or pleasure will be sadly reduced. This makes a nonsense of current claims that Britain is to be the best place in the world to own or operate one.

I am sorry to end with stressing a need for positive action, but I must mention that I have been actively involved on a full-time basis with general – including historic – aviation for more than sixty years, during which I have participated in exactly thirty public planning inquiries and ten court cases in support of our aircraft cause.

Several people have asked if I have a favourite aeroplane. The answer is no, but the one with the most nicely balanced controls is the Gladiator and the one that made the greatest impression is the Mosquito. Neither is available for the asking, but someone seeking a machine that is a delight to fly from the handling aspect is the Chipmunk, and to experience the vintage appeal of the open cockpit try the Tiger Moth. More than 100 examples of each are on the UK register so it should not be very difficult to find one.

FLYING AND PRESERVING HISTORIC AIRCRAFT

I hope you have found the book interesting, and if you are a pilot, helpful. I may have at times sounded pessimistic but let me make clear that so long as suitable action is taken, especially on the aerodrome closures, the future can be bright and I hope that you will have many hours of enjoyable and/or useful flying.